RESEARCHING

Constitutional

Law

Albert P. Melone

Southern Illinois University, Carbondale

SCOTT, FORESMAN/LITTLE, BROWN HIGHER EDUCATION
A Division of Scott, Foresman and Company

Glenview, Illinois   London, England

Dedicated to the best teacher I know, Jody DeGenaro. Friend for thirty years, he is the model for what we should all aspire to as educators and human beings. He really cares.

Library of Congress Cataloging-in-Publication Data
Melone, Albert P.
   Researching constitutional law / Albert P. Melone.
      p.   cm.
   Includes bibliographical references.
   ISBN 0-673-52086-2
   1. United States—Constitutional law—Legal research. I. Title.
KF241.C66M455   1990
342.73'0072—dc20
[347.302072]
                                                                    90-8018
                                                                      CIP

1 2 3 4 5 6—PAT—95 94 93 92 91 90

Preface

Educated persons are able to think and act independently. A goal of liberal arts education is to help individuals acquire the skills necessary for living an independent life. It is not enough to know the right answers to pre-programmed questions, nor is it sufficient to know what the right questions might be. The ability to study issues outside a structured classroom setting is the training for life that distinguishes the truly educated from those condemned to the follower ranks. *Researching Constitutional Law* reflects the view that all persons living in a democratic culture should possess the tools to research questions that guide how they must live. The law belongs to the people and each member of the polity should know how to investigate questions of law and society. *Researching Constitutional Law*, then, is meant for general lay public use, for students enrolled in law-related courses, and for professionals who may find parts of this book suitable for their purposes.

Researching Constitutional Law is a considerable revision of an earlier text, *Primer on Constitutional Law*, coauthored with Carl Kalvelage. It follows the same format as the earlier volume, but is up-to-date and contains more material. Each chapter is thoroughly revised and expanded, and there is an additional chapter summarizing landmark Supreme Court decisions.

Students of constitutional law will find this book useful because it acquaints them with legal research skills necessary for getting the most from their classroom experiences. Before writing research papers on constitutional law topics, students may turn to this text for descriptions and explanations of general legal research materials as well as literature especially pertinent to the topics. *Researching Constitutional Law* examines specific legal materials and relevant literature found in law libraries or legal collections at general college or community libraries. It explains the correct reference forms for citing materials in research papers, and the reasons and methods for briefing court opinions. It contains summaries of leading decisions of the U.S. Supreme Court, a glossary of legal terms, and a substantial bibliography on constitutional law and related topics.

A poorly researched law-related term paper is a living nightmare of students and instructors alike. Too often students read a few books and articles and their finished papers erroneously purport to fully explore the subject. Because laws are constantly changing, even relatively current publications cannot give the reader a contemporary understanding or a complete historical appraisal of legal topics. Students must be able to find the latest words on subjects and relate given legal issues to other matters of social and historical concern. This book can help researchers understand their topics comprehensively.

Because most constitutional law instructors do not have the time to teach their students about legal research, they can save valuable time by assigning selected chapters or parts of chapters in this text for students to read outside the classroom. Chapter One, for example, describes how legal opinions are reported by official and unofficial sources; it also details numerous sources available to conduct legal research. Chapter Two contains annotations of books which consider the relationship of judicial review to constitutional interpretation, the problems encountered in studying the lives of Supreme Court justices, historical accounts of the Supreme Court and subject-specific expository works, and the variety of approaches and methods used when studying public law topics. Chapter Four provides students with a description and sample of the ways to brief court opinions. The glossary will help students answer definitional questions.

Students may use chapters of this volume without reading the book cover to cover. For example, students may use Chapter Three when writing and documenting research papers for any social science or humanities course. Chapter Five contains summaries of leading Supreme Court decisions. Anyone needing to recall the facts and holdings of particular landmark opinions will find this chapter handy. The Contents and Index should be used to guide readers to the answers for their specific questions.

Persons without legal training or individuals without specific course work in constitutional law should find this work to be a handy research guide. The previous version of this work won high praise from former students who entered the worlds of business and education. Students who earned law degrees commented that the *Primer on Constitutional Law* was a fine introduction to legal research and proved invaluable to them particularly during their first year of law school; it gave them a significant head start over their struggling peers. Practicing paralegals noted they used the previous edition on a daily basis. Residents of Illinois correctional centers commented that the *Primer* helped them understand and deal with legal processes more fully than was permitted by their personal experiences alone. This new text will be an even more helpful reference work for personal libraries. However, anyone with a genuine legal problem is best advised to consult an attorney. *Researching Constitutional Law* can help clarify legal issues and language, but it should not take the place of professional advice.

I owe thanks to many individuals who helped me write this text. The professional staff of the law library at the Southern Illinois University School of Law has been cooperative. In particular, law librarians Kathy R. Garner and Elizabeth W. Matthews have been helpful in answering my questions and those of my students. I am especially grateful to Laurel Anne Wendt for her assistance over many years in helping me track down sources and better understand legal literature. Always professional, engaging, charming, and witty, she has made visits to the law library pleasant and fruitful. My research assistants over several semesters have helped locate materials and shape up this manuscript in a variety of important ways; Scott Myers and Timothy Millmore performed yeoman service. Aline Davis Wilson and Cathy Croquer were responsible for the final word processing of the submitted manuscript, and Darren Nix typed revisions. They all did a good job. Professor John R. Schmidhauser of the University of Southern California and Professor Steven Cann of Washburn University of Topeka provided cogent and in-depth criticisms of the manuscript. In one way or another, I used most if not all of their fine suggestions. Special appreciation goes to Cecilia G. Lause for bringing my manuscript to the attention of Richard Welna at Scott, Foresman and Company. The treatment afforded me by Dick Welna and his staff has been superb. They prove that a modern corporation can be productive, innovative, and humane. Further thanks go to Sean Leman, Bob Cooper, and Barbara Tompkins for their careful help in producing the text.

Consistent with good manners and the truth of the matter, I relieve any of the above-named individuals from responsibility for the inevitable shortcomings of this book. Hopefully, owing to the collective efforts of all involved, the practice of chanting *"mea culpa, mea culpa"* will prove little more than a customary ritual.

A.P.M.

Contents

_____

_____

1 Conducting Legal Research *1*

Introduction *1*

Opinions of the United States Supreme Court *1*
> United States Reports (U.S.) *2*
> United States Supreme Court Reports—Lawyers' Edition
> (L. Ed.) *3*
> Supreme Court Reporter (S. Ct.) *4*

Briefs Filed with the U.S. Supreme Court *4*
> Landmark Briefs and Arguments of the Supreme Court of
> the United States: Constitutional Law *5*
> U.S. Supreme Court Records and Briefs *5*
> Supreme Court of the United States Petitions and Briefs *6*
> LEXIS *6*

Lower Federal Court Reports *6*
> Federal Cases (Fed. Cas.) *6*
> Federal Reporter (F.), (F.2d) *7*
> Federal Supplement (F. Supp.) *7*

State Court Reporters *8*

American Law Reports (ALR) *9*

Keeping Current *10*
> U.S. Law Week *11*
> U.S. Supreme Court Bulletin (S. Ct. Bull.) *12*
> West's Federal Case News *13*

Legal Encyclopedias *13*
> The Guide to American Law: Everyone's Legal
> Encyclopedia *14*
> Encyclopedia of the American Judicial System *14*
> American Jurisprudence 2d (Am. Jur. 2d) *15*
> Corpus Juris Secundum (C.J.S.) *16*
> Encyclopedia of the American Constitution *17*

Codes *18*
  United States Code (U.S.C.) *19*
  United States Code Service (U.S.C.S.) *19*
  United States Code Annotated (U.S.C.A.) *20*
Administrative Agency Reporting *20*
  Federal Register *21*
  Code of Federal Regulations (C.F.R.) *21*
Digests *22*
  American Digest System *22*
    Key Number System *22*
  Specialized Digests *24*
    Federal Practice Digest *24*
      U.S. Supreme Court Digest (West Publishing Company) *24*
      U.S. Supreme Court Reports Digest: Lawyers' Edition *24*
Citators *26*
  Shepard's United States Citations: Cases *26*
  Shepard's United States Citations: Statutes *30*
Legal Periodicals and Indexes *31*
  Index to Legal Periodicals *32*
    Subject and Author Index *32*
    Table of Cases Commented Upon *33*
    Table of Statutes Commented Upon *33*
    Book Review Index *33*
  Current Law Index *33*
  Legal Trac *34*
  Index to Foreign Legal Periodicals *34*
  Index to Periodical Articles Related to Law *34*
  Criminal Justice Periodical Index *35*
  Public Affairs Information Service Bulletin *35*
  Social Science Index *35*
  Reader's Guide to Periodical Literature *35*
  The New York Times Index *35*
Law Dictionaries *36*
Computer Terminal Research-Aids *36*
Legal Research Exercises *37*
    Exercise 1—Legal Encyclopedias *37*
    Exercise 2—Legal Codes *38*
    Exercise 3—Digests *38*
    Exercise 4—Citators *39*
    Exercise 5—Legal Periodicals *39*
Answers for Legal Exercises *39*

2 Survey of Book Literature *41*
Introduction *41*
Expository Works *41*
Historical Accounts of the Supreme Court *45*
Judicial Review and Constitutional Interpretation *51*
Judicial Biographies *55*
Case Studies *59*
Compliance and Impact Analysis *61*
Judicial Process and Behavior *64*

3 Writing and Documenting Research Papers *73*
Introduction *73*
Choosing a Topic *73*
Using the Library *74*
The Format for a Paper *75*
Citations *75*
    What to Cite *75*
Footnoting Form *76*
    Footnoting Books *77*
    Footnoting Journal and Magazine Articles *80*
    Footnoting Encyclopedias, Almanacs, and Other Works *81*
    Footnoting Legal Sources *83*
    Footnoting Government Documents *85*
Later References to the Same Footnote or Endnote
Source *88*
    Second References with Intervening Citations *88*
Bibliography Form *89*
    Bibliography Entries for Books *89*
    Bibliography Entries for Journal and Magazine Articles *92*
    Bibliography Entries for Encyclopedias, Almanacs, and Other
    Works *93*
    Bibliography Entries for Legal Sources *95*
    Bibliography Entries for Government Documents *97*
Scientific Reference Form *100*

4 Why and How to Brief a Case *104*
Introduction *104*
Elements of a Brief *106*
Model Brief *112*

5 Summaries of Leading Supreme Court Decisions *115*

Introduction *115*
Summaries *116*
 Baker v. Carr *116*
 Barenblatt v. United States *116*
 Barron v. Baltimore *117*
 Bolling v. Sharpe *118*
 Brown v. Board of Education of Topeka I *118*
 Brown v. Board of Education of Topeka II *119*
 Buckley v. Valeo *120*
 Butchers' Benevolent Association v. Crescent City Livestock Landing and Slaughterhouse Co. (Slaughterhouse Cases) *120*
 Civil Rights Cases *121*
 Cooley v. Board of Wardens of the Port of Philadelphia *122*
 Dennis v. United States *122*
 Ex Parte McCardle *123*
 Ex Parte Milligan *123*
 Fletcher v. Peck *124*
 Furman v. Georgia *125*
 Garcia v. San Antonio Metropolitan Transit Authority *125*
 Gibbons v. Ogden *126*
 Gideon v. Wainwright *127*
 Gitlow v. New York *127*
 Griswold v. Connecticut *128*
 Hammer v. Dagenhart *128*
 Heart of Atlanta Motel v. United States *129*
 Home Building and Loan Association v. Blaisdell *129*
 Hurtado v. California *130*
 Immigration & Naturalization Service v. Chadha *131*
 Katz v. United States *131*
 Katzenbach v. McClung *132*
 Korematsu v. United States *132*
 Lochner v. New York *133*
 Luther v. Borden *133*
 McCulloch v. Maryland *134*
 Mapp v. Ohio *134*
 Marbury v. Madison *135*
 Milliken v. Bradley *136*
 Miranda v. Arizona *136*
 Missouri v. Holland *137*

Munn v. Illinois   *137*
National Labor Relations Board v. Jones and Laughlin Steel
Corp.   *138*
New York Times Co. v. Sullivan   *139*
New York Times Co. v. United States   *139*
Nixon v. Fitzgerald   *140*
Palko v. Connecticut   *140*
Plessy v. Ferguson   *140*
Pollock v. Farmers' Loan and Trust Co.   *141*
Powell v. Alabama   *142*
Regents of the University of California v. Bakke   *142*
Reynolds v. Sims   *143*
Roe v. Wade   *144*
Schechter Poultry Corp. v. United States   *145*
Schenck v. United States   *146*
School District of Abington Township v. Schempp   *146*
Shelley v. Kraemer   *147*
Smith v. Allwright   *148*
Stuart v. Laird   *148*
Tinker v. Des Moines Independent Community
School District   *149*
Trustees of Dartmouth College v. Woodward   *149*
United States v. Butler   *150*
United States v. Curtiss-Wright Export Corp.   *151*
United States v. Darby   *151*
United States v. E. C. Knight Co.   *152*
United States v. Nixon   *153*
United States v. United States District Court for Eastern
District of Michigan   *154*
Walz v. Tax Commission of the City of New York   *154*
West Coast Hotel v. Parrish   *155*
West Virginia State Board of Education v. Barnette   *156*
Youngstown Sheet and Tube Co. v. Sawyer   *156*

6 Glossary of Terms and Phrases   *158*

Bibliography   *177*
The Judicial System   *177*
Jurisprudence   *181*
Constitutional Law—General   *183*
Constitutional History   *184*
Federalism   *190*

Congress *193*
Presidency *196*
Civil Rights and Liberties *200*
Law and Society *213*
Legal Profession *219*

Index *221*

Chapter One

Conducting Legal Research

Introduction

The purpose of this chapter is to familiarize students with the basic legal research tools. These materials, presented here with no unnecessary legal jargon, can help students to do legal research for undergraduate and graduate assignments. Many examples in this chapter are from the constitutional law field; however, they are applicable to many law-related undergraduate and graduate courses,—business law, criminal justice, consumer affairs, and planning law, for example.

The primary sources for all legal research in the United States are the reported opinions of law courts. Without such opinions it is impossible to cite cases as precedent and the principle of *stare decisis*—stand by past decisions—has little meaning. With this in mind, understanding where and how to locate the sources of court opinions is important.

Most college and university libraries have much of the legal-research material discussed in this chapter. Those institutions with law schools naturally will provide the most research materials. Some readers may discover inadequate library sources; many community libraries, however, have adequate law collections, and many state governments provide law libraries for public use.

Opinions of the United States Supreme Court

Because government and private firms publish judicial opinions, there is often more than a single citation to the same case—for example, Dennis v. United States, 341 U.S. 494, 71 S. Ct. 857, 95 L. Ed. 1137 (1951). These multiple citations to a single case are called *parallel citations*. For the case of *Dennis* v. *United States*, there are three citations. The first, 341 U.S. 494, refers to the official government publication, *United States Reports* (U.S.).

The number preceding the letters U.S. (341) refers to the volume, and the number following U.S. (494) indicates the first page in Volume 341 of *United States Reports* at which *Dennis* appears. The citation to the *Supreme Court Reporter* (S. Ct.) is 71 S. Ct. 857. It indicates that the *Dennis* case is located in Volume 71 and begins on page 857. The final citation, 95 L. Ed. 1137, refers to the place in the *United States Supreme Court Reports—Lawyers' Edition* (L. Ed.) where the *Dennis* case may also be located; that is, Volume 95 beginning on page 1137. Because students often have access to only one set of court reports, it is convenient to provide parallel citations.

All three of these court reports have one common feature—they each present the written opinions of the Supreme Court. The *United States Reports* (U.S.) is an official report, whereas the *Supreme Court Reporter* (S. Ct.) and the *Lawyers' Edition* (L. Ed.) are unofficial publications of private firms. Each source has its own special features.

United States Reports (U.S.)

The first ninety volumes of this official report contain the names of the respective court reporter. From 1790 to 1874 the court reporter's name is on each volume and is cited—Marbury v. Madison, 5 U.S. (Cranch) 137 (1803). The following is a list of the full names of the seven reporters along with their name abbreviations as they appear in legal citations, the volume number designations of the *U.S. Reports* for which they each contributed, and the corresponding years of service.

A. J. Dallas (Dall.)	1–4 U.S. (1789–1800)
William Cranch (Cranch)	5–13 U.S. (1801–1815)
Henry Wheaton (Wheat.)	14–25 U.S. (1816–1827)
Richard Peters (Peters)	26–41 U.S. (1828–1842)
Benjamin C. Howard (How.)	42–65 U.S. (1843–1860)
J. S. Black (Black)	66–67 U.S. (1861–1862)
John William Wallace (Wall.)	68–90 U.S. (1863–1874)

The designation for the *United States Reports*, changed in 1875, is now by volume number only, beginning with Volume 91 and the letters *U.S.*

Besides the official opinions of the Supreme Court, *United States Reports* contains summaries of facts, syllabi, and indexes. Syllabi (or syllabuses), sometimes called headnotes, are brief summaries of the important aspects of cases and contain references to the pages of the written opinions containing significant legal points. These features provide a quick reference for the contents of each case and can save valuable research time.

Shortly after a Supreme Court opinion is handed down, the Government Printing Office releases a *slip opinion*, the Supreme Court's initial issue; most libraries that have *U.S. Reports* receive slip opinions. At the end of the Court's term, permanently bound volumes replace the slip opinions.

When citing a U.S. Supreme Court opinion, legal authorities prefer the official report (U.S.) alone without parallel citations. For social science purposes, however, it is desirable to include unofficial and official reports. The following are sample citations: Testa v. Katt, 330 U.S. 386 (1947); United States v. Klein, 80 U.S. (13 Wall.) 128 (1872). When citing a case in the body of a text, the case name should not be underlined or placed in italics. When a case name with citation appears in a footnote or bibliographic entry, it should not be underlined or placed in italics (printers treat an underline entry as italics). If the name of the case or a case name and date of the opinion are written in the body of the text, then underline the case name.

United States Supreme Court Reports—Lawyers' Edition (L. Ed.)

United States Supreme Court Reports—Lawyers' Edition, an outstanding private organ, is published by the Lawyers Co-operative Publishing Company and the Bancroft-Whitney Company. It contains all Supreme Court decisions in two series beginning with Volume 1 with accompanying tables of parallel references to the official *United States Reports.* In addition to the opinions rendered in the official reports, the *Lawyers' Edition* contain features valuable to the practicing attorney and student researcher, including summaries of each case with headnotes (syllabi), and abbreviated versions of the briefs of counsel with annotations discussing important legal developments reported in the official cases. For example, the case of Nixon v. Administrator of General Services, 53 L. Ed. 2d 867 (1976) gave rise to an annotation on Bills of Attainder. The twenty-nine-page essay at the back of the volume provides a thorough and current treatment of the topic. Beginning with Volume 32 of the *Second Series,* each volume contains pocket supplements placed at the back cover. This service provides brief summaries of holdings from later Supreme Court decisions making reference to decisions published in the in-hand *L. Ed. 2d* volume. In this way, it is possible to learn how a case just read is treated many years later.

A useful *Desk Book,* which accompanies the *Lawyers' Edition, Second Series,* contains a *Table of Cases* for those instances when the researcher knows only the case name, without benefit of a volume number, page number, and reporter name. By looking up the case name, the researcher can find the parallel legal citations as well as other references keyed to other Lawyers Co-operative Publishing Company material. This annual supplement also contains a *Table of Justices of the Supreme Court,* a *Table of Federal Laws, Rules and Regulations Cited and Construed,* and an *Index to Cases and Annotations* arranged alphabetically by subject matter.

When the Supreme Court is in session, the *Lawyers' Edition* is kept current with the twice-monthly publication of Advance Sheets, which contain the most recent decisions of the Supreme Court with various research aids furnished by the editors. Together with other Lawyers Co-operative publications, the *Lawyers' Edition* becomes an outstanding research tool.

Supreme Court Reporter (S. Ct.)

Supreme Court Reporter, issued by the West Publishing Company, is an unofficial law reporter that contains many of the same features as the *Lawyers' Edition*. For example, headnotes and other references correlate with other West publications. It is also supplemented with semimonthly advance sheets when the Supreme Court is in session. The Court's opinions are first placed in temporary volumes before final publication, making it convenient to access decisions.

Unfortunately, in contrast to the *Lawyers' Edition*, *Supreme Court Reporter* offers one disadvantage: it begins with the Supreme Court's 1882 term and therefore does not contain the cases reported in volumes 1–105 of the official *United States Reports*. Nonetheless, the *Supreme Court Reporter* remains a useful reference.

Briefs Filed with the U.S. Supreme Court

Supreme Court rules require legal counsel to present written arguments, or *briefs*, to support their respective cases. Attorneys file such briefs, which vary from several pages to several hundred pages, with the explicit intent to convince justices how they should decide the case. Briefs contain detailed legal justifications with appropriate citations to existing precedents and extralegal materials in support of client interests.

Supreme Court justices are free to reject any or all the arguments found in the written briefs. Careful reading of briefs and opinions written by justices, however, show that justices often rely on briefs for arguments in support of a given position. Interested third parties may also file *amicus curiae* briefs with the Court to provide material, information, and arguments that assist in decision making.

Researchers use briefs to gain a greater understanding of the issues and possible outcomes in cases than they receive from reading only Court opinions. Because legal counsel commonly presents in writing a wide range of ideas, lines of legal reasoning, and social and political justifications, even when they appear contradictory, briefs of counsel are particularly useful when exploring such addendum. If the researcher is conducting an in-depth study of a particular case, then a careful reading of the submitted briefs will add much to understanding. In addition, it is interesting to note whether the Court accepts, rejects, or ignores the arguments contained in the briefs.

The following citation is an example of how to cite one of the several sources where Supreme Court arguments and briefs can be found: Appellant's

Brief at 112, Roe v. Wade, 410 U.S. 113 (1973), in vol. 75, *Landmark Briefs and Arguments of the Supreme Court of the United States: Constitutional Law*. A discussion of these sources will follow. See Chapter 3 for additional illustrations.

Landmark Briefs and Arguments of the Supreme Court of the United States: Constitutional Law

Before the middle of the nineteenth century, oral arguments were the principal form of advocacy. In 1849, the Supreme Court ruled that counsel could not be heard at oral argument unless they first filed a formal brief.[1] As a result, briefs are not uniformly available for many early cases of the Supreme Court. However, the editors of *Landmark Briefs and Arguments of the Supreme Court of the United States* have made a significant contribution by locating existing briefs including notes and summaries of oral arguments held by the National Archives and private sources.

Landmark Briefs and Arguments of the Supreme Court of the United States: Constitutional Law, edited by University of Chicago law professors Philip B. Kurland and Gerard Casper and published by University Publications of America, Inc., is usually available in law libraries. The first eighty volumes of this impressive work appeared in 1978; by 1986 the set numbered 159 volumes and will continue to grow as additional landmark cases are handed down by the high court. Notable examples of briefs in this set include: *McCulloch v. Maryland* (1819) in Volume 1, *Carter v. Carter Coal Co.* (1936) in Volume 32, *Baker v. Carr* (1962) in Volume 56, and *Garcia v. San Antonio Metropolitan Transit Authority* (1984) in Volume 159.

U.S. Supreme Court Records and Briefs

Unfortunately, the Kurland and Casper work contains briefs and oral arguments of only landmark decisions. To satisfy research needs on lesser decisions, several publishers have made available on microfilm or microfiche *U.S. Supreme Court Records and Briefs*, which begins with cases decided in 1832 and extends to the present day. This work contains the extant briefs and other materials pertinent to each Supreme Court opinion. The following publishers were associated at one time or another with the production of these materials: Congressional Information Service (CIS), Scholarly Resources, Information Handling Services, Microcard Editions Services, and the United States Printing Office. Ask your law librarian to determine whether the briefs of specific research interest are available in microtext format. If a law library

---

[1]Philip K. Kurland and Gerard Casper, eds., *Landmark Briefs and Arguments of the Supreme Court of the United States: Constitutional Law*, 159+ vols. (Washington, D.C.: University Publications of America, Inc., 1978), preface to Vols. 1–4.

has all or some of these materials, hard copy indexes will probably be on hand as well.

Supreme Court of the United States Petitions and Briefs

The Bureau of National Affairs (BNA) publishes *BNA's Law Reprints*. Having begun in 1967, the company publishes in six series *Supreme Court of the United States Petitions and Briefs*, which includes: *criminal law, labor law, securities regulation, tax law, trade regulation,* and *Patent, Trademark and Copyright*. Each series appears in paperback format, and case indexes are available by Court Term (year).

LEXIS

Finally, briefs recently filed before the Supreme Court are accessible through LEXIS, a computer-based legal service (see discussion of computer-based materials at the end of this chapter). Beginning with the October 1979 Term, all brief filings for all Supreme Court cases are on-line.

Lower Federal Court Reports

Until recently, social scientists placed almost exclusive emphasis on decisions of the U.S. Supreme Court. There is a growing awareness, however, that preoccupation with the Court unduly blinds us to how the entire judicial system operates. Besides setting the stage for Supreme Court determination of issues, district courts and courts of appeal deal with issues which, for one reason or another, never are adjudicated by the Supreme Court. Because such decisions may have far reaching policy implications for the political system at large, they should not be ignored. Students must be aware of developments in the inferior federal courts, and should be familiar with the reporter system for federal cases.

Federal Cases (Fed. Cas.)

Before 1880, opinions of the federal district courts and the circuit courts of appeal were scattered through a variety of law reports. In 1880, this situation was remedied when the West Publishing Company reprinted all previously reported federal cases in a thirty-one-volume set named *Federal Cases*. Although cases are usually reported in chronological order, *Federal Cases* is an exception; cases are arranged alphabetically by the name of the case.[2] The following is a sample citation: United States v. Burr, 25 F. Cas. 1 (C.C.D. Kent. 1806) (No. 14,692).

---

[2]J. Myron Jacobstein and Roy M. Mersky. *Fundamentals of Legal Research* (Mineola, NY: The Foundation Press, 1987), p. 34.

Federal Reporter (F.), (F.2d)

Federal Reporter, also published by West Publishing Company, contains decisions of federal courts with appellate jurisdiction other than the U.S. Supreme Court delivered since 1880. In addition, *Federal Reporter* also contains decisions of specialized federal courts having original and appellate jurisdiction. Reported here are the opinions of the following courts: (1) U.S. Court of Appeals (1891–present); (2) U.S. Circuit Court (1880–1912); (3) Commerce Court of the U.S. (1911–1913); (4) U.S. District Courts (1880–1932); (5) U.S. Court of Claims (1929–1932 and 1960–1982); (6) U.S. Court of Customs and Patent Appeals (1929–1982); (7) U.S. States Emergency Court of Appeals (1943–1961); and (8) Temporary Emergency Court of Appeals (1972).[3] The following is a sample citation for decisions of the thirteen judicial bodies which comprise the United States Court of Appeals: Kadala v. Amoco Oil Co., 820 F.2d 1355 (4th Cir. 1987).

Federal Supplement (F. Supp.)

Federal Supplement contains U.S. District Court decisions for the current era (1932–present). There is a minimum of one court with original federal jurisdiction in all fifty states, the District of Columbia, Puerto Rico, Guam, Virgin Islands, and the Northern Mariana Islands. These courts also have local jurisdiction in Guam, Virgin Islands, and Northern Marina Islands. For U.S. District Court opinions before 1932, it is necessary to consult the *Federal Reporter* (1880–1932) and *Federal Cases* (1789–1880).

The *Federal Supplement* also contains decisions of the United States Court of International Trade (formerly named the United States Customs Court), and the decisions of the Judicial Panel on Multi-District Litigation.[4]

The following is a sample citation for a United States District Court opinion: Republic of Philippines v. Marcos, 665 F. Supp. 793 (N.D. Cal. 1987).

There are a few reporters that publish opinions of federal courts unlikely to receive much attention from constitutional law students. First released in 1982, the *United States Claims Court Reporter* contains opinions and speaking orders for the new United States Claims Court, and opinions of the U.S. Courts of Appeals and the Supreme Court on appeal from the U.S. Claims Court. *Federal Rules Decisions* reports cases involving U.S. District Court

---

[3]*West's Law Finder: A Research Manual for Lawyers* (St. Paul: West Publishing Co., 1985), p. 6.

[4]Ibid. Not all or even a majority of the opinions of federal district court judges are reported. But it is believed that opinions dealing with important matters find their way into print. See, Robert A. Carp and C. K. Rowland, *Policymaking and Politics in the Federal District Courts* (Knoxville: University of Tennessee Press, 1983), p. 17.

opinions interpreting the Federal Rules of Civil and Criminal Procedure that are not found in the *Federal Supplement. West's Military Justice Reporter* contains decisions of the United States Court of Military Appeals and the Army, Navy, Air Force, and Coast Guard Courts of Military Review. Finally, on occasion one may find use for the self-explanatory *West's Bankruptcy Reporter*. Opinions published in these reporters should be cited as suggested in each volume by the publisher.

State Court Reporters

The American federal system presupposes that a majority of human relations are governed by the states. Indeed, most legal activity takes place at state and local levels. Although it is true that some federal court cases are first processed through state judicial systems, state courts are important policy making centers independent of the federal judiciary. Some state court systems are generally perceived as trail blazers and are often cited as authority in other American courts. Therefore, a working knowledge of state court reporters is a prerequisite for comprehending policy making in the entire judicial system.

Almost one-half of the states publish their own official court reports. Some have elected to report only opinions of the highest state court while others report all appellate courts and some publish only decisions of trial courts.[5] As part of its National Reporter System, the West Publishing Company has made available state appellate decisions for all the states, and trial court opinions for some states. It divides the nation into seven geographical regions. See Table 1-1 for a listing of each regional reporter describing the states covered with a sample citation for each.

Probably reflecting case volume and market considerations, West Publishing Company also produces two state-specific reporters. First released in 1887, the *New York Supplement* reports all opinions of the New York Court of Appeals, all decisions of the Appellate Division of the Supreme Court, and all opinions of the lower courts of record. In 1960, the *California Reporter* made its debut, reporting all decisions of the California Supreme Court, the California District Courts of Appeal, and the California Supreme Court, Appellate Department.

All West Publishing Company law products contain attractive reference features not found in official government reports. Most importantly, there is the West Key Number System (discussed later in this chapter). All West publications are coordinated to provide an interlocking research network. Mastering this system is not particularly difficult and the payoffs are worth the effort.

---

[5]Jacobstein and Mersky, *Fundamentals of Legal Research,* pp. 684–685.

TABLE 1-1

Reporter	States Covered and Sample Citation
North Western Reporter 1879–1940 (1st series) 1940–present (2d series)	Iowa, Michigan, Minnesota, Nebraska, North Dakota, South Dakota, Wisconsin. General Homes, Inc. v. Tower Insurance Co., 67 Wis. 2d 97, 226 N.W.2d 394 (1975).
Pacific Reporter 1883–1931 (1st series) 1931–present (2d series)	Alaska, Arizona, California, Colorado, Hawaii, Idaho, Kansas, Montana, Nevada, New Mexico, Oklahoma, Oregon, Utah, Washington, Wyoming. Byrd et al. v. Peterson et al., 66 Ariz. 253, 186 P.2d 955 (1947).
Atlantic Reporter 1885–1938 (1st series) 1938–present (2d series)	Connecticut, Delaware, Maine, Maryland, New Hampshire, New Jersey, Pennsylvania, Rhode Island, Vermont, and District of Columbia Municipal Court of Appeals. Adams v. Barrell, 132 A. 130 (Me. 1926).
North Eastern Reporter 1885–1936 (1st series) 1936–present (2d series)	Illinois, Indiana, Massachusetts, New York, Ohio. People v. Savino 44 N.Y.2d 669, 376 N.E.2d 196 (1978).
South Eastern Reporter 1887–1940 (1st series) 1939–present (2d series)	Georgia, North Carolina, South Carolina, Virginia, West Virginia. Greer v. Greer, 128 S.E.2d 51 (Ga. 1962).
Southern Reporter 1887–1940 (1st series) 1940–present (2d series)	Alabama, Florida, Louisiana, Mississippi. Long v. Woollard, 163 So.2d 698 (Miss. 1964).
South Western Reporter 1886–1940 (1st series) 1940–present (2d series)	Arkansas, Kentucky, Missouri, Tennessee, Texas, Indian Territory. Hunt v. State, 48 S.W.2d 466 (Tx. 1932).

American Law Reports (ALR)

American Law Reports does not neatly fit the description of a court reporter. Although it contains judicial decisions, its primary function extends beyond the reporting of court opinions and is best employed as an excellent annotation elaborating on important judicial opinions.

Published by a Lawyers Co-operative and Bancroft-Whitney publication, the *American Law Reports*, in fact, is a highly selective case reporter. The editors choose for inclusion those cases that illustrate important legal developments. An impartial treatment of the law relevant to the particular case follows each judicial opinion. Each annotation includes a detailed treatise on the specific legal topic that discusses the inception, development, and contemporary applicability of the law relating to the reported judicial opinions.

First published in 1919, *American Law Reports* is now in its fifth series. The first series covers the period from 1919 to 1948 and contains 175 volumes. The second series (ALR 2d) deals with legal topics for 1948 to 1965 and appears in one hundred volumes. The third series (ALR 3d) contains both state and federal topics from 1965 to 1969, but from 1969 to 1979 deals only with state law topics. Introduced in 1980, the fourth series (ALR 4th) covers state topics only. The fifth series (ALR *Federal*) reports only federal law topics beginning in 1969[6] and is the most useful series for those conducting research on contemporary federal law issues and constitutional law matters. However, it is unwise to ignore the other series, especially when research entails historical analysis.

Until recently, the research process was complicated by the existence of several indexes for each *ALR* series. As a result, researchers were often compelled to consult more than one of the indexes and sometimes all of them to be certain they had discovered pertinent cases and annotations. In 1986, however, this awkward situation was remedied by the publication of a five volume *Index to Annotations*, which provides a unified treatment of annotations to most of the *ALR* system. The comprehensive A–Z index is arranged around significant words and facts.[7]

Each constitutional law topic follows a similar format. First, the summary of the court decision is followed by headnotes, abbreviated briefs of counsel, and the court opinion. An annotation, written by a legal expert, explains the opinion of the court. Readers are also provided with information about related legal matters. Finally, the article indicates the location of additional analyses with references to other Lawyers Co-operative Publishing Company publications and law review articles.

The *ALR* series can save the researcher considerable time and effort. However, for those interested in locating a large body of cases, the West National Reporter System is probably the superior tool. While the editors of the Lawyers Co-operative Company do provide an excellent treatment for selected cases, the West Publishing Company has elected to provide more cases without elaborate editorial annotations. A sample citation for an *American Law Reports* annotation is: Annot., 5 A.L.R. 4th 708 (1981).

Keeping Current

Persons interested in legal topics should be aware of recent developments in constitutional law. However, keeping abreast of recent developments involves a concentrated and comprehensive effort.

---

[6]*The Living Law 1987–1988: A Guide to Modern Legal Research* (The Lawyers Co-operative Publishing Company and Bancroft-Whitney Company, 1987). p. 18.
[7]Ibid.. p. 28.

Newspapers and other media are the most obvious sources for accurate and current information about legal developments. For example, *The New York Times* and a growing number of leading newspapers often print the entire text or at least substantial parts of important Supreme Court opinions, but these are the exceptions. Most newspapers print summaries that are provided by news services and often edited by local newspapers reflecting space and cost considerations. The result is often misleading information. The different electronic media, although they employ highly qualified personnel, often present misleading coverage due primarily to the short time allocated for such coverage, and often confuse dicta pronouncements for rules of law.

Newspapers specializing in legal and business news are available, however. The *Chicago Daily Bulletin*, the *Los Angeles Daily Journal*, and the *New York Law Journal* are notable examples of large-circulation legal newspapers that provide daily information of particular importance for the practicing bar. Information about court calendars, changes in court rules, classified advertisements, and stories on members of the bench and bar are common features. These newspapers also print important court opinions of wide interest to the readership. The *Legal Times* and the *National Law Journal* are weekly newspapers with a national circulation, and *The American Lawyer* is a monthly publication also with a national readership.

Because legal newspapers are sources of current information on court opinions they are useful for staying current with court developments. However, from a social science perspective, these newspapers can be used to understand the sociology and politics of the legal profession. Legal newspapers will provide insight into what motivates lawyers, professional priorities, and bar stratification.

Many of the leading legal newspapers are indexed in the standard indexes to legal periodicals discussed later in this chapter. Libraries typically keep back copies of newspapers for no more than a few weeks. However, thanks to microtext technologies, it is possible to access wanted stories through microfiche. The following is a sample citation for newspaper articles: Charley Roberts, "Public Interest Law By Conservatives Enjoys Resurgence," *Los Angeles Daily Journal*, 2 December, 1988, p. 6.

Caution is advised when accepting news stories as accurate presentations of the action that occurs in courtrooms. It pays to read a court decision yourself. Unfortunately, it may take weeks or months to obtain a copy of a court decision. To circumvent this problem, read *United States Law Week*, *U.S. Supreme Court Bulletin*, or *West's Federal Case News*.

U.S. Law Week (U.S.L.W.)

U.S. Law Week, a publication of the Bureau of National Affairs, Inc., is a weekly looseleaf service designed to keep readers current. Its general features include: (1) a summary and analysis of new law and leading court cases of the preceding week, (2) new court decisions reported earlier than any of the court reporters, (3) full text of federal statutes of general interest, and (4) a general news section providing readers with advance notice of developments in pending or proposed legislation, administrative regulations, and litigation.

U.S. Law Week is divided into two parts: "General" and "Supreme Court." The special binder devoted to the Supreme Court includes among its features:

1. full text and digests of Court opinions;
2. Supreme Court docket information;
3. orders granting or denying appellate review;
4. summaries of significant oral argument; and
5. summer issues, usually in July and August, that analyze the work of the Court during the preceding term.

Both the "General" and "Supreme Court" parts include a topical descriptive index and a table of cases which are easy to use. A sample citation to a case read in *U.S. Law Week* is: Richardson v. Marsh, 55 U.S.L.W. 4510 (April 21, 1987).

U.S. Law Week is more than a valuable aid in keeping current on Supreme Court decisions, however. The oral argument feature is particularly useful in gaining insight into the nature of judicial argument. Because justices regularly interrupt attorneys during oral argument with questions and comments which Court observers interpret as clues to probable patterns of judicial voting and case outcomes, oral arguments can reveal conflicts and problems the Court may be having with the respective case. While presentations of oral arguments here are not transcripts of proceedings but well-done summaries composed by editors, they are faithful renditions nonetheless. If a researcher wants to read the unvarnished record, then consult *The Complete Oral Arguments of the Supreme Court of the United States*, published by University Publications of America, Inc. First issued with the 1953 Supreme Court term and continued to the present, full transcripts of existing oral arguments are available on microfiche. A helpful looseleaf index is available at most law libraries. *Landmark Briefs and Arguments of the Supreme Court of the United States: Constitutional Law*, by Kurland and Casper, also contains transcripts of oral arguments.

U.S. Supreme Court Bulletin (S. Ct. Bull.)

U.S. Supreme Court Bulletin, published by Commerce Clearing House, Inc., is a topical publication that features newly decided opinions. In fact, the publisher usually sends the opinions to its subscribers on the day the Court issues them. This service contains indexes to the Court's opinions and to its docket, a table of cases, a status table, and it also reproduces and indexes the

Rules of the Supreme Court. Finally, each issue features a *Report Letter* which contains summaries of Court opinions and other pertinent matters affecting constitutional law. The following is a sample citation of a U.S. Supreme Court opinion reported in the *U.S. Supreme Court Bulletin:* Honig v. Doe, 48 CCH S. Ct. Bull. p.B606 (Jan. 20, 1988).

West's Federal Case News

West's Federal Case News, a new weekly publication in pamplet form, promises to be a helpful aid in keeping up with current developments. *West's Federal Case News* summarizes the latest federal cases even before they are published in regular advance sheets. Each federal court jurisdiction, including the U.S. Supreme Court, is in a different section. By reading several paragraphs, one can quickly decide whether a newly decided case is worthy of further attention. Besides summaries of federal cases, it also contains summaries of leading cases from state courts, and congressional and administrative highlights.

Legal Encyclopedias

Encyclopedias are elementary research tools commonly employed by students. Yet most students are unaware that legal encyclopedias are available and represent a convenient research tool for those interested in legal questions.

Legal encyclopedias are of three varieties: general, local, and specialized. For constitutional law students, general and specialized encyclopedias are most useful. Local law and most special subject encyclopedias are of particular interest to legal practitioners. Local law encyclopedias cover the case and statutory law of specific state jurisdictions. Unfortunately, fewer than a third of the fifty states have them. Special subject encyclopedias contain comprehensive discussions of specific legal topics, for example, automobiles, private corporations, evidence, and constitutional law.

The four general encyclopedias commonly held by law libraries include: *The Guide to American Law: Everyone's Legal Encyclopedia*, the *Encyclopedia of the American Judicial System, American Jurisprudence 2d (Am. Jur. 2d)*, and *Corpus Juris Secundum (C.J.S.)*. Published in 1983, *The Guide to American Law* was created explicitly for laypersons. The remaining two general encyclopedias are designed and marketed for attorney use. *American Jurisprudence 2d* replaces *American Jurisprudence*, and *Corpus Juris Secundum* likewise supersedes the old *Corpus Juris*. All law-related encyclopedias are publications of private companies that employ subject experts to write on various topics, and are not official government documents.

For the most part, encyclopedia articles on general or specific legal topics differ from legal treatises or articles appearing in legal periodicals in that there is no overt attempt to argue the merits of particular legal rules or principles. Unless otherwise indicated, the writers attempt to present clear, concise, and *objective* statements on the law of a particular topic or law-related matter. For laypersons, *The Guide to American Law* is an excellent first source in the research process. Both *Am. Jur. 2d* and *C. J. S.* are also appropriate tools for beginning research into a specific legal question when the emphasis is on understanding legal rules. Besides an exposition on the law, the topical discussions have cross-references to other legal research materials including, for example, cases, digests, statutory provisions, and annotations. Researchers should go from the encyclopedia exposition to the other-cited sources for a complete understanding of the subject matter.

The Guide to American Law: Everyone's Legal Encyclopedia

The Guide to American Law: Everyone's Legal Encyclopedia, produced by West Publishing Company, is a twelve-volume set containing essays on a variety of law and law-related topics. Because it cultivates the nonspecialist audience, it is ideal for college students in the liberal arts. Containing over 500 signed articles, it covers legal topics not likely to be of direct interest to students of constitutional law—for example, canon law, Privy Council, and Marxist jurisprudence—yet it contains many essays directly relevant to the subject matter with topics ranging from "Abortion" to "Impeachment" to "Earl Warren."

Volume 12, which contains a Quotation Index by Topic, Author Index, Name Index, and a Subject Index, also features a Table of Cases Cited and a Special Topics List. In 1987, the publisher introduced a *Yearbook* that functions as an integrated up-to-date accompaniment to the set. *The Guide to American Law* is found in general purpose college, city, and law libraries. A sample citation is: *The Guide to American Law*, s.v. "Apportionment," by Robert B. McKay.

Encyclopedia of the American Judicial System

The *Encyclopedia of the American Judicial System*, published in 1987 by Charles Scribner's Sons, is a comprehensive, three-volume reference work on all aspects of the legal system. Students of constitutional law and judicial process will find this set particularly useful for beginning their research. Covered are such broad generic topics as legal history, substantive law, institutions and personnel, process and behavior, constitutional law and issues, and methodology. There is a comprehensive, seventy-five-page index. A sample citation is: *Encyclopedia of the American Judicial System*, s.v. "The Burger Court and Era," by Richard Funston.

American Jurisprudence 2d (Am. Jur. 2d)

American Jurisprudence 2d is a discussion of both substantive and procedural aspects of American law arranged under more than 430 headings. This encyclopedia emphasizes federal statutory law and procedural rules, and although detailed references to state laws are few, *Am. Jur. 2d* does make extensive references to the *Uniform State Laws*.

Volumes are arranged alphabetically by title. For researchers already familiar with a particular legal topic, access is easy. Abstracts and subject outlines precede the exposition of each legal topic. By reading the brief abstract and perusing the subject outline, the researcher can easily determine if he or she has turned to the appropriate discussion. This method, however, presupposes a sophistication sometimes lacking in undergraduate students. If necessary, refer to the *General Index* for locating the subject matter of interest.

Using the eight-volume *General Index* involves simple procedures. For example, assume that a student wants to research housing discrimination for a course in civil rights, which may be the first topic that comes to mind. Turning to the index item, "Civil Rights," appearing in Volume C, page 276, of the *General Index*, the researcher finds the entry: "Housing Laws and Urban Redevelopment, (this index)." The researcher then knows that the topic of housing discrimination is most likely contained under this heading and, turning to this index item, he or she will find the topic. Of course, one could have avoided this initial effort by having more carefully specified the subject of interest. If the researcher had focused immediately on the subject, housing discrimination, he or she would have turned to the *General Index*, Volume F-1. On page 855 of this particular index is the entry: "Housing Laws and Urban Redevelopment," with the subheading entry, "discrimination." One will also find a subheading termed, "generally, . . ." Immediately below this entry are 34 additional subheadings. If the researcher begins the search with a broad or a specific subject category in mind, and does not locate the topic immediately, he or she should use the available cross-referencing for easy access to substantive discussions of law.

Having located the correct subject entry in the *General Index*, the researcher then turns to the appropriate volume of *Am. Jur. 2d*. For the case of housing discrimination, there is a general discussion under Civ. R. §§ 249–256. Most will immediately realize that the abbreviation "*Civ. R.*" refers to Civil Rights. For more difficult or uncommon abbreviations, consult the "Table of Abbreviations" appearing at the front of each copy of the *General Index*. The symbol (§) refers to the section under Civil Rights where the discussion of the topic is found. Thus Volume 15 of *Am. Jur. 2d* contains materials ranging in alphabetical order from Charities to Civil Rights. Turning to §§ 249–256 under "Civil Rights" there is a discussion of housing discrimination, beginning on page 775 and ending on page 797.

The legal exposition contains extensive references to original source material such as statutes, executive orders, and case law. Secondary sources are also cited including annotations to the *American Law Reports*. *American Jurisprudence 2d* is especially useful in obtaining a general overview of the law on a particular subject. Students will want to consult additional research materials often cited in this encyclopedia.

Most publishers who market research tools for practicing attorneys keep their publications up-to-date. Each *Am. Jur. 2d* topic is written with current legal issues in mind. However, the legal environment will change and so each volume is updated annually by cumulative pocket supplements. Always check these supplements for new materials. In addition, there is a special binder volume of *Am. Jur. 2d* called *The New Topic Service*, which provides discussions of new laws developed after publication of the volume in which they would have appeared. Finally, as the law changes replacement volumes are published so that the *Am. Jur. 2d* set is constantly undergoing change, allowing researchers to be reasonably certain that they are aware of recent developments in the law. A sample citation is: 15 AM. JUR. 2D *Civil Rights* §250 (1976).

Corpus Juris Secundum (C.J.S.)

Corpus Juris Secundum is a massive statement of U.S. case law. It has 101 numbered volumes with many more the actual total—lettered volumes (for example, 29A) are added to numbered volumes when the editors decide to expand treatments on given topics. This encyclopedia features over 400 separate titles, many of which are specifically labeled "constitutional law," and a five-volume *General Index*.

Included in *C.J.S.* are references to reported cases decided as long ago as the mid-seventeenth century and extensive references to state as well as federal law. Each subject essay is made current with an annual pocket supplement found at the back of each bound volume. Whole volumes are occasionally replaced with totally updated versions.

Written primarily for practicing attorneys, the publisher (West Publishing Company) has devised time-saving methods for finding the law on any given subject. However, the use of these methods presupposes a general knowledge of law not usually possessed by undergraduates. Yet by using elementary techniques similar to those described for *Am. Jur. 2d*, any student can successfully use this impressive encyclopedia.

First, consult the five-volume *General Index*, which lists all topics alphabetically. Beginning with the most general title, researchers can then proceed to locate a more specific subtitle. The *General Index* is designed to be used in close conjunction with the indexes to each *C.J.S.* subject matter title. Therefore, before turning to the specific subject essay, it is advisable to examine carefully the *Analysis* which appears at the beginning of each subject title. Consult the appropriate volume of the encyclopedia itself for a detailed description of the subject matter discussion contained therein.

The *Analysis* provides a brief description of a topic and an outline of its related parts. By studying this aid, students can acquire an overview of the subject matter and how the specific research topic fits into the general legal framework. In addition to legal essays, each volume contains its own index. Moreover, at the back of each volume is an index to words, phrases, and legal maxims found there with dictionary-type definitions.

A simple example illustrates the research procedure. In a course on the criminal justice system the question arises of whether prison officials may search inmate mail. Because no one knows the answer to the question, the instructor asks one of the students to investigate and report his or her findings to the class at its next meeting.

Turning to the *General Index M–Q*, the student finds "Prisons" beginning on page 777 and ending on page 783. Since there are many subheadings, it is necessary to narrow the investigation further. On page 782 the researcher finds: "Searches and seizures, prisoners' mail, Searches §30," and turns from the *General Index* to the appropriate subject matter volume. Since "Searches" falls alphabetically within Volume 79—"Schools, etc. 323 to End Sessions," one finds "Searches," with §30 located on page 798. Directly under the title heading, in bold print, there is a brief statement on the general rule of law. A paragraph follows explaining applications of the rule with citations to a number of state and federal cases. In addition the student carefully checks the *Cumulative Annual Pocket Part* for updated references and analyses. Because the researcher has also taken the time to consult the *Analysis* under "Searches and Seizures," he or she can discuss searches of prisoners' mail within the general context of search and seizure law. The following is a sample citation: 79 C.J.S. *Searches and Seizures* §30 (1952).

Encyclopedia of the American Constitution

Encyclopedia of the American Constitution, a four-volume set for laypersons, was published by Macmillan in time for the Bicentennial celebration of the United States Constitution. It contains over 2,000 original signed articles by 262 distinguished contributors.

The scope and organization of this specialized encyclopedia permit students to access information on the history of the Constitution, its concepts and terms, U.S. Supreme Court cases, biographical data on its authors, and public acts helpful for understanding the basic document. Thus, researchers can find entries, for example, on the Constitutional Convention of 1787, the infamous *Dred Scott* case, Sandra Day O'Connor, and the Sherman Antitrust Act.

Encyclopedia of the American Constitution offers a variety of indexes to consult, including an *Index of Subjects, Index of Names*, and an *Index of*

Cases. A sample citation is: *Encyclopedia of the American Constitution,* s.v. "Commercial Speech," by Benno C. Schmidt, Jr.

Codes

Codes are systematic compilations of statutes made by legislators. To avoid duplication and ambiguity, statutory law is codified in its various parts. Codification is helpful because it permits access to the law of particular subjects quickly and efficiently. Also, just as the situation for case law, statutory law is initially arranged chronologically rather than by subject matter. These compilations are a valuable research tool for students interested in public law. In particular, the annotated codes are useful because they contain illuminating statutory histories and judicial interpretations.

In the United States there are federal, state, and municipal codes that contain texts of pertinent statutes, constitutions, legislative histories, annotations to judicial decisions, various tables, and useful indexes. When investigating constitutional rights guaranteed by states, state and municipal codes are useful. For example, the Illinois School Code contains within one volume all the statutory rules governing the operations of the state's complicated school system. These prescriptions and proscriptions include due process rights, such as those attendant to school board personnel hearings. Although such state and municipal codes may be useful depending upon one's research topic, they are analogous in form to the various federal codes, and so only codes dealing with federal law will be considered here.

While codes are arranged by subject matter, they are also compilations of statutory laws in chronological sequence. As a result, when a legislative bill becomes a law it is initially found in a place other than an appropriate subject matter code. Where might these laws be found?

When a bill becomes a law, the United States Government Printing Office issues it as a *slip law,* which is available at government depository and other libraries around the country. Private publishers also print slip laws; these are available at most law libraries. At the end of each session of Congress, the slip laws are republished in the *United States Statutes at Large,* which arranges numerically all laws enacted since the first Congress in 1789. Because each volume contains a subject index, it is possible to look up bills on a given subject. However, if a researcher wants to know a law on a particular subject and no code is available, it is conceivable that the researcher would begin with the first session of the first Congress in 1789 and proceed through each volume noting changes, modifications, repeals, expirations, and superseded laws through the years—an extremely onerous and unnecessary task. Codes greatly simplify the search.

There currently exist three widely available federal codes: The *United States Code, 1988 Edition (U.S.C.)* is the official statement of the law. The

United States Code Service (U.S.C.S.) and the *United States Code Annotated (U.S.C.A.)* are products of private companies, and both possess features not available in the official *United States Code*.

United States Code (U.S.C.)

Every six years Congress causes the publication of a new edition of this official code for laws of the United States, with cumulative supplements available for the intervening years. The Code arranges U.S. laws under 50 separate titles, including: Title 2, the *Congress*, Title 18, *Crimes and Criminal Procedure*, and Title 49, *Transportation*. The titles are further subdivided into subtitles, parts, chapters, subchapters, and sections. The extensive multivolume *General Index* to the *U.S. Code* permits researchers to locate the statutory law in codified form quickly. A sample citation for the *United States Code* is: 18 U.S.C. §1028(a) (1982).

United States Code Service (U.S.C.S.)

The *United States Code Service* is even more useful. Among its many features are the exact language from the *Statutes at Large*, legislative histories, annotations of interpretive case law, and references to pertinent law review articles. A six-volume *General Index* is accompanied by a looseleaf *Update Service*. This set also contains an excellent four-volume annotation of the U.S. Constitution. Supplements inserted at the back of each volume keep the entire set current.

Editors have arranged *U.S.C.S.* exactly as the official *U.S.C.* For example, the codification of law dealing with federal crimes and criminal procedure are in Title 18 of both the official *U.S.C.* and the unofficial *U.S.C.S.* Because most students are too unfamiliar with the various official titles to turn directly to the code when beginning their research, it is advisable to consult the *General Index* first. If the researcher knows the popular name of a law, however,—for example, the Taft-Hartley Act—then consult the special volume index containing popular names.

What makes *U.S.C.S.* particularly useful are the extensive research aids. It contains the text of the statutory law, makes reference to amendments, and features a complete research guide. For example, it points out the location in the legal encyclopedia *American Jurisprudence 2d* of a related discussion. Its many annotations also discuss how the law has been construed by judicial bodies. An attractive feature is its bibliographic reference to law review articles on the various topics.

For students of constitutional law, the four volumes containing the Constitution's articles and amendments provide an extensive research guide. These volumes contain many of the same research aids as in the code. Under the Nineteenth Amendment, for instance, one finds the exact wording of the constitutional provision, cross references, a research guide, annotated references to court cases, and statutory law. In addition, there are interpretative notes and references to germane law review articles. *United States Code Service* also contains volumes on court rules including, for example, the Federal Rules of Civil Procedure, the Federal Rules of Criminal Procedure, the Rules of the U.S. Supreme Court, the Rules of the Courts of Appeal, and the Administrative Rules of Procedure. Students assigned the task of writing a paper on particular constitutional provisions will find the special features of this Lawyers Co-operative and Bancroft Whitney publication valuable. A sample citation is: 18 U.S.C.S. §3661 (Law. Co-op. 1988).

United States Code Annotated (U.S.C.A.)

The *United States Code Annotated (U.S.C.A.)*, produced by West Publishing Company, features pertinent statutory law with annotations to judicial interpretations. Collateral references to many other West Publishing Company products are a secondary feature. This fine set also contains an annual multivolume index and a ten-volume treatment covering the provisions of the U.S. Constitution. As with *U.S.C.S.*, the best way to research a statutory topic employing *U.S.C.A.* is to consult the *General Index* or the *Popular Name Table* found in the last volume of the *General Index*.

Students interested in bringing their research up-to-date should consult the pocket supplements placed at the back of each volume. Students should also inspect the *Supplementary Pamphlet* for each title when made available by the publisher. Finally, when it is important to treat the subject in a current fashion, consult the last published pamphlet of the *U.S. Code Congressional and Administrative News*, which cumulates the changes in U.S. statutory law since the last publication of the *U.S.C.A.* pocket supplements and the latest *Supplementary Pamphlet*. A sample citation is: 2 U.S.C.A. §441(b) (West 1988 Supp. Pamph.).

Administrative Agency Reporting

Government agencies, bureaus, commissions, districts, and offices exert considerable authority in the regulation of most aspects of life. Whether it is the protection of the physical environment from air pollution, the payment of social security benefits, or the issuances of marriage licenses, administrative agencies possess considerable authority. Administrative law consists of the norms creating and governing public bureaucracies, the rules and regulations made by these entities, and the judicial review exercised by courts that define and limit agency discretion.[8]

---

[8]H. B. Jacobini, Albert P. Melone, and Carl Kalvelage, *Research Essentials of Administrative Law* (Pacific Palisades, CA: Palisades Publishers, 1983), p. 1.

Administrative rules and regulations do not appear in court reports. However, these materials are accessible and available through the U.S. government and private publishing companies. Students wishing an overview of the many printed materials should consult H. B. Jacobini, Albert P. Melone, and Carl Kalvelage's, *Research Essentials of Administrative Law* (Pacific Palisades, CA: Palisades Publishers, 1983). Two government publications with which students need to be familiar are the *Federal Register* and the *Code of Federal Regulations*.

Federal Register

The *Federal Register* has published on a daily basis all federal administrative rules and regulations since 1936.[9] Ordering materials chronologically, the *Federal Register* contains newly adopted rules and regulations, notice of proposed regulations and rules, dates of administrative hearings, and decisions of administrative bodies. It also contains presidential executive orders and proclamations. It is indexed monthly, quarterly, and annually.

Code of Federal Regulations (C.F.R.)

Because it is arranged chronologically and not by subject, the *Federal Register* is practically impossible to use when attempting to ascertain rules and regulations by subject matter or agency. The *Federal Register* must be used with the *Code of Federal Regulations*, which is arranged under fifty separate titles and published annually in pamphlet form. Revised each year C.F.R. enables the researcher to learn which rules and regulations are currently in force. C.F.R. also contains an easy to use annual index accompanied by monthly updates.

Therefore, when attempting to update rules and regulations, use the *Code of Federal Regulations* together with the daily *Federal Register*. After consulting the annual C.F.R. index, look at the monthly cumulative issue entitled, *LSA: List of CFR Sections Affected*. This procedure will provide the researcher with an up-to-date account for the year and month. Because rules and regulations are altered and promulgated daily, it is necessary to find the latest possible changes. To do so, turn to the most recent daily issue of the *Federal Register* and examine the section titled, "Cumulative List of Parts Affected." This research procedure will yield a complete and current understanding of agency rules and regulations.

---

[9]For a history and full explanation of the *Federal Register* system see: National Archives and Records Service, General Services Administration, *The Federal Register: What it is and How to Use it*, rev. ed. (Washington, D.C.: Government Printing Office, 1978).

Digests

It is usually impressive when an attorney rattles off numerous precedents in support of a client's claim. Did the attorney spend the many hours necessary to locate all those cases? A digest is a research tool designed to access cases on a particular legal topic without having to read all reported cases in American law. Obviously, the ability to use a digest can ease the research process and lead to an up-to-date and thorough presentation.

A digest provides brief abstracts of the facts or holdings in a case. Digests are also valuable because court opinions are reported chronologically. A digest, however, is not like an encyclopedia and does not present a full legal narrative with accompanying footnotes. Because a digest acts as a subject index to reported cases, identifying only cases that deal with particular facts or legal problems, it is necessary to read and analyze the full court opinions.

Digests are available to fit a variety of needs. A national digest is available if a researcher wants to know all the reported cases in the United States on a given topic. If a researcher is interested in a particular part of the country, then regional digests are appropriate tools. Digests also exist for a number of state jurisdictions. Finally, there are digests which cover particular court systems.

Because digests are such a useful research tool, it is necessary to examine the digest system for all of American law, and specialized court systems of interest to constitutional law scholars. The regional and state digests are segments of the national digest system, and are used in the same way.

American Digest System

The *American Digest System*, a massive work consisting of over 430 volumes, classifies by subject all reported cases appearing in the *National Reporter System*. The first set in this system, the *Century Digest*, covers the period from 1685 to 1896. For each succeeding ten-year period there are decennial digests from the *First Decennial* (1897–1906) to the *Ninth Decennial* (1976–1986, Parts 1 and 2). The *General Digest*, a monthly bound supplement to the last *Decennial*, should be used if a complete enumeration of pertinent cases is desirable. In other words, use the *General Digest* as an updating service beginning in 1987. All the abstracted cases are ordered according to the West Publishing Company's "Key Number System."

Key Number System   The "Key Number System" is a scheme for assigning cases or sections of cases to appropriate subject categories. This system first divides the law into seven main classes. Each class is then divided into subclasses and each subclass is further divided into topics. Finally, each topic is divided into subtopics to which a key number—not a word label—is assigned.[10] By first identifying the appropriate topic and key number, the researcher can locate all known reported cases on a specific legal topic during a particular time period. In fact, by going through each *Decennial* and *General Digest*, it is possible to identify all the reported cases known to the publisher on a given topic. Two indexes to the "Key Number System" are best suited for layperson use: the *Table of Cases Index* and the *Descriptive-Word Index*.

An example is provided to describe how to use the *Table of Cases Index*. After reading the Supreme Court's decision in *Griswold v. Connecticut* (1965), the researcher may become interested in the right to privacy. Among other things, the researcher may want to identify all the cases dealing with the constitutional protection of privacy. Each *Decennial* and *General Digest* contains an alphabetical listing of cases by plaintiff, for example, Griswold. Since *Griswold v. Connecticut* was decided in 1965, the correct reference is the *Table of Cases Index* for the *Seventh Decennial*. By looking up *Griswold v. Connecticut* the researcher can find its legal citation and the various Topic and Key Numbers under which the case is digested. After deciding upon the appropriate Topic and Key Number, the researcher need only consult each *Decennial* and *General Digest* for a complete abstract of all reported cases under the selected Topic and Key Number.

Although the *Descriptive-Word Index* sometimes provides a quicker method for locating Topics and Key Numbers than the case index approach, it requires more thought. There is a separate *Descriptive-Word Index* for each unit of the *Decennials* and *General Digest*. By thinking of a catch word, a researcher may consult this index to determine whether there is such an entry. For this example, "privacy" is an obvious catch word for cases involving the doctrine found in *Griswold v. Connecticut*. Selecting the right word usually proves more difficult, however. But because there are hundreds of word entries, the researcher can try additional catch words until one finds the appropriate entry.

It must be reemphasized that the West Publishing Company has devised a variety of ways to find cases, but their methods were created for those who have had legal training, not undergraduate students. Use the tables of cases and the descriptive word indexes because these tools require little advanced legal training. Although the "Key Number System" may seem difficult to comprehend at first, working with the material builds confidence.

---

[10]*West's Law Finder*, pp. 16–18; Jacobstein and Mersky, *Fundamentals of Legal Research*, pp. 65–66.

Specialized Digests

As previously indicated, the West Publishing Company also publishes several regional, state, and federal digests.[11] It is important to note that each of these more specialized digests is a segment of the *American Digest System*. Therefore, if the researcher has access to the parent *American Digest System*, there is no great need to consult the specialized digests. Sometimes, reflecting academic interests, college or university libraries will have one or more of the specialized digests and not the extensive *American Digest System*. Students of constitutional law will find the *Federal Practice Digest* and the *U.S. Supreme Court Digest* well suited for most research purposes.

Federal Practice Digest   There are four sets of digests produced by West Publishing Company which index only federal court opinions. All use the "Key Number System." Because this series includes all reported federal opinions of the ninety-four U.S. District Courts, the thirteen U.S. Courts of Appeals, and the U.S. Supreme Court, it is a valuable aid to those interested in ascertaining the known corpus juris of the federal judicial system.[11] The special features of the *Federal Practice Digest* include entries indicating whether a case has been affirmed, reversed, or modified, and references to secondary sources such as *Corpus Juris Secundum*.

Federal Practice Digest 3d indexes cases since 1975 to the present day. *Federal Practice Digest 2d* indexes case from 1961 to 1975. For earlier cases (1939–1961), consult *Modern Federal Practice Digest*. For all opinions before 1930, the *Federal Digest* is available. The series is made current by *Cumulative Pocket Parts* and by subsequent pamphlet supplements.

U.S. Supreme Court Digest (West Publishing Company)   The *U.S. Supreme Court Digest*, indexes only decisions of the U.S. Supreme Court. It uses the "Key Number System" and duplicates the cases found in the *American Digest System* and the four sets comprising the *Federal Practice Digest*. In addition, it is brought up-to-date by cumulative annual pocket supplements. Comprising over 30 volumes, this set is ideal for research projects requiring the identification of only U.S. Supreme Court decisions.

U.S. Supreme Court Reports Digest: Lawyers' Edition   *U.S. Supreme Court Reports: Lawyers' Edition Digest* is a publication of the Lawyers Co-operative and Bancroft-Whitney Publishing Company, the same firm that issues *United States Supreme Court Reports—Lawyers' Edition, American*

---

[11]The regional digests correspond to the regional reporter system of the West Publishing Company. The regional digests are: *Atlantic Digest, North Western Digest, Pacific Digest, South Eastern Digest* and *Southern Digest*. Some include second series digests.

Law Reports, American Jurisprudence 2d, and *United States Code Service.* Because it is not a West Publishing Company product it does not use the "Key-Number System." Nonetheless, because *U.S. Supreme Court Reports Digest* contains both a *Table of Cases* and a *Word Index,* it is easy to use.

The *Table of Cases* lists U.S. Supreme Court decisions under both plaintiff and defendant names as well as the popular names by which cases are sometimes known. Below the alphabetical listing for each case, there is a full case citation, followed by the digest topic and section number(s). Instead of proceeding directly to the digest topic and number designation, it is advisable to consult first the scope-note and outline preceding each topic title. The scope-notes define the nature of each topic which enables researchers to determine whether they have chosen correctly. For example, the case of *Abrams v. U.S.* has four different digest topics: Appeal and Error, Constitutional Law, Criminal Law, and Evidence. As is common for all digests, the editors abstract cases under many different topics. The researcher can choose the topic title of greatest research interest by consulting the scope-notes and outlines before reading each of the digest entries. By doing so, effective researchers save time and considerable effort.

Use the *Word Index* to *U.S. Supreme Court Reports Digest: Lawyers' Edition* in the same way as West Publishing Company's *Descriptive Word Index.* Simply attempt to think of those catch words which best describe the pertinent subject matter. With practice, the researcher may find this method preferable to the *Table of Cases* approach.

In addition to the abstracts of each Supreme Court case, the editors have included references to the *Am. Jur.* series and to annotations pertinent to the case. As a result, this digest is used easily with other Lawyers Co-operative publications.

Volume 17 of this numbered twenty-volume set contains several features particularly valuable to constitutional law students. First, each article, section, and clause of the Constitution appears with digest references. For example, listed under article 1, section 8, clause 3 (the commerce clause), is the digest reference: Commerce §§1–360. In this way, all Supreme Court opinions dealing with the commerce clause are readily identified.

In Volume 17 is a second useful feature: the *Revised Rules of the Supreme Court of the United States.* It answers such common questions as what constitutes a Court quorum, or what rules govern the granting of the writ of certiorari. This *Rules* section also includes a research guide with references to the *U.S. Supreme Court Reports Digest: Lawyers' Edition,* and *American Jurisprudence 2d.*

As with most legal research material, the *U.S. Supreme Court Reports Digest: Lawyers' Edition* is brought up-to-date by pocket supplements inserted at the back of each bound volume. Always consult the supplements.

Citators

A citator is an additional research tool designed to determine the extent to which cases have been cited by subsequent court opinions, or used in concurring or dissenting opinions. By using a citator, it is possible to quickly determine the status of a rule of law.

The attorney needs a citator for an obvious reason: to argue a case from a precedent that has long been overruled or modified would, most certainly, jeopardize the client's standing in the eyes of the court. Although professional consequences differ, the researcher and teacher of constitutional law also need to know the standing of legal opinions. For example, if after reading Minersville School District v. Gobitis 310 U.S. 586 (1940) a student concludes that compulsory flag salutes are constitutionally permissible, he or she would surely be wrong. In West Virginia State Board of Education v. Barnette 319 U.S. 624 (1943), the Supreme Court overruled its 1940 decision. Using a citator would have prevented this gross error.

Citators, like digests, are aids in locating opinions with similar subject matter, because the editors of citators list a case whenever an opinion writer cites it. The citator will pinpoint the exact page of those cases which cite the main case as precedent. However, caution is advised when using citators for this purpose. Jurists sometimes cite a case to make a point on a minor issue. Opinion writers do not always cite opinions particularly germane to their argument. Indeed, some cases they cite may be highly debatable precedent. Therefore, researchers should understand that the listed cases may be only tangentially related to the topic at hand. For this reason, a digest is more appropriate for finding cases of a similar nature.

Citators are available for several different jurisdictions and subjects. Shepard's Citations, Inc., a division of McGraw-Hill, is the publisher of the widely known citators. Those citators most likely to be of use to constitutional law students include: Shepard's United States Citations: Cases; Shepard's United States Citations: Statutes; Shepard's United States Administrative Citations; Shepard's Acts and Cases by Popular Names, Federal and State; and Shepard's Code of Federal Regulations Citations. Citators are also available for lower federal court cases, state cases, criminal justice cases, and law reviews. For illustrative purposes only, the citator for U.S. Supreme Court cases will be examined here.

Shepard's United States Citations: Cases

Students commonly experience frustration when opening one of the huge volumes in this multivolume set for the first time. The blur of tiny legal citations placed on tissue-thin pages seems unwieldy, to say the least. A first reaction is to put the volume quietly back on the shelf and to forget the whole idea. But wait! Like most legal research material, the citator is easy to use.

To use the citator, start with a legal citation to a court case and locate those cases that cite this central case in a significant fashion. Because a researcher may have a citation for only one reporting system, editors at Shepard's Citations have separate sections of each volume reserved for each of the three parallel citations for each case: *United States Reports* (U.S.); the unofficial *Lawyers' Edition* (L. Ed.); or West Publishing Company's unofficial *Supreme Court Reporter* (S. Ct.). Beginning with a citation to a particular case (for example, 310 U.S. 586), locate the volume number of the citation (310) at the upper corner of each printed page of the citator—an easy task because case citations are in numerical order. On the body of each page, printed in bold numerals, is the page number of each case, in our example (586). Once the desired case is located by volume and page number, the task of identifying the citing cases begins. See the sample pages included on pages 28 and 29.

Because the editors have included a case citation whenever a judge cites another case in his or her written opinion, the number of citations is often great. The result of this editorial decision is to list a case whenever a judge mentions a cited case, even vaguely or incorrectly. Obviously, reading each one of these opinions would be an enormous and wasteful task. To circumvent this problem, the editors provide cues whenever a cited case is treated in a significant manner—for example, when a case is distinguished or overruled. These cues take the form of lower case letters appearing at the left edge of the cited or citing cases in the form of abbreviations: these abbreviations will indicate how the case is treated by the citing authority. A complete listing of abbreviations and definitions appear at the front of each volume. By running a finger down the left edge of the columns, the researcher may note the cues. To determine the context of the case and the argument of the court in its decision, read the citing case in either the official or unofficial reports.

The compulsory flag salute cases provide an uncomplicated example to illustrate further the use of this citator. Here the research problem is to determine the rule of law about the flag salute question. Armed with the *Gobitis* decision, the search begins. The official citation for *Minersville School District v. Gobitis* is 310 U.S. 586; 310 refers to Volume 310 in which *Gobitis* appears. Note that Volume 2C of *Shepard's United States Citations* contains citations for Supreme Court cases reported in Volumes 290–313 of *United States Reports*. Because the cases are in numerical order, turn directly to 310. On page 507 of *Citations* we locate 310 U.S. 586 (see page 28).

Under 586, the researcher first sights the parallel citations which include the *Lawyers' Edition* (84 LE 1375), West Publishing Company's *Supreme Court Reporter* (60 SC 1010), and the *American Law Reports* (127 ALR 1493). Immediately below these citations are several references describing the judicial history of the *Gobitis* case. At the left of these case citations are editor cues in the form of the lower case "s." To see what the various abbreviations signify, turn to the front of each Shepard's volume locating the page titled:

UNITED STATES SUPREME COURT REPORTS*
Vol. 310

430US¹605	128F2d224	345FS³88	314A2d568	j366US¹62
444US¹337	264F2d713	ECA	P R	j366US¹561
Cir. 5	319F2d²27	529F2d³1026	73PRR383	392US¹246
112F2d²948	d47FS²947	536F2d²385	77PRR364	q430US714
e220F2d²355	160FS²164	536F2d³385	Tenn	438US290
Cir. 9	319FS732	536F2d⁵385	178Ten537	450US153
811F2d1254	400FS29	536F2d⁵1384	184Ten421	457US¹882
Cir. 10	406FS365	485F2d²515	29TnA539	53USLW
558FS²744	602FS³1532	585F2d⁵515	160SW415	[4669
Ala	Cir. 3	f598F2d¹603	198SW292	j54USLW
266Ala178	465F2d¹242	f598F2d²603	199SW122	[4697
94So2d778	641F2d116	2TCt1031	555SW400	j54USLW
Calif	105FS⁴618	35FPC860	Tex	[4927
14C3d276	221FS846	Calif	152Tex447	Cir. DC
123CaR57	319FS²413	19C2d858	162Tex289	120F2d¹735
537P2d1306	372FS¹952	164CA3d99	162Tex302	j421F2d1103
Mich	Cir. 4	210CaR337	146SW1086	206FS¹373
347Mch184	101FS²563	123P2d472	161SW1047	288FS443
79NW621	312FS716	Colo	165SW503	Cir. 1
Miss	Cir. 5	168Col165	170SW570	117F2d¹664
240So2d140	113F2d²906	176Col140	186SW311	33FS¹846
Mo	118F2d²847	451P2d272	193SW834	Cir. 2
528SW161	e124F2d²468	490P2d278	215SW642	122F2d²514
S D	e128F2d²336	Me	259SW177	j122F2d¹524
71SD65	j128F2d²337	329A2d170	335SW432	c172F2d¹409
21NW64	e130F2d²14	Mass	346SW811	q380F2d448
	130F2d²19	328Mas683	346SW821	638F2d⁴414
—573—	155F2d954	106NE262	380SW602	712F2d¹1542
(84LE1368)	229F2d²199	Mich	387SW43	q307FS¹30
(60SC1021)	247F2d²893	389Mch650	Wash	325FS808
s309US646	253F2d²381	209NW221	10Wsh2d219	334FS594
s311US570	255F2d²778	Miss	116P2d521	387FS122
s311US614	322F2d¹600	190Mis253		Cir. 3
s311US727	j330F2d²7	199So304	—586—	130F2d¹656
s34LE999	53S²178	N Y	(84LE1375)	j130F2d¹662
s85LE358	218FS¹620	296NY383	(60SC1010)	d39FS²32
s85LE390	218FS²621	296NY387	(127AR1493)	310FS⁴580
s85LE473	353FS⁵584	270NYAD63	s309US645	Cir. 4
s60SC613	Cir. 6	36NYAD266	s84LE998	47FS¹252
s61SC66	j43FS²1022	73NE708	s60SC609	q47FS¹253
s61SC167	56FS³284	73NE711	s108F2d683	q391FS447
s61SC343	577FS524	58NYS2d824	s21FS581	Cir. 5
s107F2d70	Cir. 7	320NYS2d	s24FS271	124F2d¹70
s28FS131	178F2d²908	[284	316US²593	j653F2d188
314US546	513F2d¹187	N C	d316US¹598	103FS207
319US318	513F2d²187	222NC315	j316US¹623	q142FS¹716
319US²330	Cir. 8	275NC497	319US¹587	q314FS¹294
j319US²338	113F2d²701	22SE900	319US¹625	Cir. 6
320US352	132F2d²659	168SE388	319US³640	114F2d²914
329US³4	474F2d¹935	Okla	o319US¹642	178F2d¹41
334US¹67	165FS²898	199Ikjl173	j319US643	766F2d¹946
j334US²98	194FS²934	203Okl141	j319US¹643	766F2d²946
336US²351	Cir. 9	184P2d963	j319US¹664	529FS37
340US¹185	d35FS³110	220P2d285	j321US²113	638FS²579
343US392	Cir. 10	229Ore473	j340US¹308	j170F2d259
Cir. 1	36FS³69	365P2d1037	j341US¹592	44FS²818
202F2d²704	119FS³862	Pa	j343US¹268	*Continued*
Cir. 2	j147FS²645	11PaC612	j365US¹214	

Abbreviations—Analysis*

History of Case

a	(affirmed)	Same case affirmed on rehearing.
cc	(connected case)	Different case from case cited but arising out of same subject matter or intimately connected therewith.
m	(modified)	Same case modified on rehearing.
r	(reversed)	Same case reversed on rehearing.
s	(same case)	Same case as case cited.
S	(superseded)	Substitution for former opinion.
v	(vacated)	Same case vacated
US reh den		Rehearing denied by U.S. Supreme Court.
US reh dis		Rehearing dismissed by U.S. Supreme Court.

Treatment of Case

c	(criticised)	Soundness of decision or reasoning in cited case criticised for reasons given.
d	(distinguished)	Case at bar different either in law or fact from case cited for reasons given.
e	(explained)	Statement of import of decision in cited case. Not merely a restatement of the facts.
f	(followed)	Cited as controlling.
h	(harmonized)	Apparent inconsistency explained and shown not to exist.
j	(dissenting opinion)	Citation in dissenting opinion.
L	(limited)	Refusal to extend decision of cited case beyond precise issues involved.
o	(overruled)	Ruling in cited case expressly overruled.
p	(parallel)	Citing case substantially alike or on all fours with cited case in its law or facts.
q	(questioned)	Soundness of decision or reasoning in cited case questioned.

ABBREVIATIONS—COURTS*

Cir. Fed.–U.S. Court of Appeals, Federal Circuit
Cir (number)–U.S. Court of Appeals Circuit (number)
CIT–United States Court of International Trade
CCPA–Court of Customs and Patent Appeals
Cl Ct–Claims Court (U.S.)
Ct Cl–Court of Claims Reports (U.S.)
Cu Ct–Customs Court Decisions
DC–District of Columbia
EC or ECA–Temporary Emergency Court of Appeals
ML–Judicial Panel on Multidistrict Litigation
RRR–Special Court Regional Rail Reorganization Act of 1973

ABBREVIATIONS-ANALYSIS (see page 29). There note that the lower case "s" refers to "(same case), same case as case cited." The researcher knows at once that the citations accompanied by lower case "s" trace the history of the *Gobitis* controversy in the courts. Thus, the original federal district court opinion in *Gobitis* is 21 FS 581, and the second opinion in that same court is at 24 FS 271. For the opinion of the U.S. Circuit Court of Appeals the researcher must consult, 108 F.2d 683. The Supreme Court's order for the grant of the petition for the writ of certiorari is referenced as 309 U.S. 645.

The next marginal notation sighted is a lower case "d" followed by the citation, 316 U.S. 598. The ABBREVIATIONS-ANALYSIS page indicates that "d" signifies that an opinion writer indicates that the case at bar is different either in law or fact from the case cited; in this particular example, *Gobitis* is distinguishable from 316 U.S. 598. Thumbing down to the next entry the researcher finds a lower case "j" adjacent to the citation, 316 U.S. 623. This means that on page 623 of Volume 316 of the *U.S. Reports* a dissenting opinion cited *Gobitis*. Next, the researcher finds an entry for 319 U.S. 642 accompanied with the notation, "o." The lower case "o" means that 310 U.S. 586 *(Gobitis)* is overruled by the Supreme Court at 319 U.S. 642: the case is West Virginia State Board of Education v. Barnette, 319 U.S. 624.[12] Following the *Barnette* entries are many citations to federal and state cases which cite *Gobitis* in some way.

Up to this point, it is apparent that Shepard's editors indicate that *Gobitis* has been overruled by *Barnette*. To verify the editors' conclusion, and to determine the precise reasoning of the court, turn to the actual opinion for reading and analysis. Yet, having done this, the researcher cannot report that *Barnette* is the contemporary rule of law. Once again, turn to the citator, repeating the research procedure this time for the *Barnette* case. In *Volume 3* of *Shepard's United States Citations-Cases*, locate on page 122 the citation for 319 U.S. 624, where there are numerous references to judicial opinions citing *Barnette*, but there are no editor notations indicating that *Barnette* has been overruled. Consulting the later supplements indicates the same. The researcher can be satisfied that *Barnette* is still the law of the land.

Shepard's United States Citations: Statutes

The *Statutes* edition of *Shepard's United States Citations* contain citations to the *United States Code*, the *United States Code Annotated*, the *Federal Code Annotated*, the *United States Code Service*, the *United States Statutes at Large*, the *United States Treaties and other International Agree-*

---

[12]The reader will note that the page number citation for *Barnette* differs from the one presented earlier. The reason is that the Shepard's editors provide the exact page within the *Barnette* opinion where *Gobitis* is directly overruled.

ments, and the *General Orders in Bankruptcy*. It also contains citations to the U.S. Constitution and the rules for several courts including the U.S. Supreme Court.

This five-volume set with supplements contains a variety of references including citations to court decisions. If, for example, the researcher wants to know how the courts have construed the Eleventh Amendment, this citator provides a listing of cases citing the amendment. The same is true for the codes and other special features of this citator. For discussion and illustration, consult the preface and other explanatory remarks at the front of these volumes.

Legal Periodicals and Indexes

Law journal articles are useful for those researching a constitutional law topic. First, legal periodicals contain secondary source material for understanding what the law has been, what it is at any given historical moment, and what it might become. Second, law review articles reflect conflicting expert opinion about what the law should become. Third, law articles can teach students of the judicial process about the more subtle attempts to influence the bench and bar. Finally, law journals are publishing social science research at an increasing rate. Such articles assess the impact of court rulings on society, intracourt politics, and interinstitutional conflicts between and among the various branches and divisions of government.

Law journal articles are usually well-documented, meticulous discussions on a variety of legal or law-related topics. They often provide researchers with the history of the law and its more recent developments. A common error, however, is to treat these articles, no matter when they were written or by whom, as authoritative, impartial statements on the law. Although law articles are substantial treatments, they are often written from a distinct point of view. By such articles, authors often attempt to shape the future direction of the law. The views expressed, therefore, are not necessarily those of the bench and bar. It is common for particularly controversial legal issues to have several competing perspectives. To obtain a balanced outlook, make every effort to read as many law review articles on the subject as possible. As indicated earlier in this chapter, legal encyclopedias are usually an excellent source for impartial treatments of legal topics.

It is also advisable to list those articles that are useful for research. The various indexes to legal, public affairs, social science, and popular periodicals make such a procedure possible.

Some legal periodicals are particularly useful for those conducting research on a constitutional law topic. The *Harvard Law Review* publishes an annual review of U.S. Supreme Court opinions. *Constitutional Commentary*, *Hastings Constitutional Law Quarterly*, and *Saint Louis University Public Law Review* focus on constitutional law topics. *Judicature*, the journal of the

American Judicature Society, contains articles which bear on many judicial process topics. *Law and Society Review* and *Law & Policy Quarterly* provide forums that bring together legal experts from related academic disciplines. Journals devoted to specialized legal subjects include *American Journal of Legal History*, the *Journal of Psychiatry and Law*, and the *Journal of Law and Economics*.

All law journals contain valuable material. Significant articles appear in the most famous as well as the most obscure journals, and to ignore them is perilous. For a first rate research effort, always consult the various indexes. Consult Chapter Three of this volume for the methods of citing legal and other periodical literature.

Index to Legal Periodicals

A source of some confusion is the existence of three indexes with the same or similar titles. Two of these are useful for identifying old materials.

An Index to Legal Periodical Literature contains six volumes, the first of which specifies English language legal articles and related materials published before January, 1887. The remaining five-volumes treat materials up to 1937. The editor, Leonard A. Jones, includes references to articles, papers, correspondence, annotated cases, and biographical notices in journals published in the United States, England, Ireland, and the English Colonies. For research requiring vintage sources, this is an excellent tool. The *Index to Legal Periodicals*, published by the American Association of Law Libraries, is a second set of interest to those engaging in historical research. This eighteen-volume set covers the period, 1910–1925.

Index to Legal Periodicals, published by the H. W. Wilson Company, is the most accessible and widely known index at large. It contains entries beginning with the year 1926, and continues with periodic supplements to this day. It is the most complete index of legal periodicals published in the United States. It also contains entries for articles appearing in selected law journals of Canada, Great Britain, Ireland, Australia, and New Zealand. The *Index to Legal Periodicals* contains four main features: (1) subject and author index, (2) table of cases, (3) table of statutes, and (4) book review index.

Subject and Author Index   Each cumulative volume and supplement contains a "List of Subject Headings." By first determining the subject heading that best describes the research topic, the student can save considerable effort. For example, if the student is interested in articles dealing with presidential impoundment of funds, he or she can find "impoundment" in the list of subject headings. By turning alphabetically to "impoundment" in the subject and author index, numerous relevant articles can be located.

Those interested in locating articles published before 1983 and found by author and not subject matter may do so by a slightly more complicated process. For each volume of this index from 1926 to 1982, use the following method. First, locate in alphabetical order the last name of the author. Under the author's name is a listing of the subject headings under which his or her article(s) are classified. By turning to the appropriate subject heading(s), the author's name and article title are easily located. Depending on the scope of the research project, it is advisable to consult past and current volumes and to check all paperback supplementary indexes. Beginning in 1983, the subject and author listings are in alphabetical order with complete citations for each and so it is not necessary to follow the steps outlined above for index volumes before 1983.

Following the article listing under each subject heading, case notes or discussions of recent cases pertinent to the subject classification are found under the title, "Cases." For example, in Volume 17 (September 1973– August 1976) following the list of articles under the subject heading "freedom of press," there is a list of four different case notes dealing with the topic, which includes case names, followed by law journal names, volumes, pages, and dates of publication. These case notes, varying in length from a few to many pages, are often helpful in interpreting what a particular case might mean.

Table of Cases Commented Upon   The *Table of Cases Commented Upon* lists articles that focus on particular judicial opinions. At the back of each volume and supplement, this table lists each case alphabetically by plaintiff, followed by law journal entries. This table is an excellent tool for researchers interested in finding what is written about specific cases.

Table of Statutes Commented Upon   If issues surrounding the history or meaning of a statute are pertinent, then the *Table of Statutes Commented Upon* is an excellent tool. For instance, this table yields no less than twelve law review articles for the statutory topic listed as the "Victim and Witness Protection Act of 1982."

Book Review Index   This separate section of the *Index of Legal Periodicals* lists book reviews on legal subjects by name of author or title if the author's name is unknown.

Current Law Index

The *Current Law Index (CLI),* first appearing in 1980 is sponsored by the American Association of Law Libraries, references more than 700 periodicals. This useful index, a product of the Information Access Corporation, features a *Subject Index,* an *Author/Title Index,* a *Table of Cases,* and a *Table of Statutes.* When statutes are discussed in an article, they are indexed by both their popular and official names. A listing of the titles of reviewed books appears in the *Author/Title Index*. Each book is graded according to the reviewer's evaluation on a scale of A to F. As with other contemporary indexes, *CLI* is brought up-to-date with periodic supplements. *Current Law Index* has an easy-to-use companion microfilm service, *Legal Resource Index*. It has several more features than does its parent publication, but its greatest asset lies in the user's ability to locate materials by pushing buttons. It is preferable to thumbing through heavy volumes.

Legal Trac

Legal Trac, a legal periodical index, is a computer terminal system offered by the Information Access Company. Sitting at a keyboard with on-line instructions, researchers may access over 800 legal periodicals. Coverage begins with January 1980, and is updated every month. *Legal Trac* includes all the major law reviews, seven legal newspapers, specialty publications, and bar association publications. The search process begins by entering a subject heading, author, case name or statute name. By pressing the keyboard print function, the user will have a dot matrix bibliographical listing within seconds.

A growing number of law libraries and law firms are subscribing to *Legal Trac*. However, *Legal Trac* only contains entries beginning in 1980 and will be of no use to researchers interested in obtaining earlier periodical sources.

Index to Foreign Legal Periodicals

Index to Foreign Legal Periodicals is a tool for locating articles dealing with international law, comparative law, and the municipal law of non-common law countries. Published by the Institute of Advanced Legal Studies of the University of London in cooperation with the American Association of Law Libraries, this index contains article listings from 1960 to the present. It has an author index, subject index, geographical index, and book review index. The growing interest in comparative legal topics makes this index invaluable.

Index to Periodical Articles Related to Law

Index to Periodical Articles Related to Law, begun in 1958, meets the growing recognition among lawyers of a need to apply the social and behavioral sciences to law. It includes English language articles that are of research value but do not appear in the *Index to Legal Periodicals* or the *Index to Foreign Legal Periodicals*. The *Index to Periodical Articles Related to Law* is published quarterly. It contains a subject index, an index to articles, and an author index. It lists articles that have legal significance, but appear in journals not normally concerned with legal topics. For instance, this index includes articles from such unlikely places as the *Journal of Psychology*, the *Journal of Pastoral Care*, and the *Prison Journal*.

Criminal Justice Periodical Index

Many constitutional law research projects require investigation into the criminal justice literature. Much of this literature is not in law journals. Therefore, there is a need for an index specializing in periodicals with a criminal justice orientation. *Criminal Justice Periodical Index*, published by University Microfilms International, is useful for those conducting research in any facet of criminal justice research. Since 1975, this publication indexes over 100 United States, British, and Canadian journals. If the research may be subsumed under any of the broad categories covering criminal justice— corrections, criminal law, criminology, drug abuse, family law, juvenile justice, police studies, prison administration, rehabilitation, and security systems—then this index is especially practical.

Public Affairs Information Service Bulletin

The law operates in a social, economic, and political context. There are articles and books written which take a broad perspective on the law. Such publications are often indexed in *Public Affairs Information Service Bulletin (PAIS)*, which lists periodicals, books, pamphlets, and government documents useful for those conducting research on constitutional law topics. Most index entries include concise explanations of the item. Listings begin with 1915 and continue to the present.

Social Science Index

Social Science Index is among the best sources for developing an academic focus for a research paper. Students majoring in a social science discipline know this index well. It contains references dating from 1916 to the present. Constitutional law students will find that it contains many items of interests. In a recent volume, over twenty subheadings are listed under the constitutional law subject heading. Before the mid-1960s, the name of this valuable tool was *International Index to Social Science and Humanities Index*. Today, there is a separate *Humanities Index*.

Reader's Guide to Periodical Literature

The *Readers' Guide to Periodical Literature* is the index of preference for citing popular articles such as those that appear in *Time, Newsweek, New Republic* or *National Review*. This index is particularly valuable when the research topic has wide-spread public interest. It contains items dating from 1901 to the present, and features a single author and subject index.

The New York Times Index

The *New York Times* newspaper is among the best sources of information about developments in American law. For years, its editors have paid special attention to the decisions of the U.S. Supreme Court. Within academic circles, the *Times* is widely respected. Access to law-related articles is made possible through *The New York Times Index*. News items are indexed for the periods from 1851 to 1906, and 1912 to the present.

Law Dictionaries

A common complaint against a legal profession is that it has a language understandable only by lawyers. There is some truth to this charge, but law dictionaries are available to aid lay people and students as well. Most law dictionaries define a word or phrase in their legal sense and give citations to court decisions or other references. In this sense, law dictionaries are elementary research tools. Although they tend to be expensive, a law dictionary can be a useful acquisition.

Three widely known and employed law dictionaries are: (1) Ballentine, *Law Dictionary with Pronunciations*, 3d Edition, Lawyers Co-operative Publishing Company, 1969; (2) Black, *Law Dictionary*, 5th Edition, West Publishing Company, 1979; and (3) Bouvier, *Law Dictionary* (3rd revision), 8th Edition, West Publishing Company, 1914. An excellent, less technical, and inexpensive dictionary is Oran's *Law Dictionary for Non-Lawyers*, West Publishing Company, 1975.

There is a two-volume dictionary that focuses especially on constitutional law and it contains hundreds of key cases, terms, and concepts: *The Constitutional Law Dictionary* by Ralph C. Chandler, Richard A. Enslen, and Peter G. Renstrom, (Santa Barbara, CA.: ABC-CLIO, 1987, 1988). Volume 1 deals with governmental powers, and Volume 2 relates to individual rights.

A glossary of terms and phrases is provided at the end of this volume, *Researching Constitutional Law*. It contains terms constitutional law students are most likely to encounter during their studies.

Computer-Terminal Research Aids

As with most aspects of contemporary life, computers are having an impact on legal research because of their speed in gathering materials. A variety of legal research materials available on library shelves are also accessible through computer terminals. For-profit publishing houses are now engaging in a high-stakes competition for hegemony in this relatively new market.

There are three widely known services available and in use in law offices and law libraries: AUTO-CITE, LEXIS, and WESTLAW. AUTO-CITE is a product of the same firm responsible for *American Jurisprudence 2d*, and other fine publications imprinted under the Lawyers Co-operative and Bancroft-Whitney label. LEXIS is sold to subscribers by Mead Data Central of New York City. WESTLAW is a service of the most noteworthy legal publishing house in the country, West Publishing Company.

Each computer system has a different data base, and each employer user input commands along with key names, concepts, terms, words, cases, authors, courts, judges, and so on. Within minutes, the service prints out the desired information. The clear attraction of these services is the reduction in the time and pain associated with long hours in the library. However, one cannot intelligently use computer services unless there is a preexisting understanding of the organization and functions of law research materials. Computers are not a substitute for learning how to use the library. In any event, to use the computer approach one must consult a trained law librarian or have access to an institution or law office which subscribes to a service.

Legal Research Exercises

The best way to learn how to use legal source materials is by really researching a problem. The following exercises are designed to acquaint students with many of the legal research materials discussed in this chapter. Upon completion of these short assignments students can feel confident that they are capable of initiating a research effort. The correct answers for the five exercises appear at the end of this chapter.

Exercise 1—Legal Encyclopedias

Part I   Employ *American Jurisprudence 2d*.

1. Under what subject title name and section number(s) is the right to bear arms found?
2. Do private individuals have a constitutional right to bear arms?
3. Under what subject title name and section number(s) is there a discussion of the registration and licensing of firearms?

Part II   Use *Corpus Juris Secundum*.

4. Have "slungshots" been defined as weapons? (Give title name and section number where the answer may be found).
5. In what title and section is a discussion of civil liability for the manufacture of weapons found?

Exercise 2—Legal Codes

Part I   Use the *United States Code (USC)*.

1. The research topic is the use of the mails to transport firearms capable of being concealed. Under what title name and section number is this subject located within the code?

Part II   Employ *United States Code Service (USCS)*.

2. Select the volume from the *USCS* set which features a discussion of the U.S. Constitution, Amendment 2. What ALR 3d annotation contains a discussion of the validity and construction of gun control laws?
3. What 19th century U.S. Supreme Court opinion held that the Second Amendment is a limitation upon the national government, and not upon the state governments?

Part III   Use *United States Code Annotated (USCA)*.

4. You want to know the legislative history of Title 18, section 1715. What source is cited as relevant?
5. Within the terms of Title 18, section 1715, is a combination cap pistol and BB gun defined as a firearm?

Exercise 3—Digests

Part I   Use the *Century Digest*.

1. Turn to the *Century Digest* index. What is the volume number and what are the topic numbers for the subject, "weapons"?
2. You want to study the right to bear arms. (a) What Key Name and Number covers this topic? (b) What 1840 case held that the right to bear arms refers to such as are usually employed in "civilized warfare."

Part II   Use the *Eight Decennial Digest*.

3. What 1973 case held there is no absolute constitutional right of an individual to possess a firearm?

Part III   Employ West's *Federal Practice Digest 3d*.

4. Turn to the *Table of Cases*. Under what Key Name and Number is *U.S. v. Vice* located?

Part IV   Use *U.S. Supreme Court Digest: Lawyers' Edition*.

5. The case is *Rider v. U.S.* Under what topic(s) and number(s) is this case located?

Exercise 4—Citators

Part 1

1. What are the parallel citations for 336 U.S. 440?
2. What is the name of the case for the citation in question 1?
3. What is the citation of the first U.S. Supreme Court opinion in which the decision in 336 U.S. 440 is cited in a dissenting opinion?
4. As of May 1988, has 336 U.S. 440 been expressly overruled?
5. What is the meaning of the abbreviation, Dk9?

Exercise 5—Legal Periodicals

Part 1   Use the *Index to Legal Periodicals*.

1. A symposium on firearms legislation and litigation was published in 1983. In what law review does this symposium appear?
2. List all articles written by Joe Beavers that appeared between August 1949 and July 1955.
3. Sometime in the late 1980s, R. G. Steinhardt wrote a book review of R. M. Dworkin's *Law's Empire*. What is the volume number, name, page numbers, and date of the law journal in which the review appears.
4. How many case comments were written on Burton v. U.S. (175 F.2d 960, 176 F.2d 865) between August 1949 and July 1955?

Part II   Use the 1974–78 volume of the *Index to Periodical Articles Related to the Law*.

5. Under what subject heading is an article on gun related crimes in Boston indexed?

Answers for Legal Exercises

Exercise 1—Legal Encyclopedias

1. Const. L. section 484; Weap. sections 4, 8.
2. No; Weapons, section 4.

3. Weapons and Firearms, sections 31–34.
4. Yes; Weapons, sections 1, 6.
5. Weapons, section 33.

Exercise 2—Legal Codes

1. Title 18, Crimes and Criminal Procedure, section 1715.
2. 28 ALR3d 845.
3. *Presser v. Illinois* (1886), or *U.S. v. Cruikshank* (1876).
4. 1949 U.S. Code Cong. Service, page 1248.
5. No, Stanford v. Lunde Arms Corp., 211 F.2d 464.

Exercise 3—Digests

1. Volume 48, Weapons 1–35.
2. Weapons §1, or Right to Bear Arms §1. Aymette v. State, 21 Tenn (2 Humph.), 154.
3. U.S. v. Day. 476 F.2d 562.
4. Crim Law 1147, 1213–8(3); Weap 4, 17(8).
5. App, section 339f; conf I, section 9b; Waters, sections 17(1)I, 17(3)I.

Exercise 4—Citators

1. 93 LE 790, 69 SC 716.
2. *Krulewitch v. United States*
3. 336 U.S. 626.
4. No.
5. United States Court of Appeals for the Ninth Circuit, Slip Opinion Docket Numbers.

Exercise 5—Legal Periodicals

1. 6 Hamline L. Rev. 277–487 July 1983.
2. One only: Mo. L. Rev. April 1949.
3. 56 Geo. Wash. L. Rev. 431-60 Ja. '88.
4. Three.
5. Gun Control.

Chapter Two

Survey of Book Literature

_____
_____

Introduction

Exclusive reliance on court reports, legal encyclopedias, digests, codes, and periodical literature tends to narrow the scope of legal research. A constitution is a guide for conduct, regulating a government and its important human affairs. Understanding the United States Constitution requires extra intellectual effort because the basic document is more than a set of rules—it is a statement of principles. Analysis and comprehension of its principles requires less concentration on the legal minutiae than on the larger scope of law in society. Researchers must become aware of the origins, politics, and impacts of judicial decisions, and the competing ideas about the proper mode of constitutional interpretation. Books on such subjects are necessary tools without which the student would gain only a myopic vision of the judicial system.

Classifying available books on constitutional law topics is a risky business. Because authors use eclectic approaches, there is considerable overlap between systems and methods. In the most general and introductory way, the classification presented here is intended only to steer students toward literature useful when researching a topic for an undergraduate constitutional law course. The book annotations to follow are not a complete list of available titles in constitutional law, judicial process, or behavior. Works of some favorite authors may be omitted. It is not possible to list all the noteworthy books in a volume of this size. Therefore, the annotations should be viewed as a sample of available titles, to be supplemented by the bibliography located at the end of this book and the reader's own search for references.

Expository Works

Instructors often assign casebooks as the sole text. These textbooks typically include brief introductions to each constitutional law topic, followed by several edited judicial opinions. Although casebooks possess pedagogical merit, they often fail to adequately tie together disparate materials. Expository works remedy this problem by describing, explaining, and interpreting the entire field or subfield of constitutional law. They do so without reliance on the reproduction of judicial opinions to tell the story. Thus, expository works are valuable because they integrate the subject matter in a clear and succinct fashion.

New judicial opinions may render old precedents obsolete. Consequently, descriptions, explanations, and interpretations found in expository books may no longer prove valid. Therefore, these books cannot be the sole source for legal research. If a particular exposition has been well received, however, new editions or supplements updating the previous edition are often published. The entries for this and for each category of books listed in this chapter are in alphabetical order by author. Because of the changing nature of the law, researchers will want to locate the most current volumes by date of publication.

Abraham, Henry J. *Freedom and the Court: Civil Rights and Liberties in the United States*, 5th ed. New York: Oxford University Press, 1988.

This book offers an analysis of the conflict between individual rights and community welfare. Specific features include: an historical discussion of the process of incorporation of the Bill of Rights by way of the Fourteenth Amendment; a discussion of religion, speech, due process, and political and racial equality; and an overview of the political development of civil liberties and rights in the United States. For those interested in locating other sources, the author includes pertinent bibliographic notes.

Bartholomew, Paul C. and Menez, Joseph F. *Summaries of Leading Cases on the Constitution*. 12th edition. Totowa, NJ: Rowman Littlefield, Helix Books, 1983.

This paperback book contains summaries of almost 500 Supreme Court decisions. For each case it briefly states the facts, the legal issues, and the Court's decision and reasoning.

Congressional Quarterly. *Guide to the U.S. Supreme Court*, 2d ed. Washington, DC: Congressional Quarterly, Inc., 1989.

This guide is an outstanding reference work on all aspects of the Supreme Court. Topics include: the Court's history, the Court and federalism, the Court and presidential power, the Court and judicial power, the Court and the states, the Court, civil liberties, and rights, the political pressures on the Court, the internal operations of the Court, and the major decisions of the Court.

Congressional Research Service, Library of Congress. *The Constitution of the United States of America: Analysis and Interpretation*. Washington, DC: U.S. Government Printing Office, 1987.

This book, first published in 1913, offers a lengthy, authoritative, and narrative exposition of the Constitution, clause by clause. Annual pocket supplements are included.

Curry, James A., Riley, Richard B., and Battistoni, Richard M. *Constitutional Government: The American Experience*. St. Paul: West Publishing Company, 1989.

This book offers a readable exposition on almost every aspect of the American constitutional system. Part I contains the history and the theory of constitutional government. Part II presents an indepth discussion of the structure and processes of American constitutional government. Part III provides analyses of the Bill of Rights, civil liberties, and civil rights. Throughout this book, the authors summarize U.S. Supreme Court decisions and interpretations of the constitution.

Fellman, David. *The Defendant's Rights Today*. Madison, WI: The University of Wisconsin Press, 1976.

This book offers a pertinent discussion of the Supreme Court's handling of criminal justice cases with historical explanations of why criminal justice is tilted in favor of defendants. Topics covered are: arrests, preliminary hearings, bail, habeas corpus, trial by jury, right to counsel, searches and seizures, self-incrimination, double jeopardy, and cruel and unusual punishment. Although somewhat out-of-date, this book is still useful.

Halpern, Stephen, ed. *The Future of Our Liberties: Perspectives on the Bill of Rights*. Westport, CT: Greenwood Press, 1982.

This book offers a collection of essays that focus on both individual and state liberties. Diverse everyday topics are considered.

Kurland, Philip B. and Lerner, Ralph. *The Founders' Constitution*, 5 Vols. Chicago: University of Chicago Press, 1987.

This set is useful for analyzing the Constitution and the first twelve amendments, section by section, and clause by clause. The editors provide relevant records of the Federal convention, letters and commentary of the Founding Fathers, scholarly commentary and court cases interpreting each constitutional provision.

LaFave, Wayne R., *Search and Seizure: A Treatise on the Fourth Amendment*, 2d ed. St. Paul: West Publishing Company, 1987.

This book offers in four volumes a thorough treatment of all aspects of the Fourth Amendment and the exclusionary rule. The book contains a useful table of cases and an annual pocket supplement to keep the volumes up-to-date. It is the best available source on search and seizure law.

Landynski, Jacob W. *The Living U.S. Constitution*, 2d rev. ed. New York: New American Library, 1983.

An inexpensive and handy paperback, this book features character sketches of the delegates to the Philadelphia Convention, a complete text of the Constitution, and abbreviated versions of landmark U.S. Supreme Court decisions.

Miller, Arthur S. *Presidential Power in a Nutshell*. St. Paul, MN: West Publishing Co., 1977.

This book offers a brief exposition on the law and politics of the presidency. It covers important legal topics and emphasizes that presidential power cannot be understood through a purely legal approach. Use of this book must be supplemented with additional research.

Peltason, J. W. *Understanding the Constitution*, 11th ed. New York: Holt, Rinehart and Winston, 1988.

This book offers a thorough analysis of each provision of the Constitution and Supreme Court cases through 1987. The author examines how Supreme Court decisions as well as lower court decisions affect the interpretation of the Constitution.

Pritchett, C. Herman *Constitutional Civil Liberties*. Englewood Cliffs: Prentice-Hall, 1984.

This book covers both the adoption of civil rights and liberties and the Court's interpretations of those rights.

Pritchett, C. Herman. *The American Constitutional System*. 5th ed. New York: McGraw-Hill Book Company, 1981.

This book offers a succinct account of the entire constitutional system. Exemplary features include an overview of the subject matter.

Rossiter, Clinton and Longaker, Richard P. *The Supreme Court and the Commander in Chief*. Ithaca, NY: Cornell University Press, 1976.

A classic study of how the Supreme Court has interpreted presidential war powers.

Rotunda, Ronald D., Nowak, John E., and Young, J. Nelson. *Treatise on Constitutional Law: Substance and Procedure*. St. Paul: West Publishing Company, 1986.

This three-volume set contains accounts of all aspects of U.S. constitutional law. It contains an excellent table of contents, table of cases, and index for determining what the law is on a given topic. Each volume contains annual pocket supplements.

Smith, Edward C. and Spaeth, Harold J. *The Constitution of the United States—With Case Summaries*. Bicentennial edition. New York: Barnes and Noble, 1987.

This source book contains copies of the Constitution, the Virginia Bill of Rights, the Declaration of Independence and the Articles of Confederation. It describes over 250 Supreme Court rulings.

Tribe, Laurence H. *American Constitutional Law*, 2d ed. Mineola, NY: The Foundation Press, Inc., 1988.

This book examines numerous aspects of constitutional interpretation. The author builds several analytical models of constitutional law providing summaries of Supreme Court decisions and a system for considering them. While the author does not hide particular value judgments, he does present opposing views.

Way, H. Frank. *Liberty in the Balance: Current Issues in Civil Liberties*, 5th ed. New York: McGraw-Hill Book Company, 1981.

This book offers a substantive treatment of racial discrimination, women's rights, gay rights, press and censorship, speech, religion, and criminal justice. In addition, the author integrates case law with relevant social, political, and economic data and analysis.

Witt, Elder, ed. *The Supreme Court and Individual Rights*, 2d ed. Washington, DC: Congressional Quarterly, Inc., 1988.

This book offers a substantive treatment of the Court's role in protecting individual liberties and rights. Topics include: speech, religion, political participation, due process, racial, alienage, sexual, and income discrimination. In addition, the editor provides excellent narratives with citations to relevant cases.

Historical Accounts of the Supreme Court

Students of constitutional law soon learn that the meaning of the Constitution is not fixed in time. Rather, it has changed with each Court making its own contribution. The values and attitudes of the members of the Supreme Court, from the time of John Jay and John Marshall to Warren Burger and William Rehnquist, have left their own imprints upon the constitutional edifice. Possessing leeway but not license, Courts have looked to the past, present, and future for guidance in their decision making.

Books dealing with constitutional law must necessarily consider historical evolution. Yet, histories of the Supreme Court usually attempt to understand the development of the law through an analysis of how various courts have contributed in their own manner to the meaning of the Constitution.

Such histories may attempt to understand the Constitution in several ways: by discussing the entire history of the Supreme Court from the formation of the Union to the present; as in-depth studies of particular Courts or comparisons of various Courts; and as descriptions of how various Courts have dealt with particular constitutional provisions or doctrines. Whatever the variation, Court histories are valuable because they provide an overall perspective other books often fail to convey.

Allen, W. B. and Lloyd, Gordon eds. *The Essential Antifederalist*. Lanham, MD: University Press of America, 1985.

Antifederalists opposed the ratification of the document framed at Philadelphia in 1787. Like the Federalists, the Antifederalists wrote articles in newspapers. In recent years a new interest has grown in their thinking. An interpretative essay and other chapters are organized around the themes of the origins of Antifederalist thought, Antifederalist views of federalism, Antifederalist views of republicanism, and Antifederalist support of capitalism and democracy.

Beard, Charles. *An Economic Interpretation of the Constitution of the United States*. New York: Free Press, 1986.

First published in 1913, and subject to attack ever since, this book maintains that the authors of the 1789 Constitution were motivated in large part by vested economic interests. In this particular edition there is an introduction that traces the history of the controversy surrounding this seminal work.

Biasi, Vincent. *The Burger Court: The Counter-Revolution that Wasn't*. New Haven: Yale University Press, 1982.

This book analyzes the first thirteen terms of Chief Justice Warren Burger and the Supreme Court under him. The author proposes that the Burger court, contrary to popular belief, has not made major changes in the doctrines set forth by the Warren court.

Bowen, Catherine Drinker. *Miracle at Philadelphia: The Story of the Constitutional Convention May to September 1787*. Boston: Atlantic-Little Brown, 1986.

This book reconstructs the daily events of the Philadelphia Convention. The author writes her account by piecing together the letters and spoken utterances of the delegates.

Collier, Christopher and Collier, James Lincoln. *Decision in Philadelphia: The Constitutional Convention of 1787*. New York: Random House, Ballantine Books, 1987.

This book offers an account of the personalities responsible for the famous convention in Philadelphia and its concluding document.

Currie, David P. *The Constitution in the Supreme Court: The First Hundred Years*. Chicago: University of Chicago Press, 1985.

The author examines in chronological order constitutional decisions of the Supreme Court during its first hundred years.

Earle, Edward Meade, ed. *The Federalist: A Commentary on the Constitution of the United States*. [Alexander Hamilton, James Madison, and John Jay]. New York: The Modern Library, 1941, 1964.

Alexander Hamilton, James Madison, and John Jay authored under the title "Publius" eighty-five essays that advocated the adoption of the Constitution. Appearing in New York newspapers, these essays became widely known and had an impact on the ratification debates then occurring in the United States. These articles, the Federalist papers, are sometimes cited by courts and others as evidence of the Framers' intent. This book is available in several editions.

Elliot, Jonathan. *Elliot's Debates*, 5 Vols. Philadelphia: J. B. Lippincott, 1836, 1937.

These volumes contain a collection of the debates and proceedings which took place in the various state conventions which ratified the 1787 Constitution. The volumes are useful when trying to understand what those who ratified, as opposed to those who drafted the Constitution, might have had in mind. Also contained in the volumes is the Journal of the Federal Convention, and other documents and letters of interest.

Faber, Doris and Faber, Harold. *We the People: The Story of the United States Constitution Since 1787*. New York: Charles Scribner's Sons, 1987.

This book offers a lively constitutional history beginning with the Philadelphia Convention; it describes the amendments to the Constitution and concludes with a discussion of contemporary issues.

Farrand, Max, ed. *The Records of the Federal Convention of 1787*, 4 Vols. New Haven, CN: Yale University Press, 1986.

This four-volume set contains the daily records of the Constitutional Convention providing researchers with the ability to trace the origin and development of particular clauses. The index found in Volume 4 includes references for all clauses finally adopted.

Funston, Richard Y. *Constitutional Counterrevolution? The Warren and the Burger Courts Judicial Political Making in Modern American*. New York: Halsted Press, 1977.

This book critically analyzes the judicial decisions of the Warren and Burger Courts and contains a discussion of the uses of judicial self-restraint.

Grier, Stephenson, D. Jr. *The Supreme Court and the American Republic: An Annotated Bibliography*. New York: Garland Publishing, Inc. 1981.

This volume lists books and writings covering the following topics: research aids, general Supreme Court works, origins of the Supreme Court, and its institutional development, and also works on constitutional interpretation. Two appendices list justices of the Supreme Court and the number of years they served.

Haines, Charles Grove. *The Role of the Supreme Court in American Government and Politics 1789–1835*. New York: De Capo Press, 1957.
Haines, Charles Grove, and Sherwood, Foster H. *The Role of the Supreme Court in American Government and Politics 1835–1864*. Berkeley and Los Angeles: University of California Press, 1973.

In two volumes of careful scholarship, the authors attempt to demonstrate that the Supreme Court is fundamentally a political institution.

Hall, Kermit L. *A Comprehensive Bibliography of American Constitutional and Legal History, 1896–1979*. New York: Kraus International Publications, 1984.

This four-volume set is an exhaustive annotated bibliographic reference of several thousand books. A separate index volume is included as well.

Hentoff, Nat. *The First Freedom: The Tumultuous History of Free Speech in America*. New York: Delacorte Press, 1980.

This book offers a pertinent history and detailed discussion of leading Supreme Court cases involving speech, press, and religion.

Kelly, Alfred, Harbinson, Winfred A., and Belz, Herman. *The American Constitution: Its Origins and Development*, 6th ed. New York: Norton, 1983.

Now in its sixth edition, this volume offers a basic history of the U.S. Constitution. It covers materials from colonial days through much of the Burger era.

Ketcham, Ralph, ed. *The Antifederalist Papers and the Constitutional Convention Debates*. New York: New American Library, 1986.

The celebration of the Bicentennial of the U.S. Constitution has given rise to renewed interest in the debates surrounding its ratification. Although the *Federalist Papers* are well-known to students and scholars, the ideas and writings of ratification opponents are not. This publication contains the complete texts of the Antifederalist writings and the Constitutional Convention debates. It also contains a table on page 27 correlating the arguments of the Federalists and the Antifederalists by numbered papers.

Kurland, Philip B. *Supreme Court Review*. Chicago: University of Chicago Press, 1960–.

An annual publication since 1960, this book reviews the major work of the Supreme Court for each succeeding term. Included are essays written on pertinent topics by law professors and political scientists. It may also be classified as a law review.

Manley, John F., and Dolbeare, Kenneth M., eds. *The Case Against the Constitution: From the Antifederalists to the Present*. Armonk, NY: M. E. Sharpe, Inc., 1987.

Particularly during periods such as the Bicentennial of the U.S. Constitution, the document itself becomes an object of adoration and uncritical praise. However, there are democratic criticisms worth serious attention. The editors present a score of classic and modern writings including those of J. Allen Smith, Charles A. Beard, and Jackson Turner Main.

McDonald, Forrest. *Novus Ordo Seclorum: The Intellectual Origins of the Constitution*. Lawrence: University Press of Kansas, 1985.

This book offers an account of the intellectual thought influencing the authors of the U.S. Constitution.

Millett, Stephen M. *A Selected Bibliography of American Constitutional History*. Santa Barbara, CA: Clio Books, 1975.

A bibliography covering all facets of constitutional history, this source book also contains a section on judicial biographies.

Morris, Richard B. *Witnesses at the Creation: Hamilton, Madison, Jay, and the Constitution*. New York: New American Library, 1985.

This book examines the letters and other writings of the authors of the Federalist Papers, Hamilton, Madison, and Jay. Richard B. Morris offers insights into the personalities of these three key figures and how they contributed to the ratification process.

Murphy, Paul L. *World War I and the Origin of Civil Liberties in the United States*. New York: W. W. Norton, 1980.

This book argues that the development of civil liberties as a body of law did not occur before the coming of World War I.

Pritchett, C. Herman. *The Roosevelt Court*. New York: Macmillan, 1948.

This book is recognized as having revolutionized the study of the judicial process. The author focuses on the Supreme Court from 1937–1947. Analyzing the nonunanimous votes of the justices, the author studies the politics, attitudes, and values of the Roosevelt Court.

Reams, Bernard D. Jr., and Haworth, Charles H., comps. *Congress and the Courts: A Legislative History 1787–1977, 1978–1984.* Buffalo: William S. Hein and Company, 1978, 1985.

This is a multivolume set in two series that brings together congressional documents including hearings and reports, and other materials regarding the creation, structure, and organization of the federal judicial system. Those interested in studying the interaction between Congress and the federal courts will find this set a convenient research tool. An extensive table of contents and an index reference historic congressional/court interactions and conflicts such as the Judiciary Act of 1789, President Roosevelt's Court-packing scheme, and hearings on Supreme Court workload.

Rodell, Fred. *55 Men: The Story of the Constitution.* Washington, DC: Liberty Lobby, 1987.

This is a recently updated version of a classic account of the 1787 Constitutional Convention. The author relies on Madison's notes as the foundation for his version of the events during the summer of 1787.

Rodell, Fred. *Nine Men: A Political History of the Supreme Court from 1790–1955.* New York: Random House, 1955.

A history of the Supreme Court from the era of John Jay to Earl Warren. This book views the Court primarily as a political institution most often reflecting conservative values.

Rossiter, Clinton. *1787: The Grand Convention.* New York: Macmillan, 1966.

This book offers a pertinent a treatment of the Philadelphia Convention with an account of ratification politics.

Schmidhauser, John R. *Constitutional Law in American Politics.* Monterey, CA: Brooks/Cole Publishing Company, 1984.

Intended as a textbook for courses in constitutional law, this book provides an interpretation of constitutional history, including the relationship of doctrinal change to major political transformations involving critical elections theory.

Schmidhauser, John R. *Judges and Justices: The Federal Appellate Judiciary.* Boston: Little, Brown and Co., 1979.

An important book in judicial process, this book contains two chapters of particular historical interest: a study of the social and political backgrounds of the justices of the Supreme Court and federal appellate court judges, 1789–1976; and a discussion of the evolution of the Supreme Court's internal procedures.

Schwartz, Bernard. *Super Chief: Earl Warren and His Court*. New York: New York University Press, 1983.
This book offers a comprehensive study of the Supreme Court's decision-making process.

Schwartz, Herman, ed. *The Burger Years: Rights and Wrongs in the Supreme Court, 1969–1986*. New York: Viking-Penguin, 1987.
This book is a collection of essays which detail and analyze Supreme Court decisions under Chief Justice Warren Burger.

Steamer, Robert J. *The Supreme Court in Crisis: A History of Conflict*. Amherst, MA: University of Massachusetts Press, 1971.
This book offers a history of the Supreme Court as the nonelected branch pitted against the popularly elected branches of government.

Swisher, Carl B. *American Constitutional Development*. Boston: Houghton Mifflin, 1954, 1978.
As an historical treatment of constitutional issues, this book is especially useful for understanding constitutional problems during the first decades of the present century.

Twiss, Benjamin. *Lawyers and the Constitution*. Princeton: Princeton University Press, 1942.
This book is an early study that recognizes the vital relationship between the bench and the bar. It demonstrates how an elite segment of the bar had a far-reaching impact on the development of U.S. constitutional law.

Warren, Charles. *The Supreme Court in United States History*, 2 vols. Boston: Little, Brown and Company, 1987.
This book offers a perceptive constitutional history with special focus given to the interplay of politics and history with the law. It is especially sensitive to developments that took place during the 19th century. This is a re-published work.

Judicial Review and Constitutional Interpretation

Although it may be inferred, there is no explicit mention of judicial review in the Constitution. Judicial review was established in 1803 in John Marshall's famous opinion in *Marbury v. Madison*. However, from Jefferson's time to this day, the exercise of judical review has been questioned. For example, whether John Marshall usurped power is certainly debatable. What occupies greater attention, however, is the proper role of judges in interpreting the basic document. Should judges exercise judicial review with great restraint or should they actively use their power to protect rights guaranteed under the Constitution?

The most recent version of the activism versus restraint argument centers around the polar concepts of interpretivism and noninterpretivism. Interpretivists believe that judges should focus on the words and substantive intentions of the Framers of the Constitution when interpreting the document. If judges do so, judicial decisions will be objective or *principled* and not a matter of subjective value and moral judgments. Noninterpretivists argue that numerous constitutional provisions are not ascertainable from a literal reading of the Constitution or from an historical search for the intentions of its Framers. Instead, judges must exercise their discretion to protect valuable constitutional rights. Of course, the debate between these schools of thought contains variations. Also, there are other labels for the same or similar arguments, including: intentionalism versus nonintentionalism, originalism versus nonoriginalism, strict construction versus loose construction, positivism versus natural law, and mechanical jurisprudence versus realism. Articles and books on this topic exist by the score. A few of the leading books with annotations follow.

Berger, Raoul. *Government by Judiciary: The Transformation of the Four-teenth Amendment.* Cambridge: Harvard University Press, 1977.

The author argues for a jurisprudence of original intention. Jurists should attempt to find meaning in the constitutional text and if that is fruitless then a search for original intention is appropriate. Judges do not have the right to update the Constitution through their own interpretation of what it ought to be. The Constitution should be changed only through the formal amending process and not by judicial policy making.

Cannon, Mark W. and O'Brien, David M., eds. *Views From the Bench: The Judiciary and Constitutional Politics.* Chatham, NJ: Chatham House Publishers, Inc. 1985.

This book offers a collection of readings authored mainly by distinguished jurists. They deal with issues surrounding judicial restraint and activism and the problem of the judicial capability to solve societal problems.

Choper, Jesse H. *Judicial Review and the National Political Process: A Functional Reconsideration of the Role of the Supreme Court.* Chicago: University of Chicago Press, 1980.

This book examines the extent to which the Supreme Court should use its authority for judicial review. The author argues that the Supreme Court should reserve the use of its power to only those cases involving the protection of minorities.

Clinton, Robert L. *From Precedent to Myth: Marbury v. Madison and the History of Judicial Review in America*. Lawrence: University Press of Kansas, 1989.

The author argues that the precedent of *Marbury v. Madison* does not stand for the proposition that the federal courts may overturn any act of Congress thought to be unconstitutional. Instead, *Marbury* should be read narrowly to apply to those situations where judicial power is infringed. The author claims that the misuse of John Marshall's famous opinion is traceable to Progressive Era historians.

Ducat, Craig R. *Modes of Constitutional Interpretation*. St. Paul, MN: West Publishing Company, 1978.

This book offers an analysis of the principal frameworks employed by justices of the Supreme Court in justifying their opinions. The author describes and criticizes absolutism, balancing of interests, and preferred freedoms as competing modes of constitutional interpretation.

Dworkin, Ronald. *Law's Empire*. Cambridge: Harvard University Press, 1986.

By understanding history, morality, and political theory, the author argues that jurists when deciding cases must search for and apply principles found in the community's concept of fairness and justice. He argues against the approach of determining original intent to constitutional interpretation.

Ely, John Hart. *Democracy and Distrust: A Theory of Judicial Review*. Cambridge, MA: Harvard University Press, 1980.

The author believes that general principles of interpretation may be gleaned from the constitutional text and that jurists must trace their opinions to such concepts and not to their own views on political policy. Consequently, he believes that judicial policy making is permissible when it serves to maintain democratic procedures but it is illegitimate when it serves only to disturb policy decisions of politicians in the other branches of government.

The Federalist Society. *The Great Debate: Interpreting Our Written Constitution*. Washington DC: The Federalist Society, 1986.

This pamphlet features a collection of five speeches delivered by persons directly involved in the contemporary controversy over the exercise of judicial review. Attorney General Meese, Judge Robert H. Bork, and former President Ronald Reagan present their case for intentionalism and interpretativism. Justices William J. Brennan, Jr., and John Paul Stevens present the opposing arguments.

Horowitz, Donald L. *The Courts and Social Policy.* Washington, DC: The
   Brookings Institution, 1977.
   This book offers the argument that courts do not have the capacity to
shape social policy. Courts do not know how to find and apply data relevant to
such decision making so as to fashion flexible solutions and predict and
control the after affects of their decisions. The author illustrates his points
with several case studies.

McCann, Michael W., and Houseman, Gerald L. *Judging the Constitution:
   Critical Essays on Judicial Lawmaking.* Glenview, IL: Scott Foresman
   and Company, 1989.
   The editors present fifteen original essays of political scientist and lawyers. These writers move beyond the mainstream to analyze the nature of
constitutional lawmaking by the Supreme Court from predominately a critical
legal studies perspective.

McDowell, Gary L. *Equity and the Constitution: The Supreme Court, Equitable Relief, and Public Policy.* Chicago: University of Chicago Press,
   1982.
   Though equity is part of the jurisdiction of U.S. courts, in recent decades
it has been used to include the judiciary in matters previously reserved to other
political institutions. The author argues that equity jurisdiction has been
misused to promote social justice thereby contributing to the unwarranted
posture of court activism.

Melone, Albert P. and Mace, George. *Judicial Review and American Democracy.* Ames: Iowa State University Press, 1988.
   This book begins with a discussion of the scope and history of judicial
review in the United States. It then focuses on whether judicial review is a
usurpation of power and whether it is compatible with democracy. It contains
classic pro and con writings by notables such as Hamilton, Beard, Thayer,
Lurton, and Rostow. An extensive Bibliography contains both articles and
books written on the subject of judicial review.

Miller, Arthur Selwyn. *Towards Increased Judicial Activism: The Political
   Role of the Supreme Court.* Westport, CT: Greenwood Press, 1982.
   This book presents a view which rejects judicial self-restraint in favor of
judicial activism. It is an outstanding presentation of the view of the Constitution as a living document.

Neely, Richard. *Judicial Jeopardy: When Business Collides with the Courts.*
   New York: Addison-Wesley, 1986.
   The author argues that activist courts are threatening the legal status of
American business and advises business to fight back.

Perry, Michael. *The Constitution, the Courts, and Human Rights: An Inquiry into the Legitimacy of Constitutional Policymaking by the Judiciary.* New Haven: Yale University Press, 1982.

The author reasons that noninterpretivism cannot be justified by either an investigation into the intention of the Framers of the Constitution or by an analysis of the document itself. However, noninterpretivism may be sustained because judicial invention of rights is justifiable on the functional grounds of protecting precious human rights.

Wolfe, Christopher. *The Rise of Modern Judicial Review.* New York: Basic Books, 1986.

The author argues there has been a serious transformation of judicial power in America. He traces this transformation from the founding of judicial power to the present day and makes a case against judicial activism as practiced in the modern era.

Judicial Biographies

Judicial biographies are typically absorbing accounts of the life and times of individual justices. Although modern social science methods have been employed in an attempt to comprehend judicial attitudes and values, judicial biographies are often a valuable contribution in supplementing and sometimes in correcting common notions of the motivations underlying judicial opinions. Besides illuminating judicial decision making, judicial biographies are instructive as to career patterns and the character of those acceding to the Supreme Court.

Lawyers and judges in particular tend to retain personal correspondence and records. Historians and political scientists who gain access to these papers are able to fill in details surrounding the judicial environment—information which would otherwise remain unknown to the public at large. Biographers make use of published material, private papers, and personal interviews where possible. The better biographies have been written about well-known twentieth century judges and a handful of nineteenth century jurists. Some are autobiographical. However some authors do tend to idealize or at least overemphasize the accomplishments and character of the studied justice. Therefore, take some care in your reading of these materials.

Beveridge, Albert J. *The Life of John Marshall,* 4 vols. New York: Houghton Mifflin Company, 1916–1919.

This work offers a detailed account of Marshall's life employing personal letters, diaries and journals, newspapers of the time, and other sources. The author emphasizes Marshall's strong points.

Bland, Randall W. *Private Pressure on Public Law: the Legal Career of Justice Thurgood Marshall.* Port Washington, NY: Kennikat Press, 1973.

This biography examines the life of the first black to sit on the Supreme Court bench; a fascinating account of Marshall's association with the National Association for the Advancement of Colored People (NAACP) and his days as a U.S. Solicitor General. Included is discussion of Justice Marshall's judicial opinions. However, this book must be supplemented with additional information before a definitive judgment can be made about Justice Marshall's effectiveness on the Court.

Boles, Donald E. *Mr. Justice Rehnquist, Justice Activist: The Early Years.* Ames: Iowa State University Press, 1987.

Because William Rehnquist is Chief Justice of the Supreme Court, there is a keen interest in his attitudes and values. This work is an examination of Rehnquist's attitudes and actions from the beginning of his legal career until he acceded to the high bench as associate judge.

Douglas, William O. *The Court Years, 1939–1975: The Autobiography of William O. Douglas.* New York: Random House, 1980.

As an autobiography, this book is a disappointment. It is only sprinkled with short expositions on prominent public figures Justice Douglas knew during his thirty-six-year Court tenure. The book does, however, provide some insight into his judicial philosophy.

Douglas, William O. *Go East, Young Man: The Early Years.* New York: Random House, 1974.

This interesting and revealing autobiography depicts the early struggles and associates of the opinionated Douglas. His candid appraisal of Felix Frankfurter and other New Dealers is instructive.

Dunham, Allison and Kurland, Philip B., eds. *Mr. Justice.* Chicago: Phoenix Books, The University Chicago Press, 1964.

This book is a valuable collection of short biographies about twelve Supreme Court justices written by outstanding public law scholars. It contains biographies of Justices Marshall, Taney, Bradley, Harlan, Holmes, Hughes, Brandeis, Sutherland, Stone, Cardozo, Murphy, and Rutledge.

Dunne, Gerald. *Hugo Black and the Judicial Revolution.* New York: Simon and Schuster, 1977.

This book treats Black's days in Alabama, the U.S. Senate, and his long years as justice on the Supreme Court.

Duram, James C. *Justice William O. Douglas*. Boston: K. G. Hall, 1981.
In this examination of the writings of Justice Douglas, the author also provides a biographic view of Douglas' life at home and in the courtroom. It can be used as an appropriate reference to other writings by Justice Douglas.

Friedman, Leon and Israel, Fred L., eds. *The Justices of the United States Supreme Court 1789–1978: Their Lives and Major Opinions*, 5 vols. New York and London: Chelsea House Publishers, 1980.
This five-volume effort records the lives and important opinions of every member of the Supreme Court from 1798 to 1978. It is the most complete work of its kind and provides a valuable bibliography of available articles and books on each justice.

Hirsch, H. N. *The Enigma of Felix Frankfurter*. New York: Basic Books, 1981.
This book, a psychobiography, focuses on the personality of this controversial justice. The author analyzes Justice Frankfurter as a liberal New Dealer and how he became an isolated figure on the Supreme Court.

Magee, James L. *Mr. Justice Black: Absolutist on the Court*. Charlottesville, Virginia: University of Virginia Press, 1980.
This book traces Justice Black's First Amendment views from the initial preferred position doctrine to his absolutist period and finally to his less libertarian position during his later years.

Magrath, C. Peter. *Morrison R. Waite: The Triumph of Character*. New York: Macmillan, 1963.
This book offers a serious treatment of Chief Justice Waite from his early years in Connecticut and later in Ohio to his management of the Supreme Court during an important period of U.S. history, 1874–1887.

Mason, Alpheus Thomas. *Harlan Fiske Stone: Pillar of the Law*. New York: Viking Press, 1956.
In this book the author surpasses simple historical description by utilizing Stone's personal papers and interviews with Stone's associates. In addition, the book serves as an excellent history of the Supreme Court for the period 1925–1946. It is one of the finest judicial biographies extant.

Mason, Alpheus Thomas. *William Howard Taft: Chief Justice*. London: Oldbourne Book Co. Ltd., 1964.
This book offers an account of the life of the only man to be both President of the United States and Chief Justice of the Supreme Court. A conservative and opponent of government regulation, Taft was primarily responsible for revamping the federal judicial system.

Murphy, Bruce Allen. *The Brandeis-Frankfurter Connection*. New York: Oxford University Press, 1982.

This book contains an analysis of the collaboration of Justices Brandeis and Frankfurter in their extra-judicial activities, and sharing of political goals.

Newmyer, Kent R. *Supreme Court Justice Story: Statesman of the Old Republic*. Chapel Hill: University of North Carolina Press, 1985.

This book is a biography of Justice Story, his place in history, and his contributions to society. A sample of cases are explained and analyzed.

Parrish, Michael. *Felix Frankfurter and His Times: The Reform Years*. New York: Free Press, 1982.

This book offers a thorough account of the life and times of the late Associate Justice Felix Frankfurter from his early career to his later years.

Pohlman, H. L. *Justice Oliver Wendell Holmes and Utilitarian Jurisprudence*. Cambridge: Harvard University Press, 1984.

This work presents a historical view of jurisprudence, especially the views of Justice Holmes. The author contends that Holmes was a utilitarian thinker, and that his views were closely related to early utilitarian thinkers such as John Stuart Mill.

Silverstein, Mark. *Constitutional Faiths: Felix Frankfurter, Hugo Black, and the Process of Judicial Decisionmaking*. Ithaca: Cornell University Press, 1984.

In this comparative study of the philosophies of Justice Frankfurter and Justice Black, the author examines their backgrounds, and how their philosophies shaped their court decisions.

Simon, James F. *Independent Journey: The Life of William O. Douglas*. New York: Harper and Row, 1980.

This book offers an admiring portrait of the life of Justice Douglas.

Steamer, Robert J. *Chief Justice: Leadership and the Supreme Court*. University of South Carolina Press, 1986.

In this comparative analysis of the fifteen chief justices of the Supreme Court, the author discusses both their formal and informal duties while in office.

Strum, Philippa. *Louis Brandeis: Justice for the People*. Cambridge: Harvard University Press, 1984.

This book offers a thorough biography of Justice Louis Brandeis and a detailed account of his life and career, on and off the Supreme Court.

Warren, Earl. *The Memoirs of Earl Warren.* Garden City, NY: Doubleday and Co., 1977.

This book is an autobiography of how Justice Warren saw himself and the people and events that surrounded his fifty years of public service. It provides a pertinent account of his troubles with such foes as the American Bar Association and the John Birch Society. He died before the book was completed.

Case Studies

The authors of case studies endeavor to view the total environment rather than simply reporting or interpreting a Supreme Court decision. This is often accomplished by tracing the beginnings of a case—whether it originates in a police station, a corporate board room, or the picket line—then following it through its various political and judicial channels, and concluding with a discussion of its impact. Such studies provide readers with the scope and knowledge necessary to understand the dynamics of constitutional politics.

Case studies, however, suffer from a major deficiency. While fully explaining a case in all its relevant parts, it remains difficult to generalize from a particular case to the broader universe of all cases. Nevertheless, case studies can provide the reader with a feel for constitutional politics unrivaled by any other type of study. Although the potential list of case studies is long, the annotations that follow highlight some of the better works.

Baxter, Maurice G. *The Steamboat Monopoly: Gibbons v. Ogden, 1824.* New York: Alfred A. Knopf, 1972.

This book examines the first landmark commerce clause case in its political and economic context. It investigates the impact of *Gibbons* upon 19th-century America and discusses the long-range importance of the case.

Berman, Daniel M. *It Is So Ordered: The Supreme Court Rules on School Segregation.* New York: Norton, 1966.

This book offers an excellent treatment of the famous cases of *Brown v. Board of Education.* It introduces beginning students to the workings of the judicial system.

Carter, Dan T. *Scottsboro: A Tragedy of the American South.* New York: Oxford University Press, 1971.

A vivid account of the infamous Scottsboro cases, this book examines radicalism, racism, and southern justice during the 1930s.

Cortner, Richard C. *The Jones and Laughlin Case.* New York: Alfred A. Knopf, 1970.

For those interested in the history of the commerce clause, this case study is essential reading.

Cortner, Richard C. *The Supreme Court and Civil Liberties Policy*. Palo Alto, CA: Mayfield Publishing Co., 1975.

Intended as a supplementary text, the author provides six in-depth studies of Supreme Court cases, from 1960 and through the 1970s, involving the nationalization of the Bill of Rights. Cases discussed are: *Duncan v. Louisiana, Doe v. Bolton; Chimel v. California; Cohen v. California; Wisconsin v. Yoder;* and *Frontiero v. Richardson*.

Garraty, John A. *Quarrels that Have Shaped the Constitution*, rev. ed. New York: Harper and Row, 1987.

This work contains twenty case studies of landmark Supreme Court decisions. The essays focus on the real life disputes and the personalities of the persons involved in the controversies.

Irons, Peter. *The New Deal Lawyers*. New York: Princeton University Press, 1982.

This book offers an account of litigation over the constitutionality of New Deal Laws, including the National Industrial Recovery Act, the Agricultural Adjustment Act, and the National Labor Relations Act.

Lewis, Anthony. *Gideon's Trumpet*. New York: Vintage Books, 1964.

In this book, the author provides a readable account of the landmark right to counsel case, *Gideon v. Wainwright*.

Lofgren, Charles. *The Plessy Case: A Legal-Historical Interpretation*. New York: Oxford University Press, 1987.

This book offers an analysis of both political and historical issues associated with the famous 1896 *Plessy* case. It is a case study of the Supreme Court decision that created the constitutional doctrine known as separate-but-equal.

Magrath, C. Peter. *Yazoo: Law and Politics in the New Republic*. New York: Norton, 1967.

This book offers a case study of the famous case of *Fletcher v. Peck*. For those who believe corruption is new to the United States, this case study will be enlightening. It is followed by an excellent brief history of the contract clause.

Melnick, Shep. *Regulation and the Courts: The Case of the Clean Air Act*. Washington, DC: Brookings Institution, 1983.

This book examines the Supreme Court as a regulatory policymaker. The author contends that courts have created a policy making system that is ineffective at creating firm regulatory policies.

Murphy, Walter F. *Wiretapping on Trial: A Case Study in the Judicial Process*. New York: Random House, 1965.

This book offers a case study of *Olmstead v. United States* from the first trial through Supreme Court adjudication. It provides a fine, but outdated, discussion of the law involving wiretapping.

Pritchett, C. Herman and Westin, Alan F., eds. *The Third Branch of Government: 8 Cases in Constitutional Politics*. New York: Harcourt, Brace and World, Inc., 1963.

This book offers a collection of eight case studies dealing with eight Supreme Court decisions that occurred after 1937, studies including the flag-salute case, the portal-to-portal case, the electric chair case, the released time case, the NAACP in Alabama case, subversion and the cold war case, the offshore oil cases, and the Sunday closing cases.

Sindler, Allan P. *Baake, DeFunis, and Minority Admissions: The Quest for Equal Opportunity*. New York: Longman, Inc., 1978.

This book offers an in-depth treatment of two highly controversial affirmative action cases dealing with so-called reverse discrimination that initially occurred in law and medical schools. The cases illustrate the interaction between government and university bureaucracies and the courts.

Westin, Alan F. *The Anatomy of a Constitutional Law Case*. New York: Macmillan, 1958.

This book offers a portrait of the famous steel seizure case, *Youngstown Sheet and Tube v. Sawyer*. It vividly records how this case rose from a bargaining dispute to the intervention of various governmental agencies and the role of the judiciary.

Compliance and Impact Analysis

To understand what a court has said and why it has said it is one thing, but to ascertain what happens after a decision is handed down is quite another. Compliance with a judicial opinion is not automatic and simply because the Supreme Court hands down a judgment does not necessarily mean that the political controversy has ended. A cursory examination of the history of the Supreme Court's efforts to end segregation in the public schools or the public reaction to the Court's abortion decision should alert even the most casual observer to the difficulties involved in compliance. Moreover, the myth that the Supreme Court is the final place to appeal policy decisions should be arrested by the observation that Court decisions can be overturned through constitutional amendment, passage of new statutory language, or the removal of appellate jurisdiction. More broadly, impact analysis concerns how judicial decisions affect society.

Most impact and compliance studies are published in law and social science journals and do not appear in book form. Recently, political scientists have acquired a greater interest in policy analysis. There is a growing list of available books employing impact and compliance analysis. The annotated list that follows highlights some of the better impact and compliance studies.

Becker, Theodore L. and Feeley, Malcolm M., eds. *The Impact of Supreme Court Decisions: Empirical Studies*, 2d ed. New York: Oxford University Press, 1973.

This book offers a collection of articles originally appearing in law and social science journals dealing with a variety of impact topics. Articles appear under the following general headings, preceded by the editors' explanatory introductions: the Supreme Court's effect on the president and congress, the Supreme Court's impact on lower federal courts, the Supreme Court's impact on state and local government and politics, and the Supreme Court's impact on public opinion. A final section deals with the theory and methods of impact analysis.

Blaustein, Albert P. and Ferguson, Clarence Clyde Jr. *Desegregation and the Law: The Meaning and Effect of the School Segregation Cases*. New York: Vintage Books, 1962.

In this book, an early example of an impact study, the authors combine the case study feature of tracing the development of the school segregation cases through the Supreme Court with a description of the problems of compliance, avoidance, and delay. Specifically a study of the impact of legislation and judicial decisions on the rights of blacks, the book deals with voting, public accommodations, school desegregation, employment, and housing.

Bullock, Charles and Lamb, Charles M. *Implementation of Civil Rights Policy*. Monterey, CA: Brooks/Cole, 1983.

This book offers a collection of case studies and essays focusing on the implementation of civil rights policies.

Johnson, Charles A. and Canon, Bradley C. *Judicial Policies: Implementation and Impact*. Washington, DC: Congressional Quarterly Press, 1984.

This book presents a classification scheme for understanding compliance and impact.

Johnson, Richard M. *The Dynamics of Compliance: Supreme Court Decision-Making From a New Perspective*. Evanston, IL: Northwestern University Press, 1967.

The author develops an analytical framework within which to study compliance. He focuses on the politics of compliance with the Supreme Court's school prayer decisions in two rural Illinois school districts.

Milner, Neil A. *The Court and Local Law Enforcement: The Impacts of Miranda*. Beverly Hills: Sage Publications, 1971.

This book assesses the impact of the Supreme Court's decision in *Miranda v. Arizona* on four Wisconsin police departments.

Muir, William K. Jr. *Prayer in the Public Schools: Law and Attitude Change*. Chicago: University of Chicago Press, 1967.

This book offers a before-and-after study of educator reactions to the Supreme Court decisions regarding school prayer. It is an application of psychological cognitive dissonance theory to the issue of whether law can change deeply rooted attitudes.

Murphy, Walter F., Tanenhaus, Joseph, and Kastner, Daniel L. *Public Evaluation of Constitutional Courts: Alternative Explanations*. Beverly Hills: Sage Publications, 1973.

This is a highly technical and informative volume concerning the ability of constitutional courts to have an impact on public opinion. The findings, based on survey data from the mid-1960s, are generally negative. Serious students of public opinion and the courts will find this work important.

O'Rourke, Timothy G. *The Impact of Reapportionment*. New Brunswick, NJ: Transaction Books, 1979.

This book is one in a large number of studies to consider the impact of *Baker v. Carr* and other reapportionment decisions on state politics. The author uses six states as the basis for his analysis.

Rodgers, Harrell R. Jr. *Community Conflict, Public Opinion and the Law: The Amish Dispute in Iowa*. Columbus, OH: Charles E. Merrill Publishing Company, 1969.

This is a case study of a legal dispute that did not reach the U.S. Supreme Court. Employing modern political science techniques, the author examines the circumstances under which responsible officials refuse to enforce the law and what effect such refusal has upon public support for law and the political system generally.

Rodgers, Harrell R. Jr. and Bullock, Charles S. III. *Law and Social Change: Civil Rights Laws and Their Consequences*. New York: McGraw-Hill Book Company, 1972.

This book offers a study of the impact of legislative and judicial decisions on the rights of blacks. It deals with voting, public accommodations, school desegregation, employment, and housing.

Schmidhauser, John R. and Berg, Larry L. *The Supreme Court and Congress: Conflict and Interaction, 1945–1968*. New York: The Free Press, 1972.

Employing both historical and modern behavioral methods, the authors investigate the myth that the Supreme Court is protected from congressional attack by an aura of reverence. The authors discuss the role of lawyer-congressmen and the American Bar Association in Court/Congress interinstitutional conflicts.

Tarr, George Alan. *Judicial Impact and State Supreme Courts*. Lexington, MA: Lexington Books, 1977.

This book presents an empirical investigation of state compliance with U.S. Supreme Court establishment clause cases decided between 1947 and 1973. The author presents interesting alternative explanations for compliance and noncompliance.

Wasby, Stephen L. *The Impact of the United State Supreme Court: Some Perspectives*. Homewood, IL: The Dorsey Press, 1970.

In this book, an early effort to integrate the various works on impact, the author discusses problems of conceptualization and offers a series of hypotheses for future research.

Judicial Process and Behavior

The study of judicial process and behavior is an important subfield within public law. There is little doubt that studies centering on how and why judges make decisions, the demands and supports on the judicial system, and the politics and policies surrounding the judiciary are necessary to understand how government works.

Books on judicial process and behavior range from simple institutional descriptions of how the judicial process works to sophisticated treatments entailing such approaches as small group, psychometric, interest group or role analysis. The annotations that follow highlight some of these works, including collections of articles appearing in book form.

Abraham, Henry J. *The Judicial Process: An Introductory Analysis of the Courts of the United States, England, and France*, 5th ed. New York: Oxford University Press, 1986.

This book examines the judicial systems of the United States, England, France, and includes some discussion of the system in the Soviet Union. It also contains a discussion of judicial self-restraint as practiced in the United States. Bibliographies of American constitutional law, biographies, autobiographies and related works of and by writers of the U.S. Supreme Court, comparative constitutional law, and selected works on civil rights and liberties are included as well.

Auerbach, Jerold S. *Unequal Justice: Lawyers and Social Change in Modern America*. New York: Oxford University Press, 1976.

In this book, the author offers a lively and penetrating account of how the elite segment of the bar dominates the legal profession and has fought against social change.

Becker, Theodore L. *Comparative Judicial Politics: The Political Functionings of Court*. Chicago: Rand McNally and Co., 1970.

In this book, the author attempts a reconceptualization of public law by applying concepts of structure and function. He argues for a better understanding of judicial role as opposed to judicial behavior.

Becker, Theodore L. *Political Behavioralism and Modern Jurisprudence*. Chicago: Rand McNally and Company, 1964.

This book offers a pertinent critique of the work of leading judicial behavior advocates, principally Glendon Schubert and Harold Speath. The author argues that judges are constrained in their behavior by perceptions of the judicial role and reports an experiment that provides prima facie evidence for the argument.

Beckstrom, John H. *Sociobiology and the Law: The Biology of Altruism in the Court of the Future*. Champaign: University of Illinois Press, 1985.

The author examines the theory of sociobiology and its implications on the actions of courts, lawyers, and law-makers.

Cardozo, Benjamin N. *The Nature of the Judicial Process*. New Haven: Yale University Press, 1921.

This book, a classic by a leading jurist of this century, describes the process of judging by examining how historical, philosophical, and sociological factors enter the conscious and subjective considerations of judicial decision makers.

Carp, Robert A. and Rowland, C. K. *Policymaking and Politics in the Federal District Courts*. Knoxville, TN: University of Tennessee Press, 1983.

A study of judicial decision-making, this book focuses on the relationship between background characteristics and decision-making of federal district court judges.

Carp, Robert A. and Stidham, Ronald. *The Federal Courts*. Washington, DC: Congressional Quarterly Press, 1985.

This book offers a study of the policy-making role of judges and information relevant to the understanding of the federal judicial system.

Casper, Jonathan D. *Lawyers Before the Warren Court: Civil Liberties and Civil Rights, 1957–66.* Urbana: University of Illinois Press, 1972.
This book explores how private practice attorneys become involved in litigation before the Supreme Court and what goals and interests they pursue.

Chinn, Nancy and Berkson, Larry. *Literature on Judicial Selection.* Chicago: American Judicature Society, 1980.
In this book, the authors annotate judicial selection articles and books published between 1913 and 1980. Divided into three parts, the book features annotations on state judicial selection, federal judicial selection, and judicial selection in foreign nations.

Danelski, David J. *A Supreme Court Justice is Appointed.* New York: Random House, 1964.
This book offers a case study of the appointment to the Supreme Court of Pierce Butler by President Harding. Employing notions of transaction, influence, and personality, the author presents a conceptual framework for understanding the appointment process.

DuBois, Philip, ed. *An Analysis of Judicial Reform.* Lexington: Lexington Books, 1982.
This book is a collection of articles related to judicial reform, such as the structure, staffing and operation of courts. The articles focus on the study and evaluation of policies aimed at improving the administration of the judiciary.

Fairchild, Erika S. and Webb, Vincent J. *The Politics of Crime and Criminal Justice.* Beverly Hills: Sage Publications, 1985.
This book is a collection of original articles demonstrating the linkage between crime policy and politics. Major headings include: Crime and Politics, Legislative Politics and the Criminal Law, and the Politics and Accountability in Criminal Justice Institutions.

Glick, Henry R. *Courts, Politics, and Justice.* New York: McGraw-Hill, 1983.
Written as an undergraduate text, this book focuses on broad topics concerning the American judicial system. The author examines traditional issues of judicial policy as well as judges' roles as policy makers.

Glick, Henry Robert and Vines, Kenneth N. *State Court Systems.* Englewood Cliffs, NJ: Prentice-Hall, Inc., 1973.
This slim but important book focuses on a study of state judicial systems.

Goldman, Sheldon and Sarat, Austin. *American Court Systems: Readings in Judicial Process and Behavior*, 2d ed. New York: Longman, Inc., 1989.

This book offers a collection of recent articles on important topics, including: courts and their alternatives, litigation in trial and appellate courts, plea bargaining and civil settlement in trial courts, judicial gatekeeping, public opinion and the courts, lawyers and litigants, judicial selection and backgrounds, juries, judicial decisionmaking, and compliance and impact.

Goldman, Sheldon. *Constitutional Law: Cases and Essays*. New York: Harper and Row, 1987.

A textbook for constitutional law courses, this volume contains a particularly valuable feature for those interested in understanding judicial behavior: a discussion of the justices' appointments, backgrounds, voting patterns, and patterns of group interaction with appropriate data and tables. This data begins with justices from 1789 and ends with the Burger Court.

Goldman, Sheldon and Lamb, Charles M., eds. *Judicial Conflict and Consensus: Behavioral Studies of American Appellate Courts*. Lexington: University Press of Kentucky, 1986.

This book analyzes twelve cases which examine conflict and consensus among appellate judges. Specifically examined are the causes and reasons of judicial behavior and the judge's role as policy maker.

Goldman, Sheldon and Sarat, Austin, eds. *American Court Systems: Readings in Judicial Process and Behavior*. San Francisco: W. H. Freeman and Company, 1978.

This book offers a selection of fifty-four articles placed in a dispute-processing framework. It contains many of the finest articles written in the field of judicial process and behavior.

Grossman, Joel B. and Tanenhaus, Joseph, eds. *Frontiers of Judicial Research*. New York: John Wiley and Sons, 1969.

This book presents papers delivered at the Shambaugh Conference held at the University of Iowa in 1967. The conference was attended by many of the leading public law scholars at the time, and represented a high point in the study of judicial behavior.

Grossman, Joel B. *Lawyers and Judges: The ABA and the Politics of Judicial Selection*. New York: John Wiley and Sons, 1965.

In this book, the author presents a study of the efforts of the American Bar Association to influence judicial selection.

Harrington, Christine. *Shadow Justice: The Ideology and Institutionalization of Alternatives to Court*. Westport, CT: Greenwood Press, 1985.

This book focuses on dispute resolution in the United States, various types of disputes, how they are handled by the courts, and available alternatives.

Howard, Woodford. *Courts of Appeal in the Federal Judicial System: A Study of the Second, Fifth, and District of Columbia Circuits.* Princeton: Princeton University Press, 1981.

The author provides an analysis of decision making on the U.S. Courts of Appeals. In addition, he examines the evolution of the appeals courts and their role in shaping federal policy.

Kramer, Daniel C. *Comparative Civil Rights and Liberties.* Washington, DC: University Press of America, 1982.

This book offers a comparative study of civil liberties in the United States, Great Britain, India, the Soviet Union, and France. Through an examination of judicial opinions, the author points out the limits of civil liberties in these countries.

McClosky, Herbert and Brill, Alida. *Dimensions of Tolerance: What Americans Believe about Civil Liberties.* New York: Russell Sage Foundation, 1983.

This book reports the results of survey research on attitudes of Americans about civil liberties; it contains statistical findings on attitudes toward freedom of speech and press, religion, due process, privacy, and life style preferences.

Melone, Albert P. *Lawyers, Public Policy and Interest Group Politics.* Washington, DC: University Press of America, 1977, 1979.

This book offers a study of the sociology and politics of the American Bar Association and its relationship with government and other vital segments of society.

Mendelson, Wallace. *Supreme Court Statecraft: The Rule of Law and Men.* Ames, IA: Iowa State University Press, 1985.

This book contains thirty of Mendelson's previously published articles, all organized into six parts. It represents Mendelson's thoughts on the Constitution, judicial events, and the behavior of judges.

Murphy, Walter F. and Tanenhaus, Joseph. *The Study of Public Law.* New York: Random House, 1972.

In this book, the authors review the development and approaches in the discipline of public law. The authors employ cross-cultural studies.

Murphy, Walter F. and Pritchett, C. Herman, eds. *Courts, Judges, and Politics: An Introduction to the Judicial Process,* 4th ed. New York: Random House, 1986.

This book offers a collection of edited cases and articles covering most aspects of the judicial process in the United States.

Murphy, Walter F. and Tanenhaus, Joseph. *Comparative Constitutional Law: Cases and Commentaries.* New York: St. Martin's Press, 1977.

As the first of its kind, this book discusses the politics and courts of six nation-states and then presents judicial opinions of these courts classified under the following headings: horizontal and vertical distribution of power, foreign affairs, governmental regulation of economic affairs, equality under law, human dignity and public health, morals and safety, religious freedom, freedom of expression, voting and political participation, threats to a democratic order, and constitutions in times of emergency. The six countries studied are the United States, Germany, Japan, Canada, Australia, and Ireland.

Murphy, Walter F. *Elements of Judicial Strategy.* Chicago: University of Chicago Press, 1964.

This book investigates the capability of the U.S. judiciary to influence public policy, and provides an account of the small group dynamics and politics of the Supreme Court.

Nagel, Stuart, Fairchild, Erika and Champagne, Anthony, eds. *The Political Science of Criminal Justice.* Springfield, IL: Charles C. Thomas Publishers, 1981.

This book is a series of articles about criminal justice issues and the relevance of political science to understanding.

Nagel, Stuart S. *The Legal Process from a Behavioral Perspective.* Homewood, IL: The Dorsey Press, 1969.

This book offers a collection of a leading public law scholar's published articles.

Neely, Richard. *How Courts Govern America.* New Haven: Yale University Press, 1981.

Written by a judge, the thesis of this book is that U.S. courts operate to make the society democratic and not the contrary. The author argues that the judicial branch alleviates the deficiencies of the other institutions of government. However, Judge Neely also identifies deficiencies in the judicial system that need remedy.

O'Brien, David M. *Storm Center: The Supreme Court in American Politics.* New York: W. W. Norton, 1986.

This book offers an analysis of the Supreme Court, its management of caseloads, and its communication of decisions to the public.

Peltason, Jack W. *Federal Courts in the Political Process.* New York: Random House, 1955.
This book features an argument for and presentation of an interest group approach to the study of courts.

Pinkele, Carl and Louthan, William, eds. *Discretion, Justice, and Democracy: A Public Policy Perspective.* Ames: Iowa State University Press, 1985.
This book contains readings which examine how discretion is available to authorities at many levels of the legal system, including law enforcement. It explores how discretion impacts society.

Porter, Mary Cornelia and Tarr, Allan G., eds. *State Supreme Courts: Policymakers in the Federal System.* Westport, CT: Greenwood Press, 1982.
This book is a collection of essays by political scientists focusing on state–federal relations, and constitutional and nonconstitutional policy making. An introductory chapter discusses the selection of justices, their surrounding legal environments, and broad topics concerning state supreme court policy making.

Posner, Richard. *The Federal Courts: Crisis and Reform.* Cambridge: Harvard University Press, 1985.
This book addresses problems of the federal judiciary. Its main premise describes the increase in caseloads as causing a decline in the quality of the federal justice system.

Provine, Doris Marie. *Judging Credentials: Nonlawyer Judges and the Politics of Professionalism.* Chicago: University of Chicago Press, 1986.
This book offers a comparative study of lawyer and non-lawyer judges, and how they perform in the courtroom. The results are surprising.

Rehnquist, William. *The Supreme Court: How it Was, How it Is.* New York: William Morrow, 1987.
Chief Justice Rehnquist offers an inside view of how the Supreme Court works. He includes discussions of the lives of judges, analyses of the workings of the judicial process, and historical perspectives of the Court's development.

Richardson, Richard J. and Vines, Kenneth N. *The Politics of Federal Courts: Lower Courts in the United States.* Boston: Little, Brown and Company, 1970.
This book explores the lower federal courts' role in the judicial system. The authors present evidence exploding the myth of a judicial hierarchy.

Rohde, David W. and Spaeth, Harold J. *Supreme Court Decision-Making.* San Francisco: W. H. Freeman and Company, 1976.

This book offers a pertinent example of the judicial behavior approach to the study of Supreme Court decisionmaking.

Schubert, Glendon. *Human Jurisprudence: Public Law as Political Science.* Honolulu: The University Press of Hawaii, 1975.

As a leading advocate of the judicial behavior approach, the author provides here an overall view of public law and his pioneering efforts to develop public law as an exemplary social science.

Schubert, Glendon. *The Judicial Mind Revisited: Psychometric Analysis of Supreme Court Ideology.* New York: Oxford University Press, 1974.

Focusing primarily on methodology, the author develops a theory of political ideology from a synthesis of the works of leading psychologists. He studies ideological patterns of justices from the Vinson through the Warren eras.

Schubert, Glendon and Danelski, David J., eds. *Comparative Judicial Behavior: Cross-Cultural Studies of Political Decision-Making in the East and West.* New York: Oxford University Press, 1969.

As an outstanding collection of articles dealing with judicial behavior, this book includes studies of Korea, Japan, Philippines, Canada, and Australia. It also discusses methods and approaches for cross-cultural judicial behavior studies.

Schubert, Glendon, ed. *Judicial Behavior: A Reader in Theory and Research.* Chicago: Rand McNally and Company, 1964.

This book offers a collection of articles placed within the editor's intellectual framework of what constitutes the proper study of judicial behavior; it contains many of the important judicial behavior articles published before 1964.

Sheldon, Charles H. *American Judicial Process: Models and Approaches.* New York: Dodd, Mead and Company, 1974.

This book offers a discussion of the analytical models and conceptual approaches developed for studying the judiciary.

Simons, William B., ed. *The Constitution of the Communist World.* Alphen ann den Rijn, Germantown, MD: Sijthoff & Noordhoff, 1980.

This book offers translations of the constitutions of fifteen Communist nation-states. Introductory essays written by subject specialists precede each document.

Sprague, John D. *Voting Patterns of the United States Supreme Court: Cases in Federalism, 1889–1959*. Indianapolis: Bobbs-Merrill Co., 1968.
    In this book, the author evaluates bloc and scalogram analyses with a view of moving toward a small-group theory of judicial voting.

Stumpf, Harry P. *American Judicial Politics*. New York: Harcourt Brace Jovanovich, 1988.
    This author takes a modern political science approach to understanding the judiciary within the American political context. A rule-oriented approach to law is eschewed in favor of a broader sociopolitical conception of courts.

Ulmer, S. Sidney, ed. *Courts, Law, and Judicial Processes*. New York: The Free Press, 1981.
    This book is a collection of eighty articles, mostly reprinted from previous works, focusing on decision making discretion, structure, and purposes of judicial institutions, and problems in the judicial system.

Wasby, Stephen L. *The Supreme Court in the Federal Judicial System*, 3d ed. Chicago: Nelson-Hall Publishers, 1988.
    This book offers pertinent information about the operations and roles of the Supreme Court, and the effects of Supreme Court decisions on American life.

Watson, Richard A. and Downing, Rondal G. *The Politics of the Bench and Bar: Judicial Selection Under the Missouri Nonpartisan Plan*. New York: John Wiley and Sons, 1969.
    This book offers an empirical study of the most popular of merit appointment plans of judicial selection. Subjects include: bar politics, nominating commission politics, and attitudes concerning effectiveness of election versus appointment plans of judicial selection.

Wheare, K. C. *Federal Government*, 4th ed. New York: Oxford University Press, 1963.
    This book offers a comparative analysis of federalism as a governmental system.

Woodward, Bob and Armstrong, Scott. *The Brethren: Inside the Supreme Court*. New York: Simon & Schuster, 1979.
    This book offers a journalistic account about the internal politics of the Burger Court. The authors claim to rely on confidential interviews of former Supreme Court clerks.

Chapter Three

Writing and Documenting Research Papers

———
———

Introduction

Writing a paper on a constitutional law topic presents special problems including how to cite materials. In addition to examining these difficulties, this chapter contains a practical discussion useful for other courses in the social sciences and humanities.

Choosing a Topic

Student papers are usually determined by the requirements established by the course instructor. If an academic unit offers many law-related courses, most probably the instructor will narrow the range of topic choices. This range may reflect not only the specialized subject matter as defined by the curriculum, but the instructor's academic and ideological interests as well. As a result, students should pay close attention to instructor expressions of expectations.

In courses on constitutional law instructors typically ask students to write a term paper that traces or analyzes the development of doctrine. Sometimes instructors ask students to research some aspect of judicial process and behavior, including the politics surrounding particular court decisions. Whatever the case, there is a wealth of material available for student papers. Consequently, no student may legitimately claim that materials are nonexistent on a law-related topic.

For students without direct access to a law library the research task, though still possible, does pose difficulties. For students needing assistance, the interlibrary loan department of the college library is an appropriate place to start. Materials, for example, can be photocopied at no or little expense. A visit to a law library some distance from campus may be worth the additional effort too. It is wise, however, to plan the research project carefully. Because of the usual research problems just mentioned, never leave the paper to the last minute.

When choosing a topic keep it narrow. While the initial impulse of an inexperienced researcher is to choose a broad topic, it is better to keep it narrow. Remember, when dealing with law-related topics, it is easy to write an excessively long and involved paper. If the topic is conceived as open-ended from the start, it will be difficult to contain it within reasonable bounds. A common pitfall for students is to get trapped into a project with no logical conclusion. A long rambling paper usually raises more questions than it answers.

Before settling on a firm topic, conduct a preliminary investigation. Ask the following questions:

1. Am I interested in the topic?
2. Does the topic fulfill course requirements and instructor expectations?
3. Are the necessary library materials accessible to me?
4. What are my specific research questions?

Upon answering the first two questions affirmatively, then it is necessary for the student to visit the library for a careful appraisal of whether he or she may do the task in a reasonable amount of time.

Using the Library

Do not waste time and energy compiling a bibliography without first narrowing your topic. A quick way to determine the scope and practicality of the research topic is to consult legal encyclopedias and indexes to periodical literature. Because of the nearly objective nature of most encyclopedia articles, a student can determine the scope and some key citations almost immediately. By consulting periodical literature indexes for recent years, it is possible to know what questions are of contemporary interest and need researching. Once satisfied with the ability to conduct the research, write out the specific research questions of interest. Armed with this knowledge, consult the instructor for advice. Indicate the topic, specific research questions, and how you expect to conduct your research. The instructor might steer you to a better topic, a slightly different slant on the topic, or a superior way to conduct the research. Compile a complete bibliography only after narrowing the topic.

When conducting legal research leave no pertinent materials untouched. Because the nature of the research project will dictate where to begin, it is misleading to suggest that students should always begin in one place and end in another. However, consult each of the following categories of research materials. The student who does this can be reasonably certain that he or she has adequately surveyed the topic.

1. encyclopedias
2. books
3. articles
4. codes and statutory law
5. court opinions, case annotations
6. digests
7. citators
8. case updating services and newspapers

See Chapter One for a description of these research tools and a discussion on how to use them.

The Format for a Paper

Constitutional law research papers should contain the following elements: (1) *Title Page,* which includes the title given the paper, student name, instructor name and course number and title, and date; (2) *Table of Contents,* which includes chapter or section headings; (3) *Table of Cases,* listing in alphabetical order each case mentioned or cited, the legal citation for each case, and the page numbers where each appears in the body of the text; (4) *Body of the Text;* (5) *Bibliography* at the end of the paper; and (6) depending on course requirements, place notes citing authority at the bottom of each page, at the back of each chapter, at the end of the paper just before the bibliography, or within the body of the text. Note that citation formats for footnotes and so on may vary with each professor. Always type and double space all papers.

Citations

There are almost always a greater number of citations in constitutional law papers than for the average research project in the social sciences or humanities. Commonly, constitutional law research papers require much citation to authority. This is so because most facts and ideas are those of legal professionals.

What to Cite

Ordinarily, cite ideas originating from another source. It is unnecessary to cite ideas, facts, and quotations of common knowledge: for example, "The United States Constitution contains provisions for three branches of the national government."

Because there is a tendency to rely heavily on court cases, writers are obliged to note that fact. These notes may appear in the middle or at the end of a sentence: for example, "The dispute, *Hawaii Housing Authority v. Midkiff* (1984),[86] arose out of a state land reform statute. Writing for a unanimous Court Justice Sandra Day O'Connor, a Republican appointed by a Republican President, pointed out that the contract clause had never been used against the exercise of eminent domain power.[87]"

There is also a tendency to quote extensively from judicial opinions. Though often useful, long quotations can be boring and consume too much space. Learn how to use ellipses; that is, three dots indicating omission of words within a sentence. Four dots, a period followed by three spaced dots (. . . .) indicate the omission of the last part of the sentence quoted, omission of the first part of the sentence, omission of a complete sentence or more including a paragraph or more. By employing ellipses it is possible to relate the essence of what is being quoted without requiring readers to plow through unnecessary verbiage: for example, "This conclusion was based upon an important stated assumption, that is, a state cannot be presumed to surrender its power to promote . . . the happiness and prosperity of the community by which it is established.[34]" Indent and single space quotations of more than three lines in length. When using block quotations, it is unnecessary to use quotation marks unless one is quoting a quote within the quote. In such instances, use single quotation marks.

At times it is desirable to alert readers to tangential facts or quotations. However, to do so would distract the reader's attention from the flow of ideas developing in the body of the text. In such an event, use reference notes, sometimes called explanatory or discursive footnotes. It is common, for example, to place a discussion of a minority court opinion in a footnote. Methodological analyses are also appropriately found in explanatory notes.

A source of confusion when referencing court opinions is the circumstance when writers should underline (italicize) case names. This is especially the case when referencing court opinions in the body of the text. I suggest the following practice. *Do not* underline a case name if it is followed by a legal citation, for example, Roth v. United States, 354 U.S. 476 (1957). If the case name or the case name and date of the opinion are written then underline the case name including the abbreviation for versus, for example, *Roth v. United States* or *Roth v. United States* (1957). Do not underline case names in footnotes and in bibliographies where legal citations are provided.

Footnoting Form

Footnote (endnote if placed at end of the paper) form is one of the few things which can be justifiably arbitrary. There is no inherent reason to use one form rather than another, so long as the communication is clear and consistent. The works used should be cited in the same form as in indexes, bibliographies, and library catalogs. In this way, a reader will be able to locate cited sources.

What follows are examples of the most frequent types of footnote entries used in a political science paper. Most of the forms are based upon the various editions of: *The Chicago Manual of Style;* Kate L. Turabian, *A Manual for Writers of Term Papers, Theses and Dissertations;* and the 13th and 14th editions of *A Uniform System of Citation* (Cambridge: Harvard Law Review Association, 1981, 1986). Although the forms presented should meet the requirements of most instructors, there is an alternative form of citation gaining prominence in social science circles. This scientific reference format is located after the examples for the more conventional forms of footnote citation.

The examples of footnoting form that follow conform to functional customs and conventions. First, provide the reader with the name of the author(s), a full title, and the facts of publication, including for a book: the name of the publisher, the place of publication, and the publication date. For journal articles it is appropriate to indicate the name of the author, the title of the article, the name of the journal in which the article appears, the volume number, the date of publication, and the page(s) of the cited materials. The justification for providing this information is that other researchers may need to access and read for themselves the cited material. Second, when referencing unpublished material, make it possible for others to track down your source. Provide the author's name, the title of the unpublished material, the type of material (for example, a convention paper or a M.A. thesis), where the material may be found, the date appearing on the material, and lastly the page numbers if citing specific pages for a footnote.

Footnoting Books   The following are examples of footnote citations for many of the most common types of books. Listings are given for single author books, books by more than one author, books in a series, books by an editor or translator, and many others. While this is not a complete list, the researcher will be able to find most of the examples he or she will require.

Book With One Author:

1. Phillip J. Cooper, *Hard Judicial Choices: Federal District Court Judges and State and Local Officials* (New York: Oxford University Press, 1988), p. 61.

Book With Two Authors:

2. Peter C. Hoffner and N. E. Hull, *Impeachment in America, 1635–1805* (New Haven: Yale University Press, 1985), pp. 50–65.

Book With Three Authors:

3. Carl Kalvelage, Albert P. Melone, and Morley Segal, *Bridges to Knowledge in Political Science: A Handbook for Research* (Pacific Palisades, CA: Palisades Publishers, 1984), p. 138.

Book With More Than Three Authors:

4. Donald Harris, et al., *Compensation and Support for Illness and Injury* (Oxford: Clarendon Press, 1984), p. 108.

Edition of a Book Other Than the First:

5. Laurence H. Tribe, *American Constitutional Law,* 2d ed. (Mineola, N.Y.: The Foundation Press, 1988), p. 1493.

Book in a Series:

6. Lief H. Carter, *Contemporary Constitutional Law Making,* Permagon Government and Politics Series (New York: Pergamon Press, 1985), p. 44.

Book by Editor:

7. Gary McDowell, ed., *Taking the Constitution Seriously* (Dubuque, Iowa: Kendall/Hunt Publishing Company, 1981), p. 85.

Book by Translators:

8. Willi Paul Adams, *The First American Constitution: Republican Ideology and the Making of the State Constitutions in the Revolutionary Era,* Trans. Rita and Robert Kimber (Chapel Hill: University of North Carolina Press, 1980), p. 164.

When both author and translator names appear on the title page, the translator's name should appear after the title. However, if the author's name is not on the title page, the translator's name should appear first, followed by the word trans.

Multivolume Book:

9. Richard Loss, ed., *Corwin on the Constitution,* 2 vols. (Ithaca, New York: Cornell University Press, 1987), 2: 179–193.

Citation in One Book From Another Book:

10. F. Frankfurter, *The Commerce Clause under Marshall Taney and Waite,* pp. 80–82 as cited in David P. Currie, *The Constitution in the Supreme Court* (Chicago: University of Chicago Press, 1985), p. 449.

Book Review:

11. George Kannar, *Review of Constitutional Choices* by Laurence Tribe, *The New Republic* (October 14, 1985), p. 33.

The first name cited is that of the reviewer of the book. The second name cited is the author of the book reviewed.

Book in a Series, One Author, Several Volumes, Each With a Different Title:

12. Arthur M. Schlesinger, *The Age of Roosevelt,* 3 vols., *The Politics of Upheaval* (Boston: Houghton Mifflin, 1960), 3:215.

The first title is the name of the book series. The second title *(The Politics of Upheaval)* is the name of the specific cited volume.

Paperback Edition of a Book First Published in Hardcover:

13. Bob Woodward and Scott Armstrong. *The Bretheren: Inside the Supreme Court* (New York: Avon Books, paperback, 1979), p. 85–92.

Introduction or Foreword of a Book by Another Author:

14. Gilbert Y. Steiner, Foreword to *The Courts and Social Policy,* by Donald L. Horowitz (Washington, D.C.: The Brookings Institution, 1977), p. i.

The first appearing name is the person writing the foreword or introduction to the book. It is his or her comments that are regarded as important and therefore are cited, not those of the author of the book.

Book with an Association as an Author:

15. American Enterprise Institute for Public Policy Research, *Forming a Government under the Constitution* (Washington, D.C.: American Enterprise Institute for Public Policy Research, 1985), p. 35.

Author's Name Not on Title Page, but Known:

16. [Alexander Hamilton], *The Federalist Papers* (New York: New American Library, 1961), p. 471.

Article, Chapter, or Part of Another Book:

17. John R. Coen, "On Worrying About the Constitution," in *The Humane Imagination*, edited by Charles L. Black, Jr. (Woodbridge: Ox Bow Press, 1986), p. 118.

Footnoting Journal and Magazine Articles   The following are examples of footnote citations for periodical literature. Magazine, newspaper, and journal article examples are given.

Academic Journal:

18. Gregory A. Caldeira, "Public Opinion and the U.S. Supreme Court: FDR's Court-Packing Plan," *American Political Science Review* 81 (Dec. 1987): 1141.

It is preferable to reference legal articles in the same way as other academic articles when submitting a research paper in a social science or humanities course. However, sometimes instructors want students to be aware of how different legal citation style is from other academic disciplines. Therefore, they ask their students to use the legal style of citation. See footnote 20 for an example of legal style for citing a law review article.

Popular Magazine Article, No Author Given:

19. "Supreme Court Ruling is Civil Rights Roadblock [Grove City Decision], *Jet*, 7 April 1986, p. 10.

Legal Periodical:

20. Handberg, *After the Fall: Justice Fortas' Judicial Values and Behavior After the Failure of His Nomination as Chief Justice*, 15 CAP. U. L. REV. 205 (1986).

Use this legal style only if requested by instructor. See footnote 18 for preferable style.

Popular Magazine Article, Author Given:

21. Edwin Meese, "The Law of the Constitution," *The National Review*, July 17, 1987, p. 30.

Newspapers:

22. Stephen Labotan, "Judges Mark 200 Years of Constitutional Law," *The New York Times*, 19 July, 1987, p. 88.

When the author byline is given, name the reporter at the beginning of the citation. For foreign newspapers that do not indicate the city in their titles, place the city name in parentheses, e.g., *Le Monde* (Paris).

Footnoting Encyclopedias, Almanacs, and Other Works Examples of footnote citations are given here for a variety of less commonly used sources. Examples included are for encyclopedias, almanacs, dissertations, and nonprinted matter. The researcher should find that most contingencies have been addressed, or at least be able to fashion a citation from the information given.

Signed Articles:

23. *Encyclopedia of the American Judicial System*, s.v. "The Chase and Waite Courts and Era," by Jeffrey Brandon Morris.

Unsigned Articles:

24. *Encyclopedia Britannica*, s.v. "United States (of America)."

Legal Encyclopedias:

25. 70 AM. JUR. 2D *Sedition, Subversive Activities, and Treason* §15 (1987).
26. 16 C.J.S. *Constitutional Law* §1256 (1985).

Almanacs:

27. *The World Almanac and Book of Facts 1985*, s.v. "Judiciary of the U.S."

When citing encyclopedias or almanacs the place of publication, publisher, date, and page numbers are normally omitted. Editions other than the first should be specified. Page numbers should be used in the footnotes when there are more than just a few citations from the source. The letters s.v. mean *sub verbo*, "under the word"; i.e., under the designated title.

Dissertation or Thesis:

28. Allen Franklin Anderson, Jr., "Plea Bargaining Rates in North Carolina: Some Determinants of Variability" (Ph.D. Dissertation, Southern Illinois University at Carbondale, 1984), p. 50.

29. Cynthia J. Hennings-Dawson, "The Impact of First Amendment Decisions on the Political Activities of Unified Bar Associations" (M.A. Thesis, Southern Illinois University at Carbondale, 1987), p. 198.

Material from Manuscript Collections:

30. Administration of Justice and Courts, 1916–, Richard Richards Papers, Library of University of California, Los Angeles, Los Angeles, California, p. 4.

Radio and Television Programs:

31. NBC, NBC Nightly News, 9 March 1983, "President Reagan's Acceptance of Burford's Resignation," Chris Wallace, reporter.

Interviews:

32. Interview with Colleen Kay Connell, Staff Attorney, American Civil Liberties Union, Chicago, Illinois, April 23, 1983.

Letters:

33. Albert Ellery Bergh, ed., *The Writings of Thomas Jefferson* (Washington, D.C.: Thomas Jefferson Memorial Association, 1907), 15:447–48. Letter of Thomas Jefferson to Judge William Johnson, June 12, 1823.

Mimeographed or Other Nonprinted Reports:

34. Werner F. Grunbaum, "Selected Bibliography on Artificial Intelligence Applications and Expert Systems for Law," mimeographed (Law, Courts, and Judicial Process Section Newsletter, American Political Science Association, Spring, 1987), p. 12.

Booklets and Pamphlets:

35. Alice O'Conner and Mary L. Henze, *"During Good Behavior": Judicial Independence and Accountability* (Washington, D.C.: The Jefferson Foundation, 1984), p. 5.
36. Illinois Office of Education, *Study Guide, Constitution of the State of Illinois and the United States* (Springfield, Illinois: State Board of Education, 1981), p. 21.

Underscore titles of booklets and pamphlets.

Proceedings of a Meeting or Conference: Reproduced:

37. The Bicentennial Conference of the United States Constitution, "Committee II—Effectiveness of Governmental Operations," (Philadelphia, Pa.: April 5–8, 1986), p. 123.

Paper Read or Speech Delivered at a Meeting:

38. Ronald Cohen, "Procedural Justice and Participation" (Paper Delivered at the 1984 Annual Meeting of the Law and Society Association), Boston, June 8, 1984, p. 45.

Footnoting Legal Sources   Examples of footnotes for legal materials follow.

U.S. Supreme Court (U.S.):

39. City of Mobile v. Bolden, 446 U.S. 73 (1980).

If one is citing a specific point found in a judge's opinion on a particular page, then that page of the judicial opinion should be cited in the reference note. This rule applies to all judicial opinions whatever the source.

U.S. Supreme Court (U.S.) (reporter's name):

40. Shelton v. Tiffin, 47 U.S. (6 How.) 163 (1848).

Federal Cases (F. Cas.):

41. Washington Mills v. Russell, 29 F. Cas. 336 (C.C.D. Mass. 1873) (No. 17,247).

Federal Reporter (F.), (F. 2d):

42. Hong Kong Supermarket v. Kizer, 839 F. 2d 1078 (9th Cir. 1987).

Federal Supplement (F. Supp.):

43. Pestrak v. Ohio Elections Commission, 670 F. Supp. 1368 (S.D. Ohio 1987).

Federal Rules Decisions (F.R.D.):

44. Hawthorne v. Gulf Shores, Inc., 115 F.R.D. 474 (1986).

American Law Reporter (A.L.R.) Annotation:

45. Annot., 68 A.L.R. Fed. 290 (1984).

American Law Reporter (A.L.R.) Opinion:

46. Loose v. Offshore Navigation, 68 A.L.R. Fed. 318 (1984).

United States Law Week (U.S.L.W.):

47. Gulfstream Aerospace Corp. v. Mayacamas Corp., 56 U.S.L.W. 4243 (March 22, 1988).

U.S. Supreme Court Bulletin (CCH S.Ct. Bull.):

48. Langley v. Federal Deposit Insurance Corp., 48 CCH S.Ct. Bull. p. B211 (Dec. 1, 1987).

State Cases:

49. Adams v. Barrell, 132 A. 130 (Me. 1926).
50. Byrd v. Peterson, 66 Ariz. 253, 186 P. 2d 955 (1947).

When possible cite both the official and West reports. Cite the appropriate West reporter and include the state name when a state does not have its own reporter or if official reports are unavailable.

Briefs, Oral Arguments, Transcripts and Records:

51. Petitioner's Brief at 7, Mazer v. Stein, 347 U.S. 201 (1953), in 1953 FO No. 228, card 2, *Information Handling Service.*
52. Respondent's Brief at 594, Kissinger v. Halperin, 452 U.S. 713 (1981), in vol. 123, *Landmark Briefs and Arguments of the Supreme Court of the United States: Constitutional Law.*
53. Oral Argument by Harry D. Miller, Esq. on behalf of Appellants at 22, Pennell v. San Jose, 108 S.Ct. 849 (1988), on Fiche 28, *University Publications of America.*
54. Transcript of Record at 23, Mazer v. Stein, 347 U.S. 201 (1953), in 1953 FO No. 228, card 1, *Information Handling Service.*

When citing briefs, oral arguments, transcripts, and records, first describe what is being cited, followed by the page number being cited, followed by the full legal citation to the case. As a courtesy to the reader, provide the source where the information is found. Petitions, complaints, and other court records are cited in the same way. The first words describe the nature of the document.

Legal Encyclopedia:

55. see footnotes 25 and 26.

Federal Statute:

56. *Department of Defense Authorization Act, 1985,* Publ. L. No. 98-525, 98 Stat. 2492 (1984).

Federal Code:

57. 20 U.S.C. §1210 (1982).
58. 42 U.S.C.S. §1983 (Law. Co-op. 1986).
59. 28 U.S.C.A. §144 (West 1987 Supp. Pamph.).

Cite statutes commonly referred to by their official or popular name. For example: Comprehensive Employment and Training Act, 29 U.S.C. (1978) §834 (Supp. IV 1980). It is permissible to substitute the word section, or its abbreviation sec., for the section symbol(§).

U.S. Constitution:

60. U.S. Const. art. II, §3.

Federal Register (Fed. Reg.):

61. Visa Waver for Certain Cotton Terry Bar Mops, 50 Fed. Reg. 32,467 (1985).

Code of Federal Regulations (C.F.R.):

62. Standard for Nitrogen Oxides, 40 C.F.R. §60.44a (1987).

Footnoting Government Documents   The form for government documents is unlike that adopted for books and articles, and it is often a source of confusion. The best rule is to follow the card catalog as a guide. In general, references to government documents should include in the following order: (1) the country (U.S.), (2) the branch of government (legislative, executive), (3) the subbranch or branches (House, Senate, Judiciary Committee), (4) the document title (underscored), (5) the name of the document series or sequence and the facts of publication (H. Rept. 342 to Accompany H.R. 6258, 95th Cong., 1st sess., 1977). Examples follow.

Legislative Bills:

63. U.S. Congress, House, *Authorization for Childhood Immunization*, H.R. 5230, 99th Cong., 2d sess., 1986, p. 2.
64. U.S. Congress, Senate, *Violent Crime and Drug Enforcement Act of 1982*, S2572, 97th Cong., 2d sess., 1982, p. 7.

Legislative Debates:

65. U.S. Congress, Senate, Balanced Budget—Tax Limitation Constitutional Amendment, 97th Cong., 2d sess., 13 July 1982, *Congressional Record*, 128, no. 12, S15922.

Legislative Reports:

66. U.S. Congress, House, *The Changing Distribution of Industrial Profits: The Oil and Gas Industry within the Fortune 500, 1978–1980*, H. Rept. 97-390, 97th Cong., 1st sess., 1981, p. 2.

Legislative Hearings:

67. U.S. Congress, House, Committee on the Judiciary, *Immigration and Naturalization Act Amendments of 1986, Hearings before the Subcommittee on Immigration, Refugees, and International Law of the Committee on the Judiciary on H.R. 444*, 99th Cong., 2d sess., 1986, p. 23–41.

Executive Department:

68. Executive Office of the President, Office of Management and Budget, *Budget of the United States Government, Fiscal Year 1987* (Washington, D.C.: U.S. Government Printing Office, 1987), p. 5/102–5/107.
69. General Accounting Office, "The Seizure of the Mayaguez: A Case Study of Crisis Management," GAO ID-76-45, (May, 1976), p. 114–128.

Government agencies often imprint documents with publication numbers and specify publication series. If such numbers are available, include them in citations. Because author names are sometimes printed on documents it is desirable to cite the authors. However, libraries often do not catalog government documents by author name. Thus, do not neglect to include sponsoring agencies in citations.

Presidential Papers:

70. U.S. President, "Veto of War Powers Resolution," *Weekly Compilation of Presidential Documents,* vol. 9, October 27, 1973, p. 1285.

Treaties:

71. *U.S. Statutes at Large,* vol. 43, pt. 2 (December 1923–March 1925), "Naval Arms Limitation Treaty," February 26, 1922, ch. 1, art. 1, p. 1655.
72. U.S. Department of State, *United States Treaties and Other International Agreements,* vol. 27, pt. 2, "Soviet Socialist Republics, Union of- ABM treaty," TIAS No. 8276, 3 July 1974.

Beginning in 1950, U.S. treaties may be found in the publication, *United States Treaties and Other International Agreements.* The United Nations and formerly the League of Nations also publish a treaty series that includes international agreements.

International Organizations:

73. United Nations, *Report of the Secretary-General Submitted under General Assembly Resolution 39/146 of 14 December 1984, Covering the Developments in the Middle East in all Aspects* (a/40/779), 1985, p. 2.

Kate Turabian suggests that citations for international documents include: authorizing body, topic or title, document or series number when available, and publication date.

State Documents:

74. Illinois, Secretary of State, *Handbook of Illinois Government,* June, 1987, p. 23.
75. Illinois, *Constitution,* art. 2, sec. 1.

Specify the date of the constitution if the constitution cited is not the one currently in force, for example, Illinois, *Constitution* (1848), art. 1, sec. 2.

Local Documents:

76. Carbondale, Illinois, City Manager, "City of Carbondale, Illinois Annual Budget FY 1987–88," mimeographed (April 10, 1987), p. 16.

Often there is insufficient documentation for state and local materials. It may be necessary to improvise because many of these materials are not

catalogued. Citations for state and local government documents should follow
the form for U.S. government documents.

Later References to the Same Footnote or Endnote Source

A good research paper displays references to a wide variety of source
material. However, it is common to reference a single source more than once.
Shorten all second and later note references. Fortunately, the general rules for
doing so have simplified over the years into the following three:

1. For references to the same work with no intervening notes simply use
   the Latin term "Ibid.," meaning "in the same place."
2. For second references with no intervening note, but with a different
   page of the same work, use Ibid., and the page number: for example:
   Ibid, p. 101.
3. For second references with intervening notes, indicate: the author's
   last name, but not first name or initials unless another author of the
   same name is cited; a shortened title of the work; and the specific page
   number.

Below are examples of second citations following first citations of a
representative number of works.

Second References with Intervening Citations

Book, Single Volume:

1. Lawrence Baum, *The Supreme Court* (Washington, D.C.: Congressional
   Quarterly Press, 1981), p. 42.
8. Baum, *The Supreme Court,* p. 101.

Journal Article:

3. James Murray, "The Role of Analogy in Legal Reasoning," *U.C.L.A.
   Law Review* 29 (1982): 833.
9. Murray, "Role of Analogy," p. 840.

Government Documents:

11. U.S. Congress, Senate, Balanced Budget—Tax Limitation Con-
    stitutional Amendment, 97th Cong., 2d sess., 13 July 1982, *Con-
    gressional Record,* 128, no. 12, :S15922.
15. U.S. Congress, Senate, Balanced Budget, S15925.

Judicial Opinions:

2. Dames and Moore v. Reagan, 453 U.S. 654 (1981).
31. 453 U.S. at 655. *Or* 453 U.S. 654, 655.

Bibliography Form

A bibliography is a listing at the end of a research paper of all references a writer uses in preparation of his or her project. It includes all works cited in the footnotes or endnotes and other works the writer found useful in thinking about the topic. If one merely examines but does not use the work in a meaningful intellectual way, do not include it in the bibliography. However, some instructors demand that students note all references found during the course of the research.

List bibliographical entries in alphabetical order, last name first. When a person is the author of more than one work list the works chronologically, the earliest date first with the most recent scholarship listed last.

Bibliographies exist for the convenience of readers. Consequently, if a bibliography is long it is advisable to break it into categories of works, for example, books, articles, and government documents. Because they typically contain discussion of many cases, constitutional law research papers should include a separate table of cases. List the cases alphabetically together with their full legal citations, followed by the page number(s) in the text where each case is mentioned. Always cite the first page in the court reporter where the judicial opinion begins.

The researcher must understand that a bibliographic entry is a transposition of a footnote entry. Although there are exceptions, change a footnote into a bibliographical entry by transposing the author's first and last names, by removing parentheses from the facts of publication, by omitting page references, and by re-punctuating with periods instead of commas. The reader should also be aware that the bibliographical examples provided below are parallel transformations of the footnote examples found in the preceding section of this chapter.

Bibliography Entries for Books   The following are examples of bibliographic citations for many of the most common types of books. Listings are given for single author books, books by more than one author, books in a series, books by an editor or translator, and many others. While this is not a complete list, the researcher will be able to find most of the examples he or she will require.

Book With One Author:

1. Cooper, Phillip J. *Hard Judicial Choices: Federal District Court Judges and State and Local Officials.* New York: Oxford University Press, 1988.

Book With Two Authors:

2. Hoffer, Peter C. and Hull, N. E. *Impeachment in America, 1635–1805.* New Haven: Yale University Press, 1985.

Book With Three Authors:

3. Kalvelage, Carl, Melone, Albert P., and Segal, Morley. *Bridges to Knowledge in Political Science: A Handbook for Research.* Pacific Palisades, CA.: Palisades Publishers, 1984.

Book With More Than Three Authors:

4. Harris, Donald, Mavis Maclean, Hazel Genn, Sally Lloyd-Bostock, Paul Feen, Peter Corfied, and Yvonne Brittan. *Compensation and Support for Illness and Injury.* Oxford: Clarendon Press, 1984.

Edition of a Book Other Than the First:

5. Tribe, Laurence H. *American Constitutional Law.* 2d ed. Mineola, N.Y.: The Foundation Press, 1988.

Book in a Series:

6. Carter, Lief H. *Contemporary Constitutional Law Making.* Permagon Government and Politics Series. New York: Permagon Press Inc., 1985.

Book by Editor:

7. McDowell, Gary, ed. *Taking the Constitution Seriously.* Dubuque, Iowa: Kendall/Hunt Publishing Company, 1981.

Book by Translators:

8. Adams, Willi Paul. *The First American Constitution: Republican Ideology and the Making of State Constitutions in the Revolutionary Era.* Translated by Rita and Robert Kimber. Chapel Hill: University of North Carolina Press, 1980.
   When both author and translator names appear on the title page, the translator's name should appear after the title. However, if the author's name is not on the title page, the translator's name should appear first, followed by the word trans.

Multivolume Book:

9. Loss, Richard, ed. *Corwin on the Constitution,* Vol. 2. Ithaca, New York: Cornell University Press, 1987.

Citation in One Book From Another Book:

10. Currie, David P. *The Constitution in the Supreme Court.* Chicago: University of Chicago Press, 1985.
    Compare to footnote 10 on page 79.

Book Review:

11. Kannar, George. *Review of Constitutional Choices* by Laurence Tribe. *The New Republic* (October 14, 1985), pp. 33–40.
    The first name cited is that of the reviewer of the book. The second name cited is the author of the book reviewed.

Book in a Series, One Author, Several Volumes, Each With a Different Title:

12. Schlesinger, Arthur M. *The Age of Roosevelt.* Vol. 3. *The Politics of Upheaval.* Boston: Houghton Mifflin, 1960.
    The first title is the name of the book series. The second title *(The Politics of Upheaval)* is the name of the specific cited volume.

Paperback Edition of a Book First Published in Hardcover:

13. Woodward, Bob and Armstrong, Scott. *The Bretheren: Inside the Supreme Court.* Paperback. New York: Avon Books, 1979.

Introduction or Foreword of a Book by Another Author:

14. Steiner, Gilbert Y. Foreword to *The Courts and Social Policy,* by Donald L. Horowitz. Washington, D.C.: The Brookings Institution, 1977.
    The first name appearing is the person writing the foreword or introduction to the book. It is his or her comments that are regarded as important and therefore he or she is cited first, not the author of the book.

Book with an Association as an Author:

15. American Enterprise Institute for Public Policy Research. *Forming a Government under the Constitution.* Washington, D.C.: American Enterprise Institute for Public Policy Research, 1985.

Author's Name Not on Title Page, but Known:

16. [Hamilton, Alexander; Madison, James; Jay, John]. *The Federalist Papers*. New York: New American Library, 1961.

Article, Chapter, or Part of Another Book:

17. Black, Charles L., ed. *The Humane Imagination*. Woodbridge: Ox Bow Press, 1986.
    Compare to footnote 17 on page 80.

Bibliography Entries for Journal and Magazine Articles   The following are examples of bibliographic citations for periodical literature. Magazine, newspaper, and journal article examples are given.

Academic Journal:

18. Caldeira, Gregory A. "Public Opinion and the U.S. Supreme Court: FDR's Court-Packing Plan." *American Political Science Review* 81 (Dec. 1987): 1139–1153.
    It is preferable to reference legal articles in the same way as other academic articles when submitting a research paper in a social science or humanities course. However, sometimes instructors want students to be aware of how different legal citation style is from other academic disciplines. Therefore, they ask their students to use the legal style of citation. See bibliographic entry number 20 for an example of legal style for citing a law review article.

Popular Magazine Article, No Author Given:

19. "Supreme Court Ruling is Civil Rights Roadblock [Grove City Decision]." *Jet*, 7 April 1986, p. 10.

Legal Periodical:

20. Handberg, Roger. *After the Fall: Justice Fortas' Judicial Values and Behavior After the Failure of His Nomination as Chief Justice*. 15 Capital University Law Review 205–222 (1986).
    Use this legal style only if requested by instructor. See bibliographic entry number 18 for preferable style.

Popular Magazine Article, Author Given:

21. Meese, Edwin. "The Law of the Constitution." *The National Review*, July 17, 1987, pp. 30–31.

Newspapers:

22. Labotan, Stephen. "Judges Mark 200 Years of Constitutional Law." *The New York Times,* 19 July, 1987, p. 88.

When the author byline is given, name the reporter at the beginning of the citation. For foreign newspapers that do not indicate the city in their titles, place the city name in parentheses, e.g., *Le Monde* (Paris).

Bibliography Entries for Encyclopedias, Almanacs, and Other Works   Examples of bibliographic citations are given here for a variety of less commonly used sources. Examples included are for encyclopedias, almanacs, dissertations, and nonprinted matter. The researcher should find that most contingencies have been addressed, or at least be able to fashion a citation from the information given.

Signed Articles:

23. *Encyclopedia of the American Judicial System.* s.v. "The Chase and Waite Courts and Era," by Jeffrey Brandon Morris.

Unsigned Articles:

24. *Encyclopedia Britannica.* s.v. "United States (of America)."

Legal Encyclopedias:

25. American Jurisprudence, 2d. s.v. *Sedition, Subversive Activities, and Treason* (1987).
26. Corpus Juris Secundum. s.v. *Constitutional Law* (1985).

Almanacs:

27. *The World Almanac and Book of Facts 1985.* s. v. "Judiciary of the U.S."

When citing encyclopedias or almanacs the place of publication, publisher, date, and page numbers are normally omitted. Editions other than the first should be specified. The letters s.v. mean *sub verbo,* "under the word"; i.e., under the designated title.

Dissertation:

28. Anderson, Allen Franklin, Jr. "Plea Bargaining Rates in North Carolina: Some Determinants of Variability." Ph.D. Dissertation, Southern Illinois University at Carbondale, 1984.

Thesis:

29. Hennings-Dawson, Cynthia J. "The Impact of First Amendment Decisions on the Political Activities of Unified Bar Associations." M.A. Thesis, Southern Illinois University at Carbondale, 1987.

Material from Manuscript Collections:

30. Los Angeles, California. Library of University of California, Los Angeles, Administration of Justices and Courts, 1916–. Richard Richards Papers.

Radio and Television Programs:

31. NBC. NBC Nightly News. 9 March 1983. "President Reagan's Acceptance of Burford's Resignation." Chris Wallace, reporter.

Interviews:

32. Connell, Colleen Kay. Staff Attorney, American Civil Liberties Union. Chicago, Illinois Interview, April 23, 1983.

Letters:

33. Bergh, Albert Ellery, ed. *The Writings of Thomas Jefferson.* Washington, D.C.: Thomas Jefferson Memorial Association, 1907.

Mimeographed or Other Nonprinted Reports:

34. Grunbaum, Werner F. "Selected Bibliography on Artificial Intelligence Applications and Expert Systems for Law." Law, Courts, and Judicial Process Section Newsletter, American Political Science Association, Spring, 1987.

Booklets and Pamphlets:

35. O'Conner, Alice and Henze, Mary L. *"During Good Behavior": Judicial Independence and Accountability.* Washington, D.C.: The Jefferson Foundation, 1984.
36. Illinois Office of Education. *Study Guide, Constitution of the State of Illinois and the United States.* Springfield, Illinois, 1981.
    Underscore titles of booklets and pamphlets.

Proceedings of a Meeting or Conference: Reproduced:

37. The Bicentennial Conference of the United States Constitution. "Committee 11—Effectiveness of Governmental Operations." Philadelphia, Pa: April 5–8, 1986.

Paper Read or Speech Delivered at a Meeting:

38. Cohen, Ronald. "Procedural Justice and Participation." Paper delivered at the 1984 Annual Meeting of the Law and Society Association, June, 1984 at Boston.

Bibliography Entries for Legal Sources   Examples of bibliographies for legal materials follow. See Chapter One for additional examples. In most instances, footnotes and bibliographic entries for legal sources are all the same.

U.S. Supreme Court (U.S.):

39. City of Mobile v. Bolden, 446 U.S. 55 (1980).
    In a bibliography or table of cases always list the first page on which the judicial opinion appears in the reporter. Do not cite a specific point found in a judge's opinion on a particular page as one might do when footnoting an opinion. This rule applies to all judicial opinions from whatever the source.

U.S. Supreme Court (U.S.) (reporter's name):

40. Shelton v. Tiffin, 47 U.S. (6 How.) 163 (1848).

Federal Cases (F. Cas.):

41. Washington Mills v. Russell, 29 F. Cas. 336 (C.C.D. Mass. 1873) (No. 17,247).

Federal Reporter (F.), (F.2d):

42. Hong Kong Supermarket v. Kizer, 839 F.2d 1078 (9th Cir. 1987).

Federal Supplement (F. Supp.):

43. Pestrak v. Ohio Elections Commission, 670 F. Supp. 1368 (S.D. Ohio 1987).

Federal Rules Decisions (F.R.D.):

44. Hawthorne v. Gulf Shores, Inc., 115 F.R.D. 474 (1986).

American Law Reporter (A.L.R.) Annotation:

45. Annot., 68 A.L.R. Fed. 290 (1984).

Bibliography entries must list the first page on which the article begins.

American Law Reporter (A.L.R.) Opinion:

46. Loose v. Offshore Navigation, 68 A.L.R. Fed. 318 (1984).

United States Law Week (U.S.L.W.):

47. Gulfstream Aerospace Corp. v. Mayacamas Corp., 56 U.S.L.W. 4243 (March 22, 1988).

U.S. Supreme Court Bulletin (CCH S.Ct. Bull.):

48. Langley v. Federal Deposit Insurance Corp., 48 CCH S.Ct.Bull. p. B211 (Dec. 1, 1987).

State Cases:

49. Adams v. Barrell, 132 A. 130 (Me. 1926).
50. Byrd v. Peterson, 66 Ariz. 253, 186 p. 2d 955 (1947).
     When possible cite both the official and West reports. Cite the appropriate West reporter and include the state name when a state does not have its own reporter or if official reports are unavailable.

Briefs, Oral Arguments, Transcripts and Records:

51. Petitioner's Brief. Mazer v. Stein, 347 U.S. 201 (1953), in 1953 FO No. 228, card 2, *Information Handling Service.*
52. Respondent's Brief. Kissinger v. Halperin, 452 U.S. 713 (1981), in vol. 123, *Landmark Briefs and Arguments of the Supreme Court of the United States: Constitutional Law.*
53. Oral Argument by Harry D. Miller, Esq. on behalf of Appellants. Pennell v. San Jose, 108 S.Ct. 849 (1988), on Fiche 28, *University Publications of America.*
54. Transcript of Record. Mazer v. Stein, 347 U.S. 201 (1953), in 1953 FO No. 228, card 1, *Information Handling Service.*

For briefs, oral arguments, transcripts, and records, first describe what is being cited and end with a period. Follow the initial entry with the full legal citation to the case. As a courtesy to the reader, provide the source where the information is found. Petitions, complaints, and other court records are cited in the same way. The first words describe the nature of the document.

Legal Encyclopedia:

55. see bibliographical entries 25 and 26.

Federal Statute:

56. *Department of Defense Authorization Act, 1985*, Publ. L. No. 98-525, 98 Stat. 2492 (1984).

Federal Code:

57. 20 U.S.C. § 1210 (1982).
58. 42 U.S.C.S. § 1983 (Law. Co-op. 1986).
59. 28 U.S.C.A. § 144 (West 1987 Supp. Pamph.).
    Cite statutes commonly referred to by their official or popular name. For example: Comprehensive Employment and Training Act, 29 U.S.C. (1978) §834 (Supp. IV 1980). It is permissible to substitute the word section, or its abbreviation sec., for the section symbol (§).

U.S. Constitution:

60. U.S. Const. art. II, § 3.

Federal Register (Fed. Reg.):

61. Visa Waver for Certain Cotton Terry Bar Mops, 50 Fed. Reg. 32,467 (1985).

Code of Federal Regulations (C.F.R.):

62. Standard for Nitrogen Oxides, 40 C.F.R. §60.44a (1987).

Bibliography Entries for Government Documents   The form for government documents is unlike that adopted for books and articles, and it is often a source of confusion. The best rule is to follow the card catalog as a guide. In general, references to government documents should include in the following order: (1) the country (U.S.), (2) the branch of government (legislative, executive), (3) the subbranch or branches (House, Senate, Judiciary

Committee), (4) the document title (underscored), (5) the name of the document series or sequence and the facts of publication (H. Rept. 342 to Accompany H.R. 6258, 95th Cong., 1st sess., 1977). Examples follow.

Legislative Bills:

63. U.S. Congress. House. *Authorization for Childhood Immunization.* H.R. 5230, 99th Cong., 2d sess., 1986.
64. U.S. Congress. Senate. *Violent Crime and Drug Enforcement Act of 1982.* S2572, 97th Cong., 2d sess., 1982.

Legislative Debates:

65. U.S. Congress. Senate. Balanced Budget—Tax Limitation Constitutional Amendment. 97th Cong., 2d sess., 13 July 1982. *Congressional Record,* 128, no. 12.

Legislative Reports:

66. U.S. Congress. House. *The Changing Distribution of Industrial Profits: The Oil and Gas Industry within the Fortune 500, 1978–1980.* H. Rept. 97-390. 97th Cong., 1st sess. 1981.

Legislative Hearings:

67. U.S. Congress. House. Committee on the Judiciary. *Immigration and Naturalization Act Amendments of 1986, Hearings before the Subcommittee on Immigration, Refugees, and International Law of the Committee on the Judiciary on H.R. 444.* 99th Cong., 2d sess., 1986.

Executive Department:

68. Executive Office of the President. Office of Management and Budget. *Budget of the United States Government, Fiscal Year 1987* (Washington D.C.: U.S. Government Printing Office, 1987).
69. General Accounting Office. "The Seizure of the Mayaguez: A Case Study of Crisis Management." GAO ID-76-45, (May, 1976).

Government agencies often imprint documents with publication numbers and specify publication series. If such numbers are available, include them in citations. Because author names are sometimes printed on documents it is desirable to cite the authors. However, libraries often do not catalog government documents by author name. Thus, do not neglect to include sponsoring agencies in citations.

Presidential Papers:

70. U.S. President. "Veto of War Powers Resolution." *Weekly Compilation of Presidential Documents.* October 27, 1973.

Treaties:

71. U.S. Statutes at Large, vol. 43, pt. 2 (December 1923–March 1925). "Naval Arms Limitation Treaty." February 26, 1922.
72. U.S. Department of State, *United States Treaties and Other International Agreements,* vol. 27, pt. 2. "Soviet Socialist Republics, Union of- ABM Treaty." TIAS No. 8276, 3 July 1974.

    Beginning in 1950, U.S. treaties may be found in the publication, *United States Treaties and Other International Agreements.* The United Nations and formerly the League of Nations also publish a treaty series that includes international agreements.

International Organizations:

73. United Nations. *Report of the Secretary-General Submitted under General Assembly Resolution 39/146 of 14 December 1984, Covering the Developments in the Middle East in all Aspects* (A/40/779), 1985.

    Kate Turabian suggests that citations for international documents include: authorizing body, topic or title, document or series number when available, and publication date.

State Document:

74. Illinois. Secretary of State. *Handbook of Illinois Government.* June, 1987.
75. Illinois. *Constitution.*

    Specify the date of the constitution if the constitution cited is not the one currently in force, for example, Illinois, *Constitution* (1848), art. 1, sec. 2.

Local Documents:

76. Carbondale, Illinois. City Manager. "City of Carbondale, Illinois Annual Budget FY 1987–88." mimeographed (April 10, 1987).

    Often there is insufficient documentation for state and local materials. It may be necessary to improvise because many of these materials are not catalogued. Citations for state and local government documents should follow the form for U.S. government documents.

Scientific Reference Form

Because scientific notation style has been adopted by a growing number of political science and other social science journals, instructors encourage its use for referencing student papers. Instead of the conventionally numbered footnote, scientific notations use parenthetical references that indicate the author's last name, the year of publication, and pagination: for example, "In general, seminal thinkers such as Weber (Gerth and Mills, 1946: 85), Durkheim (1958: 7–8), and Tocqueville (1945: 275–276), admonish their readers to ponder the crucial or strategic position enjoyed by attorneys in the making of public policy."

This approach allows readers to discern the source of a statement instantly, and writers to edit and type a paper easily. It does, however, present a disadvantage: the interruption to the flow of ideas and sentences caused by the intrusion of author names, publication dates, and pagination. Papers of a constitutional law nature tend to exhibit more references than do papers for other academic topics. As a result, I do not recommend the scientific format for constitutional law papers. Cluttering of the body of the text with parenthetical statements makes clear communication of complex ideas only more difficult.

The format for scientific references varies from journal to journal and from one discipline to another. If this form is to be used, I recommend a hybrid variety.

Guide to Scientific References

1. All but explanatory footnotes (discursive comments) are placed in the body of the text.
2. Parenthetical references include author, year of publication, and pagination.
3. Repeat earlier citation for second or later references.
4. All sources cited in the text are listed at the end of the paper under **REFERENCES.**
5. Explanatory or discursive comments are referenced in the conventional style with footnote numbers placed in the body of the text and the comments placed together at the end of the manuscript immediately before the References. These are titled, **NOTES.**

Author Surname Not in Body of Text:

If the author's name is not mentioned in the body of the text, then the surname should be the first item in the parenthesis. The name is followed by a comma, the year of publication, colon, and page number if referencing specific pages.

Example: He regards this "Populist-Progressive" position as historically untenable (Mendelson, 1985: 264).

Author Surname in Body of Text:

If the author's name is mentioned in the body of the text, then the year of publication is first listed followed by a colon and then the page number.

Example: Mendelson (1985: 264) regards this "Populist-Progressive" position as historically untenable.

More Than One Author:

Sometimes there is need to point to several sources supporting the same or similar points. Join single references with semicolons.

Example: . . . public concern over crime and police protection have shown that these issues are tailor made for politicians aspiring to office and ill-suited to incumbents . . . (Finckenauer, 1978; Buffum and Sagi, 1983; McPherson, 1983; and Guyot, 1983).

Reference to Same Author and Same Year:

At times scholars publish more than one piece in the same year. Thus, it is necessary to distinguish among publications. This is accomplished by inserting letters "a," "b," "c," and so on in both the manuscript body and on the **REFERENCES** page at the end of the paper.

Example: . . . (Nagel, 1986a: 6).
         . . . (Nagel, 1986b: 38).
         . . . (Nagel, 1986c: 154).

Judicial Opinions Cited in Body of Text:

References to court cases and administrative agency decisions should be included in the body of the text. The case name is underscored followed by the date in parentheses. When citing a particular page of a judicial opinion, place it after the date preceded by a colon. For second and later references repeat the case name but delete the date.

Examples: . . . *United States Trust Co. v. New Jersey* (1977).
          . . . *United States Trust Co. v. New Jersey* (1977: 13).

Government Documents:

Government documents should be referenced parenthetically in the body of the text. The form is similar to other citations. List the country (U.S.), the branch of government (Congress), the subbranch or branches (House or Senate), the year of publication, followed by a colon and pagination.

Example: . . . The commission submitted its report to President Nixon in 1971, who hailed the report as a "broad comprehensive framework in which to decide the issues involved in reform of the Federal Criminal Code" (U.S. Congress, Senate, 1971: 5).

Other Legal Material:

There are other legal sources such as codes, encyclopedias, and annotations. Citation of these materials should also appear in the body of the text. Attempt to follow Guide number 2: parenthetical references include author, year of publication, and pagination. It is permissible to cite the title of the source itself when there is no author; instead of pagination, insert section numbers.

Example: . . . (20 USC, 1982: § 1210). [This citation means, Title 20 of *United States Code* for the 1982 edition at section 1210.]

References at End of the Paper:

Because parenthetical citations are brief, it is necessary to provide readers with more facts of publication. The scientific format requires the listing of all cited materials together at the end of the paper in alphabetical order by author. **REFERENCES** differ from a **BIBLIOGRAPHY** in that they do not require under any circumstance the listing of all materials consulted in researching and writing. On the contrary, a reference includes only those materials actually cited in the body of the text. Include all author names in all multiple authored works. The form for books, articles, associations as author, and dissertations or theses differ. List judicial opinions alphabetically with full citation to volume, reporter series, page, and date. When there are more than a few cases, place the list at the end of the paper under a separate title, **CASES CITED.**

Sample **REFERENCE** *page:*

Books:

Barber, Sotirios (1984). *On What the Constitution Means.* Baltimore: Johns Hopkins University Press.

Golding, Martin (1983). *Legal Reasoning.* New York: Alfred A. Knopf.

McLaughlin, Andrew Cummingham (1972a). *The Courts, the Constitution, and Parties: Studies in Constitutional History and Politics.* New York: Da Capo Press.

————. (1972b). *The Foundations of American Constitutionalism.* Gloucester, Mass.: P. Smith.

Miller, Arthur Selwyn (1982). *Towards Increased Judicial Activism: The Political Role of the Supreme Court.* Westport, Connecticut: Greenwood Press.

Articles:

Dyer, James A., (1976). "Do Lawyers Vote Differently? A Study of Voting on No-Fault Insurance." *Journal of Politics* 38 (May): 452–456.

Green Justin J., John R. Schmidhauser, Larry L. Berg, and David Brady (1973). "Lawyers in Congress: A New Look at Some Old Assumptions." *Western Political Quarterly* 26 (September): 440–452.

Association:

American Bar Association (1985). *Report of American Bar Association:* Chicago: American Bar Association.

Theses or dissertation:

Watson, Barbara Deal (1986). "History of the Legal Interpretation of Search and Seizure by the Supreme Court in Regards to the Rights of Children: Impact of these Decisions on Public Schools with Emphasis on Texas." Ed.D. dissertation. Commerce, Texas: East Texas State University.

Government Documents:

U.S. Congress, Senate (1971). Committee on the Judiciary. Reform of the Federal Criminal Laws. Hearings Before the Subcommittee on Criminal Laws and Procedures, Part I, 92d Cong., 1st sess.

Judicial Opinions:

Carson v. National Bank, 501 F.2d 1082, 1974.
Ohio v. Wyandotte Chemicals Corp., 401 U.S. 493, 1971.

Chapter Four

Why and How to Brief a Case

_____
_____
_____

Introduction

There is a major difference between *briefing a case* and *writing a legal brief*. When *briefing a case*, the task is to reduce the written opinion of a court to its most basic and essential elements. When *writing a legal brief*, the task is to assemble and present a legal argument to convince a court of the correctness of a client's conduct or argument about a disputed point of law. Because briefing cases constitutes a first step in the learning process, undergraduate students are usually asked to brief cases; it is a rare assignment to write a legal brief. Briefing is an essential skill in understanding legal thinking. This chapter, therefore, will aid students in acquiring the skill.

Full reports of court opinions are usually many pages long. Editors of instructional casebooks then reduce the full opinions to those parts of cases they believe most pertinent to conveying an understanding of the important points of each case. Although casebook editors will occasionally summarize the facts of a case, they do not change the exact words of the opinion. Rather, they delete those words, sentences, paragraphs, or sections they regard as not particularly instructive.

Instructors will sometimes send students to the library to read and brief a case from the full reported opinion of the court. However, because students are usually faced with the task of briefing edited cases that appear in a course-required textbook, much of the required analysis has been already completed by the casebook editor. As a result, students need only to further reduce court opinions to their bare bones.

Many students find it difficult to believe that it is necessary to brief cases. Rather, they attempt to short circuit the intellectual process by reading the assigned cases and writing marginal notes to help them recall pertinent points. This is a mistake! The dual act of intellectual analysis and then writing the brief is necessary. However, what are the justifications for doing so much work? There are five related purposes why it is desirable to take what is admittedly much time to adequately brief cases.

First, the number of court opinions discussed in a typical constitutional law course is impossible to recall from the memory of one or two readings. Opinions are usually complicated and the numbers are too great. By writing down the essential elements of the case, the information can be firmly retained in memory.

Second, briefs are an excellent study tool when preparing for examinations. Attempts to read, comprehend, and remember pertinent fact patterns and opinions the night before a scheduled examination almost inevitably meets with academic disaster. Read and brief the cases as the course progresses. Then sit down before an examination to review the cases. It is at this cognitive juncture that the student begins to see the relationships necessary for discerning the forest through the trees.

Third, by observing the intimate relationship between the facts and decisions of past and present cases, students gain an appreciation for the historical method of the common law. In fact, the case-method approach to legal education is supported by most law schools as the finest way to train lawyers. This viewpoint has been hotly debated because it tends to blind students to extralegal materials useful for understanding legal policy making. Political scientists are alert to this problem, and as faulty as the case-method approach may be, it is desirable to employ at least some of its aspects for two reasons: (1) It is necessary to know what the courts have said. The courts make policy and it is important to know precisely what the policy might be. By reading the written opinion, the primary and authoritative source material of judicial policy making, the student can avoid the confusion, misinformation, and improper interpretation often found in public debate about the meaning of court opinions. (2) As students of politics, it is important to understand the workings of the legal mind. This can best be done by studying lawyers and judges in their own language and on their own turf. No doubt, this can be seen as a narrow and confining task. However, unlike law students and working attorneys, a clear understanding of the case is not the conclusion of analysis, it is the beginning of explanation. Therefore, it is a necessary task for political scientists to learn what the law is, to explain why decisions are made the way they are, how cases reflect values in and out of courts, and to consider the public policy consequences of adjudication. Remember, it is not the goal of political scientists to make constitutional lawyers out of undergraduates but to enable undergraduates to understand when, how, and why the law influences the allocation of authority within the political system.

A further justification for briefing cases is that it provides students and teacher with a common point of departure for the discussion of meaningful problems. By possessing a common text, in which people are in actual conflict, a class can discuss not only what might appear to be mundane legal issues, but also the dramatic implications of decisions for government and society. Because such issues touch on numerous aspects of the social sciences and the humanities, students can appreciate the interdisciplinary nature of the subject matter. In this lively environment, a synthesis of ideas will occur.

A final justification for briefing cases concerns the task itself: It will sharpen the intellect and aid students in acquiring disciplined minds. Long after the cases are but dim recollections, the experience of rigorous reading and writing will endure. The careful and thoughtful process necessary for writing briefs will introduce an appreciation for critical thinking and prepares the student to deal with future challenges. In this sense, a rigorous constitutional law course is among the very best liberal arts courses offered on college campuses. Training the mind to discern and write carefully written analysis of actual problems in the political system remains a goal of practical value.

In the remaining sections of this chapter readers are treated to the elements of a brief. A model brief is also provided to help them in performing the task. However, students cannot learn how to brief a case by following a formula. The task is more in the nature of art than of science. When starting out, it is not unusual for students to spend two or more hours to brief a single case. With experience, however, the task becomes less time consuming and difficult. It is my experience that it takes the average student up to six weeks of intense course work to become proficient at the art of briefing cases.

At first, students exhibit stress and anxiety. They bring their briefs to class but find that the instructor and other students do not emphasize the same points. The reason for the apparent contradictions has little to do with questions of intelligence, however. Nonetheless, anxious students do request meetings with the instructor to review their briefs. Some instructors will read student briefs and sometimes briefs are assigned letter grades. Although these options may be helpful, they are unnecessary. If you experience frustration, bear with it. Continue to brief the cases and make changes in those briefs which seem dissimilar from what the instructor sanctions. Later, but only after you have expended genuine effort, you will come to understand the process and will feel confident with what you have done.

Elements of a Brief

There is no one right way to brief a case. Instructors often have their own recommendations. Although there are somewhat different styles of brief writing, all well-done briefs carefully link together each major element of a court decision. Try to remember that a brief should be just that, *brief!* In this regard, and given the understanding that court opinions often contain key words and phrases without which important ideas may be lost, I suggest that brief writers make every effort to use their own words. To reiterate: While it is desirable to write the brief independent of the legal texts of issue, there are occasions when no substitutes compare to the justices' own verbal gems.

If the student is working from a purchased private textbook, feel free to mark it up. If the student is using a reporter system found in a library, do not write in them. The reasons are obvious and need no further comment.

First, read each case quickly attempting to comprehend the general nature of the case and the problems presented. Second, read it again this time with a pencil or pen in hand. Underline pertinent parts and make notations in the margins of each page. At last you are ready to brief the case. Sit up in a hard chair and go to work. Most students use a pen and pad of paper to write their briefs. Using a typewriter or word processor, however, will speed the task. Below are elements of fundamental importance.

I. *Name or Title of Case:* The case name should appear at the top and center of the first page.

II. *Legal Citation:* Immediately below the case name place the legal citation. This information provides the location in the various court reports where the fully reported opinion is found. Usually, a single citation will suffice, for example, 369 U.S. 186 (1968). If available the student may want to include the parallel citations for the same case, 369 U.S. 186, 7 L.Ed.2d 663, 82 S.Ct. 691 (1962). Exercising this option is a good idea because at some later point in time it may become necessary to read the fully reported opinion. Knowledge of the opinion's location in the reporter systems will ease the library search. In any event, knowing at least what court has decided the case and the year it decided it is valuable information. It will help students know where the case fits in time and within the structure of authority.

III. *Statement of Facts:* The facts include the pertinent circumstances of the dispute giving rise to the lawsuit and the disposition of the case. Any legal dispute involves facts which may or may not be pertinent. Indeed, circumstances surrounding events give rise to differing interpretations of what happened. However, for purposes of brief writing and for understanding the legal reasoning in each case, it is important to note only those facts treated by the opinion writer as relevant and those facts the writer specifically mentions to be irrelevant. Facts labeled as irrelevant by the court are important to note because the court deems them consequential in some sense. For instance, when a past case is distinguishable from the present case, irrelevant commonalities between the two cases may be as important as those elements considered pertinent. It is of no consequence to the brief writer whether the facts are true or not. Nor is it of particular concern that the brief writer thinks the opinion writer has identified the wrong facts. What is important is that the court treats the facts as pertinent.

While it is usual for the facts to appear at the beginning of the written opinion, this is not always the case. It is sometimes necessary to search the court's entire opinion for the facts. This may include not only the court's majority opinion but also concurring and dissenting opinions too. Consequently, the good brief writer must be able to dissect the full opinion, separating what is important from the body of the text. Then he or she reconstructs the opinion with only the most pertinent information attached. The last lines of the fact statement should include the decisions and actions of the lower courts and how the case came before the Supreme Court: for example, writ of error, appeal, certiorari, and so on.

Before the passage of the Judiciary Act of 1925, the Supreme Court had limited discretion in the cases it heard. The writ of error required the Court to hear cases coming to it upon proper application. In 1928, Congress passed legislation resulting in the demise of this method of appeal. Owing to the extraordinary lobbying efforts of Chief Justice William Howard Taft, which culminated in the passage of the 1925 statute, the Supreme Court today has considerable control of cases it wishes to hear. The discretionary *writ of certiorari* is granted when four of the nine justices agree that a given case should be heard by the full Court. Cases usually heard by this method are previously adjudicated in a state court of last resort or in a U.S. Court of Appeals. It is important to note that most cases are settled without appeal to the Supreme Court at the lower levels of the judicial hierarchy.

Today it is fair to conclude that the U.S. Supreme Court is almost exclusively an all-certiorari tribunal. Before 1988, petitioners could bring a number of different types of cases from a variety of sources to the Court through an appeal method formally dubbed, *Appeal* (ostensibly a form of appeal not within the discretion of the Supreme Court). Yet, even on *Appeal*, the Court found a way to reject jurisdiction. In such cases, the Supreme Court could simply find that the case or controversy does not present a "substantial federal question." With this important qualification, the U.S. Supreme Court must hear certain classes of cases coming from the U.S. District Courts, from the U.S. (Circuit) Courts of Appeals, and from the state courts of last resort. In 1988, however, Congress enacted Public Law 100–352, limiting the Court's mandatory jurisdiction to cases decided by three-judge federal district courts. This law spells the virtual end of the Supreme Court's mandatory appellate jurisdiction.

A final but little used appeal method is the process called *certification*. In this instance, a lower court requests the Supreme Court to answer certain questions of law so that a correct decision may be rendered in the case before it. This method is not within the control of the parties to the suit. Only the lower court may judge whether it needs clarification of a point of law. Importantly, the Supreme Court may refuse the certificate. The Court might alternatively provide an answer which the lower court is obliged to apply, or the Supreme Court might decide the case itself without returning it to the lower court.

It is also useful for the brief writer to note if the case is heard by the Supreme Court in its original jurisdiction as spelled out in Article III, or if the case comes to the Court through extraordinary writs such as habeas corpus, writ of mandamus, or writ of prohibition. Lastly, whether petitioners pay the necessary court costs and attorney fees or the case is heard *in forma pauperis* is a noteworthy fact.

IV. *Statement of Issues:* An issue is a statement of the legal or constitutional question the opinion writer deems necessary to answer to resolve the dispute. It is common for legal opinions to contain more than one issue. Sometimes the court must answer affirmatively one issue before it can or needs to answer following issues. It should be understood that editors of instructional casebooks will often delete sections of a case they deem unimportant for understanding the topic under study. Students should be aware of this fact because cases in one context may stand for much more in another context.

Often authors of judicial opinions will place the statement of issues in one clearly identifiable place within the text—usually immediately following the recitation of the facts of the case. However, like the facts, the issues are sometimes scattered through the entire written opinion. This is another reason why it is wise to read through an opinion and to write notes in the margins of your casebook before actually writing the brief.

Follow two rules when stating issues. First, issue statements should appear as questions which can be answered yes or no. Second, phrase the issues in a precise and specific way. A case always involves answering some specific legal or constitutional question. The U.S. Supreme Court does not deal with hypothetical or general issues. The statement of issues should reflect this fact. Avoid abstract conceptualizations of the problem. For example, it is not enough to write for the case of *Baker v. Carr*, "May state legislatures fail to reapportion legislative districts consistent with population trends?" Note that the question does not raise a legal or constitutional issue; furthermore, the question is general—it deals with the general ability of state legislatures to discriminate against urban voters. No constitutional provision or legal principle is mentioned as particularly relevant. It does not address specific people with an actual controversy in law or in equity. Novice brief writers find this particular task difficult to master. It requires a careful focusing of mental energy, and a development of intellectual habits necessary for understanding judicial opinions.

A proper statement of the issues is important because it reflects an understanding of the facts, conditions the legal decision and, significantly, the reasoning of the court. Careful wording of the issues, however, often produce long conditional interrogative sentences. Though the sentence may not be elegant, the result is acceptable. Given the nature of the facts, statutes, or constitutional provisions, such sentences are often necessary because they admit of no other useful alternative. In any event, always write the issues so that they can be clearly understood. At times, copying the issue(s) as stated by the court is the best format. However, once again, whenever practical put the issues in your own words, making sure to keep those vital words or phrases of the opinion that are indispensable for understanding.

V. *Decision and Action:* For the decision, write a simply yes or no in response to each legal issue posed in the *Statement of Issues* above. No explanation or qualification is necessary at this point in the brief. The *Action* is the court ordered disposition of the case: for example, case reversed, or reversed and remanded, or affirmed, and other possibilities. This information is usually found by reading the last lines of the majority or plurality opinion of the court. Place both the court's decision and action on a single line.

VI. *Reasoning of the Court:* The reasons for the court's decision is the heart of the legal opinion. It contains the court's justification for its decision in the case. However, not everything written may be pertinent for purposes of the brief. Only that part of the opinion which is directly supportive of the decision is appropriate for inclusion in the brief. Be wary of statements and arguments not directly related to the issues and decision in the case. This verbiage is usually called *obiter dicta,* or simply *obiter,* or *dicta,* or *dictum.* It is, so to speak, excess intellectual baggage; it is argumentation unnecessary for the court to logically come to its decision in the case.

It is necessary for the good brief writer to read the court's full opinion with a view toward separating those reasons which are central for the decision and those which are not. The key for separating the wheat from the chaff is the *Statement of Issues.* Only those arguments necessary for supporting the answers to the issues should be part of the brief. Ignore the remainder. This task requires careful attention to the expressions of the opinion writers. As previously discussed, when reading through opinions, it is advisable to make special notations in the margins or underline those places in the text where the opinion writer offers essential justifications. While novice brief writers may have difficulty with this task, be assured, it will become easier with experience.

On the first line of this section of the brief note the author of the court's opinion: for example, Per Brennan. It is also wise to number the reasoning consistent with each issue statement. This permits quick eye movement between each issue, decision, and reasoning.

During the tenure of the first three chief justices—John Jay, John Rutledge, and Oliver Ellsworth—each member of the Supreme Court was entitled to write his own opinion in each case. This practice is known as *seriatim* opinion writing. Upon the accession of John Marshall to the chief justiceship, the *seriatim* practice gave way to the institutional opinion. Since Marshall's day, a single justice is assigned the task of writing the opinion of the Court.

The chief justice makes that assignment only if he is in the voting majority. If he is not, the senior-most justice in the majority makes the opinion-writing assignment. This leadership task is often delicate and complicated because it reflects conflicts and compromises on and off the Court.

VII. *Concurring Opinion(s):* A concurring opinion agrees with the result of the majority or plurality opinion but disagrees with the reasons. That is, the justice agrees with the result in the decision of the majority or plurality but for different reasons. Justices write concurring opinions because they believe it is necessary to indicate disagreement with the reasoning processes of the controlling bloc within the court. Indeed, sometimes the reasoning found in concurring opinions become adopted in later cases by a court's majority as the preferred doctrine. Also, the frequency of concurring opinions is an indicator of the degree to which a court is united on a given issue. These opinions can point the way to how a court may alter its future course.

VIII. *Dissenting Opinion(s):* A dissenting opinion expresses disagreement with the court's judgment both in terms of the result (who wins and loses) and the reasoning supporting that result. Note the justice(s) writing such opinions and the reasons for disagreement. Because dissenting justices will sometimes disagree even among themselves, when more than one dissent is filed note each dissent separately.

IX. *Voting Coalition:* If the information is available, note the justices voting together. When studying particular courts or eras it often becomes plain that some justices often vote together. The dynamics of small group interaction and ideological compatibility among certain members may aid in explaining decision making. Sometimes a court will change its approach to a subject. It may be the result of a change in court personnel and not an intellectual conversion resulting from studying case precedents.

X. *Summary of Legal Principle(s):* It is a useful exercise to summarize within a few lines the legal principles the case might stand for. This is a way to pull the elements of the case together and is a valuable study aid when preparing for examinations. Also note how the case at hand might differ from previously studied cases on the same topic.

XI. *Free Space:* Discussion of cases in class will reveal the flaws in individual briefs. Therefore, leave room at the end of the brief for classroom comments and what further revisions may be necessary or desirable. Some students prefer to use a separate notebook for such purposes.

Model Brief

I.   Baker v. Carr
II.   369 U.S. 186, 82 S. Ct. 691, 7 L. Ed. 2d 663 (1962)
III. *Facts:* The Tennessee state legislature failed to reapportion its legislative districts in both houses for sixty years. This occurred despite the enactment of a 1901 statute governing the reapportionment process on a basis of qualified voters resident in each of the state's counties as determined by the population census. During this sixty-year period, the state's population became increasingly urban and yet urban voters found themselves underrepresented in the state legislature. Baker and other urban citizens sued in U.S. District Court under federal civil rights statutes charging that they were being denied the equal protection of the laws contrary to the fourteenth amendment. The plaintiffs sought a court declaration that the 1901 law was unconstitutional and asked the court for the alternative remedies of elections of state legislators at large, or elections from districts based upon the 1950 census. The district court agreed with the plaintiffs that their civil rights had been abridged. However, the court found that it could not provide a remedy. The Supreme Court first heard arguments on appeal at the 1960 Term.

IV. *Issues:* (1) Does the district court have jurisdiction of the subject matter in this case?
        (2) Do the litigants have standing to sue?
        (3) Is the issue of malapportionment of state legislatures a justiciable question?

V. *Decision and Action:* (1) Yes, (2) Yes, (3) Yes. Reversed and Remanded.

VI. *Reasoning:* Per Brennan. (1) There is a distinction between jurisdiction of the subject matter and the justiciability of the subject matter. If there is no jurisdiction, the cause of action does not arise under the Constitution, laws, or treaties of the United States. Nor may the case come under any of the categories found in Article III, section 2 or is not a case or controversy within the meaning of that Article and section. However, the matter of equal representation arises under the equal protection clause of the Fourteenth Amendment and the U.S. District Court is authorized to hear such cases by congressional enactment (28 U.S.C. sec. 1343).

(2) Voters alleging facts which disadvantage them as individuals have standing to sue. The 1901 statute injures the appellants because they are voters in the counties which are underrepresented in the Tennessee state legislature. Voters have judicially enforceable rights against arbitrary impairment of the full enjoyment of that privilege.

(3) Simply because this suit seeks the protection of a political right does not render the case a political question and therefore nonjusticiable. The appellants' claim does not rest upon the guaranty clause of the Constitution, causes of action which the Supreme Court has declined to resolve. Rather, appellants' claims are based on a denial of equal protection of the law, a Fourteenth Amendment proscription. The political question doctrine applies to situations involving the separation of powers among the three coordinate branches of the federal government. The nonjusticiability doctrine is not applicable to the relationship between the federal judiciary and the states. The question to be decided in this case is not a conflict between coequal branches of government.

VII. *Concurring Opinion:* Per Douglas. There is no question that federal courts may restrain state agencies from violating citizen rights under the equal protection clause of the fourteenth amendment. However, the test is whether the state has made "an invidious discrimination" as when it oppresses a race or nationality. The appellants should have an opportunity to prove that an "invidious discrimination" exists.

Concurring opinion per Clark. It is not a good idea for the Supreme Court to intervene in such a delicate matter as legislative representation. However, the people in this instance have no other recourse open to them but to appeal to the courts for a remedy. The ordinary political channels are effectively closed to them.

Concurring Opinion Per Stewart. The Court's opinion is limited to three points and nothing more: (1) the Court possessed subject matter jurisdiction; (2) the case presents a justiciable cause of action; and (3) the appellants have standing to challenge the Tennessee apportionment statutes.

VIII. *Dissenting Opinion:* Per Frankfurter joined by Harlan. The Court reverses a uniformly decided set of cases on this subject. This case involves political questions and when the Court involves itself in such matters it may suffer a loss of public confidence. Moreover, the Court does not provide any guidelines for the district court to enforce the claim. Finally, this case is not a simple one of blatant discrimination. Rather, Tennessee uses a method of geographical representation that is not preferred by the plaintiffs.

Dissenting Opinion: Per Harlan joined by Frankfurter. The complaint should be dismissed for "failure to state a claim upon which relief can be granted" There is no equal protection requirement that legislative institutions must provide an equal voice for each voter. Lastly, if it is to remain a respected institution, the Supreme Court should exercise judicial self-restraint.

IX. *Voting Coalitions:* (6 to 2), For the majority Brennan, Warren, Douglas, Black, Clark, Stewart; Frankfurter and Harlan dissenting. Not participating, Whittaker.

X. *Summary:* The question of the malapportionment of state legislatures is one in which the federal courts have subject matter jurisdiction, present a justiciable cause of action, and one which citizens alleging deprivation of equal protection of the laws have standing to sue.

XI. *Free Space:* (Leave approximately one-third of a page for comments).

Chapter Five

Summaries of Leading
Supreme Court Decisions

———
———

Introduction

This chapter contains summaries of sixty-six Supreme Court decisions. These cases are presented in order to acquaint students with the essential features of each decision. These summaries are only digests of the facts and decisions in each case—a two-paragraph summary cannot do justice to the richness found in most Supreme Court decisions. These summaries are not substitutes for reading and studying each decision. Neither should these summaries be confused with a written brief of each case. Lower court holdings and actions are not typically included nor are discussions of dissenting opinions. Therefore, these summaries should be viewed as a special study tool only, not anything more.

There are several ways to use these summaries. Beginning students of constitutional law often encounter references to so-called landmark decisions. These references are sometimes made with the assumption that the readers are already familiar with the case or that they will become acquainted at a later time, perhaps after several hundred pages of reading. The summaries, arranged in alphabetical order, provide a ready reference for the essential elements of the cases. By turning to the cited decision, students may quickly obtain a working knowledge of the case. Secondly, as a quality control, these summaries may be used for comparison. Students, even after reading a case and completing an extensive written brief, may be unsure of their understanding of the case. Certitude in such matters is difficult to obtain, even for the most seasoned scholar. Although it must be reemphasized that these summaries are not the equivalent of briefs, students may wish to refer to this chapter to determine whether their understanding of the case is roughly consistent. Thirdly, both students and teachers need a quick reference when studying related topics and issues. For example, a course in political parties will often make reference to the case of *Smith v. Allwright,* which declared the Texas all-white primary system unconstitutional. The summary of this case can offer a quick refresher on the essentials of that case. Lastly, the summaries may make a valuable contribution to an individual's private reference library for the years ahead.

Summaries

Abington Township v. Schemp
(*see*: School District of Abington Township v. Schemp)

Baker v. Carr
369 U.S. 186, 82 S. Ct. 691, 7 L. Ed. 2d 663 (1962)

Utilizing the federal census of 1900, the Tennessee General Assembly in 1901 enacted legislation apportioning its two chambers and provided for subsequent reappointment every ten years. Despite the fact that the state's population continually shifted from rural to urban centers, the legislature failed for more than sixty years to redistribute the legislative seats. In 1959, charging that as urban residents they were being denied the equal protection of the laws guaranteed by the fourteenth amendment, Baker and other qualified voters brought suit under federal civil rights statutes.

Writing for the majority, Justice William Brennan first addressed the question of subject matter jurisdiction. Brennan made two points: (1) the appellants claim a denial of equal protection of the laws in violation of the fourteenth amendment; (2) since this claim was not deemed unsubstantial and frivolous, the district court, by virtue of article III, section 2, as extended by Congress to the district courts by statutory enactment, does possess jurisdiction over the subject matter. As to the second important question, standing to sue, Brennan reasoned that because Baker and the others had a personal stake in the outcome of the controversy, effective voting power, they had satisfied the standing to sue requirement. Lastly, Brennan held that this ". . . challenge to an apportionment represents no nonjusticiable 'political question'." The district court, argued Brennan, misinterpreted Colegrove v. Green, 328 US 549, and other decisions of the Supreme Court in applying the political question doctrine to this case. The political question cases refer to the relationship between the judiciary and other coordinate branches of the national government, not to the federal judiciary's relationship to the state governments.

Barenblatt v. United States
360 U.S. 109, 79 S. Ct. 1081, 3 L. Ed. 2d 1115 (1959)

Lloyd Barenblatt, a former college instructor, refused to answer questions before a subcommittee of the House Committee on Un-American Activities. The subcommittee was investigating alleged Communist infiltration in the field of education. Barenblatt claimed that compelling his testimony was neither authorized by Congress nor constitutionally permissible given the vagueness of Rule XI of the House of Representatives. Barenblatt also argued that he was not adequately apprised of the pertinency of the committee's questions to the subject matter under investigation. Lastly, he objected that the inquiry infringed on his first amendment rights. Barenblatt was convicted in federal district court of contempt of Congress. After two appeals to the District of Columbia Court of Appeals, the case was decided by the U.S. Supreme Court.

With Justice John Harlan writing for a bare majority, Barenblatt's contempt conviction was upheld. Distinguishing the Court's decision in Watkins v. U.S., 354 U.S. 178 (1957), Harlan stated that the Court reversed the Watkins conviction "solely" on the ground that he had not been adequately apprised of the committee's subject matter or of the pertinency of the questions which he refused to answer. While Rule XI of the House is rather vague, the Court did not base its decision in *Watkins* on such a "broad and inflexible holding" as is claimed by Barenblatt. Moreover, given the fact that the House of Representatives has continued to support the life of the committee, it cannot be argued seriously that the investigation of communist activities and the use of the compulsory process was beyond that which the House had intended. Barenblatt's pertinency objection was not sustained because the subject matter of the inquiry was made plain by the subcommittee at the commencement of its proceedings, and given Barenblatt's own written memorandum there is little doubt that he was fully aware of the pertinency of the questions. Additionally, unlike Watkins, Barenblatt refused to answer queries concerning his own affiliation with the Communist Party. Harlan met the first amendment argument with a balancing of interests approach. Ordinarily, argued Harlan, the activities of the Committee on Un-American Activities would be viewed as presenting a grave danger to first amendment rights. But the Communist Party, stated Harlan, is not "an ordinary political party." The goal of the Communist Party is to overthrow the government of the United States by force and violence and since the self-preservation of society is of "ultimate value," the balance between the rights of society and of individuals must be struck in favor of society.

Barron v. Baltimore
32 U.S. (7 Pet.) 243, 8 L. Ed. 672 (1833)

The City of Baltimore effectively destroyed John Barron's wharf. It redirected the course of several streams which resulted in large deposits of sand surrounding Barron's wharf. As a result, vessels could not approach Barron's wharf because of the shallow waters. A county court awarded Barron damages but an appellate court reversed the decision in favor of the city. Barron appealed to the U.S. Supreme Court arguing that Baltimore took his private property without just compensation violating the fifth amendment to the U.S. Constitution.

Writing for the Supreme Court, Chief Justice John Marshall held that the fifth amendment and the Bill of Rights in general are constraints on the national government, not the state or local governments. The people of the United States established the general government for themselves, not for the governments of the individual states. The people intended for the Bill of Rights to operate against the possible abuses of the new central government, and not against the state governments.

Bolling v. Sharpe
347 U.S. 497, 74 S. Ct. 693, 98 L. Ed. 884 (1954)

This case arose when petitioners, black children, were denied admission to a public school in the District of Columbia solely because of their race. They alleged that such segregation deprived them of due process of law under the fifth amendment.

Delivered on the same day as Brown v. Board of Education of Topeka 1, 347 U.S. 483 (1954), Chief Justice Earl Warren held for an unanimous Court that segregation in the District of Columbia public schools violated the due process clause of the fifth amendment. Because the fifth amendment does not contain an equal protection clause, the Court needed to ascertain whether the due process clause, like equal protection, was also a bar to racial segregation. Warren argued that both the equal protection and due process concepts stem from the American ideal of fairness; these concepts are not mutually exclusive. Granting that the Court had not defined "liberty" in the fifth or fourteenth amendments with any great precision, Warren reasoned that the term liberty is "not confined to mere freedom from bodily restraint." Rather, "Liberty under law extends to the full range of conduct which the individual is free to pursue, and it cannot be restricted except for a proper governmental objective." Warren then concluded that segregation of the District of Columbia public schools constituted an "arbitrary deprivation" of the liberty of black children in violation of the due process clause.

Brown v. Board of Education of Topeka I
347 U.S. 483, 74 S. Ct. 686, 98 L. Ed. 873 (1954)

This case involved several consolidated cases concerning segregation in the public schools. The black plaintiffs alleged that the denial of admission to the public schools on a nonsegregated basis deprived them of the equal protection law guaranteed by the fourteenth amendment.

Writing for an unanimous Supreme Court, Chief Justice Earl Warren struck down segregated public schools. In all but one of the consolidated cases, the public schools were found by the lower courts to satisfy the separate but equal test, first announced by the Supreme Court in Plessy v. Ferguson, 156 U.S. 537 (1896). Finding inconclusive the evidence regarding the intention of the framers of the fourteenth amendment, and concluding that consideration of only tangible factors in the separate but equal rule are inadequate, Warren framed the constitutional question. He wrote: "Does segregation of children in public schools solely on the basis of race, even though the physical facilities and other 'tangible' factors may be equal, deprive the children of the minority group of equal opportunities?" Noting that in previous cases [Sweatt v. Painter, 339 U.S. 629 (1950) and McLaurin v. Oklahoma State Regents, 339 U.S. 637 (1950)] the Supreme Court had considered the effects of intangible factors, Warren, citing social science studies, found that to separate black from white children in public schools "solely because of their race generates a feeling of inferiority as to their status in the community that may affect their hearts and minds in a way unlikely ever to be undone." Holding that segregation in public schools is a violation of the equal protection clause of the fourteenth amendment, Warren concluded "in the field of public education the doctrine of 'separate but equal' has no place. Separate educational facilities are inherently unequal."

Brown v. Board of Education of Topeka II
349 U.S. 294, 75 S. Ct. 753, 99 L. Ed. 1083 (1955)

With its decisions in Brown v. Board of Education I, 347 U.S. 483 and Bolling v. Sharpe, 347 U.S. 497 (1957), the Supreme Court declared racial segregation in public education unconstitutional. Leaving open the question of the proper implementation of these decisions, the Court asked the U.S. Attorney General and the Attorneys General of all states requiring or permitting segregation to file briefs recommending proper relief.

Writing for the Court, Chief Justice Earl Warren noted that the primary responsibilities for presenting solutions rests with local school authorities. However, the federal district courts were given the responsibility of overseeing the desegregation process because of their proximity to local conditions. The duty of the district courts were to consider whether the action of authorities constitute "good faith implementation of the governing constitutional principles" found in *Brown I*. The Supreme Court ordered the district courts to be guided by equity principles of "practical flexibility in shaping its remedies and by a facility for adjusting the reconciling public and private needs." Once a "prompt and reasonable start toward full compliance" is made, the courts may permit additional time if they find it necessary for an effective implementation; the burden of proof, however, rests upon the defendant school districts. The guiding principle for full implementation of desegregation plans is "all deliberate speed."

Buckley v. Valeo
424 U.S. 1, 96 S. Ct. 612, 46 L. Ed. 2d 659 (1976)

This case involves the constitutionality of the Federal Election Campaign Act of 1971, as amended. Characterized as the most far reaching and comprehensive reform legislation involving the role of money in federal elections, the act limited financial contributions, regulated expenditures of money, and created a commission to oversee the regulations. Senator James Buckley and former Senator Eugene McCarthy brought suit against the Secretary of the U.S. Senate, Francis Valeo and others challenging the various provisions of the act. Seeking declaratory and injunctive relief, the plaintiffs' action rested upon first and fifth amendment arguments and upon article II, section 2, clause 2 with respect to the appointment of the eight-member commission. After the Appeals Court for the District of Columbia upheld most of the act's provisions, the plaintiffs appealed to the U.S. Supreme Court.

In its lengthy Per Curiam opinion, the Court utilized a weighing process in determining whether the governmental interest in preventing corruption and the appearance of corruption justified the intrusion of the first amendment rights of expression through political contributions and expenditures. The Court decided that the individual contribution limits, the disclosure and reporting provisions, and the public financing schemes are constitutional. However, the limitations on campaign expenditures, on independent expenditures by individuals and groups, and on expenditures by a candidate from his or her personal funds were found constitutionally defective. Since several of the eight members on the election commission were not appointed by the president, consistent with the appointment clause of the Constitution (art. II, sec. 2, cl. 2), the commission, as composed, was also found unconstitutional.

Butchers' Benevolent Association v. Crescent City Livestock Landing
and Slaughterhouse Co.
(Slaughterhouse Cases)
83 U.S. (16 Wall.) 36, 21 L. Ed. 394 (1873)

The City of New Orleans, due to slaughterhouse activities there, was ineffective in its efforts to deal with pollution of the Mississippi River. To remedy this problem, the state of Louisiana enacted a statute in 1869 granting an exclusive franchise to one large slaughterhouse. The Butchers' Benevolent Association brought suit to enjoin the monopoly from operating. It contended that the Louisiana law violated the thirteenth amendment anti-slavery provision and the privileges and immunities, due process, and equal protection clauses of the fourteenth amendment. The Louisiana Supreme Court ruled in favor of the monopoly. The Association appealed its case to the U.S. Supreme Court.

Rejecting the thirteenth amendment argument as applying to slavery historically understood, Justice Samuel Miller, writing for the majority, turned to an analysis of the meaning of the fourteenth amendment. Miller opted for a dual citizenship interpretation, holding that the privileges and immunities clause refers to a citizenship of the United States and a citizenship of a state—which are distinct. The sole purpose of this clause, wrote Miller, is ". . . to declare to the several states, that whatever those rights, as you grant or establish them to your own citizens, or as you limit or qualify, or impose restrictions on their exercise, the same, neither more nor less, shall be the measure of the rights of citizens of other states within your jurisdiction." Because the suit was brought by citizens of Louisiana and not citizens of other states, the privileges and immunities clause could not justify a constitutional challenge. Refusing to recognize the notion of substantive due process, Miller expressed the majority of the Court's view that ". . . under no construction of that provision [due process] that we have ever seen, or any that we deem admissible can the restraint imposed by the state of Louisiana upon the exercise of their trade by the butchers of New Orleans be held to be a deprivation of property within the meaning of that provision." The equal protection claim was dismissed with the observation that it applies only to laws discriminating against Negroes.

Civil Rights Cases
109 U.S. 3, 3 S. Ct. 18, 27 L. Ed. 835 (1883)

The Civil Rights Act of 1875 prohibited any person from denying another the rights of access and enjoyment of accommodations, facilities, inns, public conveyances, theaters and other places of amusement. In a number of consolidated cases, known here as the Civil Rights Cases, blacks alleged that they were denied access to public facilities covered by the 1875 Act, solely because of their race.

Writing for the majority of the Supreme Court, Justice Joseph Bradley held that the Civil Rights Act of 1875 was not a valid application of the fourteenth and thirteenth amendments and consequently was an infringement of the reserved powers of the state guaranteed by the tenth amendment. The fourteenth amendment applies to state not individual action since its opening lines refers to *state* abridgments of privileges and immunities, due process and equal protection. Bradley wrote: ". . . the legislation which congress is authorized to adopt in this behalf is not general legislation upon the rights of the citizen, but corrective legislation; that is, such as may be necessary and proper for counteracting such laws as the states may adopt or enforce, . . ." Because the denial of rights to blacks by individuals cannot be regulated by Congress under the authority of the fourteenth amendment, such legislation is violative of the tenth amendment. Concluding that the thirteenth amendment refers to the abolition of slavery and that the refusal of accommodations to blacks "has nothing to do with slavery or involuntary servitude," Bradley found no constitutional authority for the Civil Rights Act.

Cooley v. The Board of Wardens of the Port of Philadelphia
53 U.S. (12 How.) 299, 13 L. Ed. 996 (1852)

In 1803, the Pennsylvania legislature enacted a law requiring ships entering or leaving the port of Philadelphia to hire a local pilot for navigation purposes. Failure to comply would result in a fine of half the pilotage fee to be levied against the vessel. An Act of Congress of 1789 provided that pilots shall continue to be regulated by state law until possible future congressional action might be taken. When Aaron Cooley violated the state law by failing to pay the fee on two of his vessels, the Board of Wardens filed suit to recover the fees. The Pennsylvania Supreme Court affirmed the lower court judgment rendered against Cooley. On a writ of error to the U.S. Supreme Court, Cooley maintained that the state statute was an unconstitutional tax on commerce.

Writing for the majority, Justice Benjamin Curtis first noted that pilots are an important part of navigation and it is well-established that navigation is part of commerce within the meaning of the commerce clause (art. I, sec. 8, cl. 3) of the Constitution. But the commerce clause does not per se deprive the states of all power to regulate pilots. Through its 1789 enactment, Congress manifested a clear intention not to regulate the subject matter, but rather to leave such regulation to the several states. Consequently, the Pennsylvania law was enacted by virtue of the power residing in the state to legislate and the law is not in conflict with congressional legislation.

Dartmouth College v. Woodward
(see, Trustees of Dartmouth College v. Woodward)

Dennis v. United States
341 U.S. 494, 71 S. Ct. 857, 95 L. Ed. 1137 (1951)

In 1948, Eugene Dennis and ten other top leaders of the U.S. Communist Party were indicted under provisions of the Smith Act for organizing the Communist Party and for willfully and knowingly conspiring to teach or advocate the overthrow of the government of the United States by force or violence. After a lengthy trial, a U.S. district court found all defendants guilty. Convictions were upheld by the Circuit Court of Appeals.

On appeal to the U.S. Supreme Court, the Court affirmed the lower court decision limiting the scope of its review to first and fifth amendment questions. Writing for the majority, Chief Justice Vinson upheld the validity of the Smith Act both inherently and as applied to the first amendment. Expanding the "clear and present danger" test, first established in Schenck v. U.S., 249 U.S. 47 (1919), the Court concluded that Congress clearly possesses the authority to protect the government from violent overthrow, even though the danger is not imminent. Adopting the test set forth by U.S. Court Appeals Judge Learned Hand, the Supreme Court rejected the notion that it must consider the success or probability of success as the criterion of clear and present danger. It stated: "In each case [courts] must ask whether the gravity of the 'evil,' discounted by its improbability, justifies such invasion of free speech as is necessary to avoid the danger." The Court also rejected the contention that the statute was too vague or indefinite so as to fail to present a clear standard of permissible behavior.

Ex Parte McCardle
74 U.S. (7 Wall.) 506, 19 L. Ed. 264 (1869)

A federal military commission arrested and detained McCardle, a Southern newspaper editor, for publishing articles alleged to be incendiary and libelous. McCardle, a civilian, argued that he was being illegally restrained and sought a writ of *habeas corpus*. A circuit court denied his petition, whereupon he appealed directly to the U.S. Supreme Court under a 1867 statute authorizing the Court to hear appeals in such cases. The Supreme Court granted review and heard the case. However, before a decision was delivered, Congress, over President Andrew Johnson's veto, repealed the statute. The resulting question before the Court was whether the Court could still exercise jurisdiction in the case.

Writing for the majority, Chief Justice Chase dismissed McCardle's appeal for want of jurisdiction. He found that appellate jurisdiction is subject to congressional regulation. Congress possesses constitutional authority to enlarge or diminish the Court's appellate jurisdiction.

Ex Parte Milligan
71 U.S. (4 Wall.) 2, 18 L. Ed. 281 (1866)

As a Civil War measure, President Lincoln on September 24, 1862, suspended the habeas corpus privilege. Later on March 3, 1963, Congress enacted a law in an attempt to modify the president's control of political prisoners. This act authorized, after the fact, suspension of habeas corpus but also required that the secretaries of state and war furnish to the federal courts lists of political prisoners. It provided that if a grand jury failed to indict the prisoners, they were to be released after taking an oath of allegiance. Milligan, a citizen of Indiana, where the administration of justice continued unimpaired in the civilian federal courts, was arrested, tried, found guilty by a military commission of disloyalty and treason, and sentenced to death. Objecting to the jurisdiction of the military commission, Milligan petitioned a U.S. circuit court for a writ of habeas corpus. The circuit court, unable to agree on a decision, certified unresolved queries to the Supreme Court for consideration.

With Justice David Davis writing for the Court, the military commission authorized by the president was found to be unlawful. A majority of five justices stated further that Congress, as well as the president, lacked the legal authority to create military commissions to try civilians in areas removed from the actual war zone and where the civilian courts remained open. Milligan was not tried by a court established by Congress; only Congress, not the president, possesses the constitutional authority to establish courts. Milligan was also denied a trial by jury guaranteed by the sixth amendment. He was entitled to the writ of habeas corpus. In a most emphatic pronouncement affirming the rule of law, Davis wrote: "The Constitution of the United States is a law for rulers and people, equally in war and in peace, and covers with the shield of its protection all classes of men, at all times, and under all circumstances. No doctrine, involving more pernicious consequences, was ever invented by the wit of man than that any of its provisions can be suspended during any of the great exigencies of government."

Fletcher v. Peck
10 U.S. (6 Cranch) 87, 3 L.Ed. 162 (1810)

In 1795, the legislature of the State of Georgia granted a large parcel of land to speculators resulting in part from bribery of several members. In 1796, the legislature declared the corrupt act of 1795 null and void. Peck took possession of the land in 1800, and in his deed which he signed over to Fletcher, he indicated that all of the past transactions involving the land were lawful. Fletcher sued Peck for breach of covenant because the original land grant was the result of an illegal agreement and, therefore, it was not Peck's to sell. A circuit court entered judgment in favor of Peck and the case was appealed to the U.S. Supreme Court on a writ of error.

Writing for the Court, Chief Justice John Marshall held that the land grant is a contract executed and because there is no constitutional difference between a contract which is executory and one which is executed, the legal agreement is one which is contemplated by article I, section 10 of the Constitution (the contract clause). The Constitution does not make a distinction between a contract between individuals and those executed between a state and individuals. Therefore, the state of Georgia was restrained from passing the repealing legislation rendering the original grant null and void. This opinion is the first major decision to strike down a state law as inconsistent with the U.S. Constitution and thus it is the state analogue to *Marbury v. Madison.*

Furman v. Georgia
408 U.S. 238, 92 S. Ct. 2726, 33 L. Ed. 2d 346 (1972)

Furman and two other petitioners, each convicted in a state court and sentenced to death, sought review of the three state appellate court decisions affirming the imposition of the death penalty.

In the U.S. Supreme Court's per curiam decision (by the court as a whole), five of the nine justices agreed that the imposition of the death penalty in *these cases* constituted cruel and unusual punishment violative of the eighth and fourteenth amendments. In a concurring opinion, Justice Douglas argued that the death penalty has been applied selectively to minorities by judges and juries. But the death penalty itself may nevertheless remain unconstitutional if a mandatory death penalty were imposed—a question he did not answer. Also concurring, Justice Brennan concluded that the death penalty does not comport with principles of human dignity. The basis of Justice Stewart's concurring opinion was that the death penalty has been wantonly and freakishly imposed. Justice White emphasized that he does not hold that the death penalty is per se unconstitutional. Rather, because the legislatures delegated to juries and judges the responsibility for determining the circumstances where the death penalty should be imposed, there is an eighth amendment violation. Justice Marshall reasoned that the purposes served by capital punishment are not realized and that the death penalty is discriminatory against certain identifiable classes of people: there is evidence that innocent people have been wrongfully executed and the death penalty ". . . wreaks havoc with our entire criminal justice system." Four separate dissenting opinions, each joined by the other dissenters, commonly invoked principles of judicial self-restraint. In *Gregg v. Georgia* (1976), the Supreme Court upheld the constitutionality of the death penalty.

Garcia v. San Antonio Metropolitan Transit Authority
469 U.S. 528, 105 S. Ct. 1005, 83 L. Ed. 2d 1016 (1985)

The Supreme Court held in *National League of Cities v. Usery* (1976) that cities were not bound by the minimum wage and maximum hours provisions of the Federal Fair Labor Standards Act (FLSA). The Court reasoned that such federal regulation impairs the integrity and ability of the states to function effectively in the federal system. Notwithstanding the Court's 1976 opinion, Garcia, an employee of the San Antonio Metropolitan Transit Authority, invoking FLSA, sued his employer for lack of payment for overtime work. However, the San Antonio Metropolitan Transit Authority relied on the Court's decision in *National League of Cities* as justification for nonpayment. The secretary of labor ruled in favor of Garcia, but a federal district court citing *National League of Cities* ruled in favor of the transit authority. The secretary of labor and Garcia took direct appeals to the Supreme Court.

Writing for the Court's 5–4 majority, Justice Harry Blackmun overruled *National League of Cities v. Usery*. He pointed out that it has been difficult to apply the principle laid down in *National League of Cities* that the national government should not invade the "traditional government functions" of the states. The boundary between that which is a traditional governmental function and that which is not has proven unworkable and inconsistent with established principles of federalism. When the Court attempted this type of distinction in the area of intergovernmental tax immunity, for example, the results were also unworkable. The regulation of state or municipal employee wages and working conditions is a valid exercise of the congressional commerce power. Therefore, it is not an invasion of the tenth amendment reserved power of the state.

Gibbons v. Ogden
22 U.S. (9 Wheat.) 1, 6 L. Ed. 23 (1824)

The New York legislature granted Robert Livingston and Robert Fulton an exclusive twenty-year franchise to operate steamboats on New York waters. Under provisions of the statute, anyone operating a steamboat in New York waters not licensed to Fulton or Livingston would be subject to forfeiting their vessel. Aaron Ogden, securing a license from the two franchise holders, operated his boats between New York and New Jersey. Gibbons, on the other hand, secured a coastal license from the federal government to operate between the same two points. Ogden, contending that the federal coastal license conflicted with New York laws, brought suit to enjoin Gibbons from continuing his business. The injunction was granted and a New York state appellate court affirmed.

The U.S. Supreme Court ruled the New York statute invalid since it conflicted with an act of Congress. Chief Justice John Marshall ruled that commerce is more than traffic; commerce he wrote: ". . . is intercourse. It describes the commercial intercourse between nations, and parts of nations in all its branches, and is regulated by prescribing rules for carrying out that intercourse." Commerce, however, does not comprehend activity which is completely internal within a state. The congressional power to regulate commerce is complete, it is plenary. Because the license granted by New York conflicts with the federal license granted to Gibbons, and since the federal Constitution is supreme (the supremacy clause), the state license is a nullity.

Gideon v. Wainwright
372 U.S. 335, 83 S. Ct. 792, 9 L. Ed. 2d 799 (1963)

Clarence Gideon was convicted of a felony under Florida law for break-ing and entering a pool hall with the intent to commit a crime. Appearing at trial, without a lawyer and without the money to obtain one, Gideon requested that the judge appoint counsel for him. Citing Florida law, the judge ex-plained that he may appoint counsel only in capital cases. Gideon conducted his own defense and was convicted and sentenced to five years in prison. After the Florida Supreme Court denied Gideon's habeas corpus petition against Wainwright, director of state corrections, Gideon proceeded *in forma pauperis* to the U.S. Supreme Court. Granting certiorari, the Court appointed well-known Washington, D.C., attorney Abe Fortas to represent Gideon.

Delivering the opinion for the Court, Justice Hugo Black directly over-ruled Betts v. Brady, 316 U.S. 455 (1942). In a similar situation to Gideon's, the Court found in *Betts* that the sixth amendment guarantee of counsel is not one of those fundamental and essential rights so necessary to a fair trial that it should be made obligatory upon the states by the due process clause of the fourteenth amendment. Black argued that the *Betts* Court had deviated from established precedent, in Powell v. Alabama, 287 U.S. 45 (1932). He held that the right to counsel is a fundamental right required by the due process clause of the fourteenth amendment.

Gitlow v. New York
268 U.S. 652, 45 S. Ct. 625, 69 L. Ed. 1138 (1925)

Benjamin Gitlow was a leader of the Left Wing Section of the Socialist Party. He was tried and convicted of the New York Criminal Anarchy Act of 1902 for distributing a document similar in character to the *Communist Manifesto*. This publication, "Left Wing Manifesto," contained writings call-ing for the overthrow of capitalism and the necessity of bringing about a socialist society through mass political strikes and industrial revolts. There was no evidence that the publication had any effect. After his conviction was affirmed by the New York Court of Appeals, Gitlow appealed on a writ of error to the U.S. Supreme Court.

Writing for a majority, Justice Edward Sanford, rejected counsel's first amendment arguments and affirmed Gitlow's conviction. In the form of *obiter dicta*, the Court agreed that the first amendment protections of speech and press are applicable to the states by way of the due process clause of the fourteenth amendment; but importantly, the Court found no first amendment infringement. The New York statute does not prohibit utterance or publication of abstract ideas. Rather, the statute prohibits language advocating, advising or teaching the advisability of overthrowing the government by unlawful means. The language in "Left Wing Manifesto," concluded the Court, is a direct incitement to action. Moreover, it is within the power of the state legislature to determine generally which utterances create a substantive evil that may be punished. In short, the clear and present danger rule first announced in Schenck v. U.S., 249 U.S. 47 (1919) is not applicable where the legislature had previously determined the danger arising from speech of a specified nature.

Griswold v. Connecticut
381 U.S. 479, 85 S. Ct. !678, 14 L. Ed.2d 510 (1965)

A long-standing but unenforced Connecticut statute made the use of contraceptives a criminal offense. Estelle Griswold, the executive director of the Planned Parenthood League, and others were convicted for having violated the law as accessories. They provided information and instruction to married persons on the use of contraceptives. A state circuit court of appeals upheld the conviction and on appeal to the Supreme Court of Errors of Connecticut the judgment was once again affirmed.

The United States Supreme Court reversed the state court decisions. Justice William O. Douglas delivered the judgment of the majority, but only Justice Clark fully accepted Douglas's reasoning. Expressly avoiding the implications of substantive due process reasoning as exemplified by Lochner v. New York, 198 U.S. 45 (1905), Douglas argued that several Court decisions established "that specific guarantees in the Bill of Rights have *penumbras,* formed by emanations from those guarantees that help them give life and substance." Five different amendments, the penumbras of which create zones of privacy, are the basis for the constitutional interpretation. They are: the first amendment's protection of the right of association; the third amendment's prohibition of quartering of soldiers in any house in time of peace without the consent of the owner; the fourth amendment's unreasonable search and seizure provision; the fifth amendment's prohibition against self-incrimination; and the ninth amendment's provision that "The enumeration in the Constitution, of certain rights, shall not be construed to deny or disparage others retained by the people."

Hammer v. Dagenhart
247 U.S. 251, 38 S. Ct. 529, 62 L. Ed. 1101 (1918)

In 1916, Congress passed the Federal Child Labor Act. This act prohibited the shipment in interstate commerce of goods produced by companies employing children under the age of fourteen; it restricted children between the ages of fourteen and sixteen from working more than eight hours a day, or more than six days a week, or at night. Dagenhart, the father of two children employed in a North Carolina cotton mill, brought suit on behalf of himself and his children against Hammer, a U.S. Attorney, to enjoin the enforcement of the act. Granting the injunction, the district court held that the act was unconstitutional.

On appeal to the U.S. Supreme Court, the district court judgment was affirmed and the federal statute was invalidated. Writing for the Court, Justice Day held that the local production of goods was a state concern and the federal attempt to regulate, even though intended for transportation in interstate commerce, was a violation of the powers reserved to the states under the tenth amendment.

Heart of Atlanta Motel v. United States
379 U.S. 241, 85 S. Ct. 348, 13 L. Ed. 2d 258 (1964)

The owners and operators of the Heart of Atlanta Motel sought a declaratory judgment that Title II of the Civil Rights Act was unconstitutional. The motel, located close to downtown Atlanta and readily accessible to interstate highways, solicited out-of-state customers and prior to the passage of the Act refused lodging to blacks because of their race. A three-judge federal court sustained the validity of the Act and issued a permanent injunction against the motel operators.

Delivering the opinion for the Supreme Court, Justice Tom Clark first noted that the history of the 1964 Civil Rights Act indicates that Congress based the legislation on both the equal protection clause of the fourteenth amendment and the commerce power. The Court, however, anchored its holding on the commerce clause (art. I, sec. 8, cl. 3) alone. Basing its finding on extensive testimony, Congress determined that discrimination in lodging for Negroes had a detrimental effect on commerce. Though Congress may have been legislating in the commerce field to deal with "moral wrongs," Clark concluded that the act is nonetheless constitutional. The "power of Congress to promote interstate commerce also includes the power to regulate the local incidents thereof, including local activities in both the State of origin and destination, which might have a substantial and harmful effect upon that commerce." How Congress may, as a matter of policy, eliminate the obstructions in interstate commerce is within the discretion of the Congress, not the courts. The only restriction on congressional power is that the means chosen must be "reasonably adapted to the end permitted by the Constitution." Finding that the legislation was reasonably related to the constitutional objective, the Supreme Court upheld the validity of the act.

Home Building and Loan Association v. Blaisdell
290 U.S. 398, 54 S. Ct. 231, 78 L. Ed. 413 (1934)

In 1933, the Minnesota legislature passed the Minnesota Moratorium Law, which was designed to prevent foreclosure of mortgages during the

Great Depression. The law provided for temporary postponement of payments on mortgages of homeowners and farmers. Under a provision of this law, John Blaisdell and his wife sought an extension of the period of redemption so they could retain ownership of their home. A state district court granted the extension but on the condition that Blaisdell make certain monthly payments to cover taxes, insurance, and interest. The Minnesota Supreme Court affirmed the judgment upholding the statute. Home Building and Loan then appealed to the U.S. Supreme Court.

Writing for the majority, Chief Justice Charles Evans Hughes, responding to the constitutional claim that the moratorium law exceeded state power, found no transgression of the contract clause (art. I, sec. 10). Noting that while emergency does not create power, emergency may furnish the occasion for the exercise of power, Hughes established five criteria for determining when a contract is not impaired: the presence of an emergency; the legislation must be addressed to a legitimate end—for the protection of the basic interests of society, not for the mere advantage of particular individuals or interests; the relief must be appropriate to the emergency, and may be granted only on reasonable conditions; the integrity of the contract is not impaired; and the legislation must be temporary in operation.

Hurtado v. California
110 U.S. 516, 4 S. Ct. 111, 28 L. Ed. 232 (1884)

Adopted in 1879, the California State Constitution provided that criminal prosecutions which previously required a grand jury indictment could be initiated by an information prepared by the prosecuting attorney. (An information is a common law device whereby the prosecutor submits charges to a trial court in the form of an affidavit supported by sworn statements.) Charged with murder, Hurtado was prosecuted through the use of an information, found guilty, and sentenced to death. Hurtado appealed arguing that the due process clause of the fourteenth amendment comprehends grand jury indictment as is found in the fifth amendment's limitation on the power of the federal government. The California Supreme Court affirmed the conviction.

The U.S. Supreme Court affirmed the state court judgment. In the decision delivered by Justice Stanley Matthews, the Court held that the due process clause of the fourteenth amendment does not provide a defendant charged with a state offense the rights to indictment by a grand jury. Due process of law refers to "Those fundamental principles of liberty and justice which lie at the base of all our civil and political institutions . . ." Since the indictment process is ". . . merely a preliminary proceeding, and can result in no final judgment," the Court ruled it a legal proceeding not within the scope of due process as found in the fourteenth amendment.

Immigration & Naturalization Service v. Chadha
462 U.S. 919, 103 S. Ct. 2764, 77 L. Ed. 2d 317 (1983)

Under a provision of the Immigration and Nationality Act either the House or Senate could reverse a decision of the attorney general to deport or refuse to deport a specific alien. The attorney general refused to deport Chadha and five other deportable aliens. This decision was transmitted to the Congress where the House of Representatives voted its disapproval. Chadha then filed for review of the deportation order with a U.S. Court of Appeals which found in his favor. The federal government then appealed to the U.S. Supreme Court.

Writing for the Court's majority, Chief Justice Warren Burger focused on the constitutional issue raised by the provision of the act authorizing one house of Congress to invalidate the decision of the executive branch pursuant to authority delegated by Congress to the attorney general. He found that the one house veto is specifically violative of the presentment clause (art. I, sec. 7, cl. 3) of the Constitution. Reading the Constitution strictly, the chief justice reasoned that the procedures in the act amount to an amendment of a law. Various provisions of article I of the Constitution require all laws and amendments thereto must be the product of the vote of the two houses of Congress, and must be presented to the president for his signature. The Court's decision in this case seriously compromises the constitutional validity of the nearly 200 statutes passed by Congress since 1932 involving the so-called legislative veto.

Katz v. United States
389 U.S. 347, 88 S. Ct. 507, 19 L. Ed. 2d 576 (1967)

Charles Katz was convicted in U.S. district court under an eight-count indictment charging him with transmitting wagering and betting information from a telephone booth in Los Angeles to Miami and Boston. During the trial, the federal government was permitted to present as evidence a recording of Katz's conversation which the FBI had obtained through the use of an electronic listening and recording device attached to the top of a public telephone booth. Katz objected to the use of the recordings as inconsistent with the fourth amendment protection against illegal searches and seizures. A U.S. circuit court affirmed Katz's conviction.

Justice Potter Stewart, expressing the views of seven members of the U.S. Supreme Court, held that the use of electronic surveillance equipment without first securing a warrant constituted a violation of Katz's general right to privacy. Overruling the underpinnings of Olmstead v. U.S., 277 U.S. 438 (1928) and Goldman v. U.S., 316 U.S. 129 (1942), on which the FBI based its conduct, the Court noted that the trespass doctrine can no longer be regarded as controlling. It is of no constitutional significance that the electronic listening device failed to physically penetrate the wall of the telephone booth.

Katzenbach v. McClung
379 U.S. 294, 85 S. Ct. 377, 13 L. Ed. 2d 290 (1964)

This case was argued along with Heart of Atlanta Motel v. U.S., 397 U.S. 241 (1964). However, unlike *Heart of Atlanta*, this case concerned the refusal to serve blacks by a restaurant in Birmingham, Alabama. Ollie's Barbecue sought injunctive relief against the United States from the enforcement of the 1964 Civil Rights Act. A three-judge district court issued the injunction.

Writing for the Supreme Court, Justice Tom Clark found that the restaurant purchased food in interstate commerce and based on a congressional finding, discrimination against black patrons had a substantial impact on interstate commerce. The district court had erred when it found "no connection between discrimination and the movement of interstate commerce." Citing numerous precedents, Clark emphasized that even though business activity may be local in nature, Congress may reach such activity if it exerts a substantial economic impact on interstate commerce. The only limitation on the commerce power is found in Marshall's decision in Gibbons v. Ogden, 22 U.S. (9 Wheat.) 1 (1824); the activities beyond congressional reach are "those which are completely within a particular State, which do not affect other States, and with which it is not necessary to interfere, for the purpose of executing some of the general powers of the government." Furthermore, Clark concluded that it is not necessary for a case-by-case determination of discrimination in restaurant service. As long as it has a rational basis for finding a regulatory scheme necessary for the protection of commerce, Congress, and not the courts, may make the determination of what constitutes a burden on commerce.

Korematsu v. United States
323 U.S. 214, 65 S. Ct. 193, 89 L. Ed. 194 (1944)

Shortly after America entered World War II, Congress enacted a law authorizing the president, by executive order, to create military areas from which residents might be restricted in order to maintain national security. Under growing concern that the Pacific Coast might be invaded by Japan, the Western Defense Command divided that entire coast into two military areas and imposed certain restrictions on those living there. The restrictions ranged from curfews that applied to aliens and persons of Japanese descent to an eventual forced removal, to relocation camps of all persons of Japanese descent. Korematsu, a United States citizen, refused to leave his home and was convicted in federal district court for violating the exclusion order. A circuit court of appeals affirmed his conviction whereupon Korematsu appealed to the U.S. Supreme Court.

Delivering the opinion of the Court, Justice Black found that exclusion was justified by the presence of an unknown number of disloyal citizens of Japanese origin. Congress and the executive branch, through the exercise of the war powers, possessed the constitutional authority to exclude citizens from certain areas during the time of war.

Lochner v. New York

198 U.S. 45, 25 S. Ct. 539, 49 L. Ed. 937 (1905)

Joseph Lochner, a bakery owner, was convicted of violating a 1897 New York statute prohibiting bakery employers from allowing employees to work more than ten hours per day or more than sixty hours per week. After two New York appellate courts affirmed Lochner's conviction, the case was appealed to the U.S. Supreme Court.

Writing for the majority, Justice Rufus Peckham held that while the state, through the exercise of its police powers, may prohibit individuals from making certain contracts, limitations on the hours a baker may work transcends the power of the state. Because it bears no reasonable relationship as a health law safeguarding the public health or the health of bakers, the legislation is in violation of the liberty provision of the due process clause of the fourteenth amendment.

Luther v. Borden

48 U.S. (7 How.) 1, 12 L. Ed. 581 (1849)

Despite the Revolutionary War, the state of Rhode Island continued to operate under its Colonial Charter of 1663. Some of the charter's provisions, particularly voting requirements, were a source of dissatisfaction among a group of citizens led by Thomas Dorr. Under Dorr's leadership, a new government was formed and a new constitution was adopted. The existing charter government appealed to President Tyler for federal troops to put down the so-called rebellion. But the president failed to dispatch troops. Dorr and his men were defeated by the state militia and the rival government collapsed. In an attempt to round up insurgents, Borden and other state militiamen were sent to arrest Luther, a Dorr supporter. Arrested at his home, Luther sued Borden for illegal trespass claiming that the charter government had been supplanted by the more representative insurgent regime, a republican form of government guaranteed under article IV, section 4 of the U.S. Constitution. Therefore, Borden had no authority to arrest him and to trespass on his property.

After a diversity of citizenship proceeding in federal circuit court, the case came before the U.S. Supreme Court. Writing for the majority, Chief Justice Roger Taney held that under the guaranty clause (art. IV, sec. 4) congress, and not the courts, has the responsibility to determine whether a state government is republican or not. Moreover, congress through statutory enactment had authorized the president and not the courts, to aid in putting down domestic violence. The case is consequently a political question and hence not within the appropriate sphere of authority of the Supreme Court.

McCulloch v. Maryland
17 U.S. (4 Wheat.) 316, 4 L. Ed. 579 (1819)

In 1816, Congress established a national bank, one branch of which was located in Baltimore, Maryland. Two years later the Maryland legislature enacted a statute taxing banks and bank branches not chartered by the state legislature. McCulloch, the cashier of the Baltimore Branch of the Bank of the United States, refused to pay the $15,000 annual fee, or the two percent tax on all notes issued by the bank. McCulloch was convicted in a Maryland County Court and a state Court of Appeals affirmed his conviction.

Reaching the Supreme Court on a writ of error, the state courts were reversed. Chief Justice John Marshall first reasoned that the powers of the national government do not emanate from the states, but rather from the people. While the powers of the national government are specifically enumerated, the "necessary and proper" clause (art. I, sec. 8, cl. 18) authorizes Congress to establish a national bank under its great powers to lay and collect taxes, to borrow money, to regulate commerce, and so on. Because the power to tax is the power to destroy, the state may not tax a federal instrumentality. The state law is inconsistent with the federal law establishing the bank. The supremacy clause (art. VI, sec. 2) makes the Constitution, Laws, and Treaties of the United States supreme over state laws. Thus, the state tax is unconstitutional.

Mapp v. Ohio
367 U.S. 643, 81 S. Ct. 1684, 6 L. Ed. 2d 1081 (1961)

Acting on information that a bombing case suspect and illegal gambling equipment might be found in the home of Dollree Mapp, three Cleveland police officers arrived at Miss Mapp's home requesting entrance. After being refused admission and without a search warrant, the officers broke into the premises, roughed up, and handcuffed Miss Mapp and conducted a search of the entire premises. In the basement, the officers discovered a trunk which they searched finding obscene materials. Ultimately the contents of the trunk were used to convict Mapp under an Ohio law for possession of obscene books, pictures, and photographs. The Ohio Supreme Court affirmed her conviction.

The United States Supreme Court reversed the lower court and overruled an earlier decision in Wolf v. Colorado, 338 U.S. 25 (1949). The Court in *Wolf* held ". . . that in a prosecution in a state court for a state crime the fourteenth amendment does not forbid the admission of evidence obtained by an unreasonable search and seizure." Establishing the exclusionary rule for state proceedings, Justice Tom Clark, writing for the majority in *Mapp v. Ohio*, held that the due process clause of the fourteenth amendment incorporates the protections of the fourth amendment. Hence, evidence obtained in a search and seizure in violation of the fourth amendment is inadmissible in state, just as in federal prosecutions.

Marbury v. Madison

5 U.S. (1 Cranch) 137, 2 L. Ed. 60 (1803)

In his last days as president, John Adams nominated William Marbury as Justice of the Peace for the District of Columbia. The nomination was confirmed by the Senate, but the commission appointing Marbury was never delivered by Secretary of State John Marshall. The next president, Thomas Jefferson, ordered Marshall's successor James Madison not to deliver the commission. Under the provisions of Section 13 of the Judiciary Act of 1789, Marbury petitioned the U.S. Supreme Court to issue a writ of mandamus ordering the secretary of state to deliver the commission.

Writing for the Court, Chief Justice John Marshall concluded that Marbury had a legal right to the commission he demands, and that where there is a legal right there must be a remedy. However, the remedy sought, a writ of mandamus, is not within the authority of the Court to grant. Marshall reasoned that Section 13 of the Judiciary Act of 1789 violates the Constitution because by granting to the Court the authority to issue writs of mandamus in its original jurisdiction it adds to that jurisdiction; Article III strictly limits the Supreme Court's original jurisdiction. Marshall based his conclusion on the following interrelated arguments. First, the Constitution established by the people a government of limit powers. Second, the Constitution is superior to legislative enactments. To hold otherwise would make a written constitution useless. Third, the Court cannot close its eyes to an unconstitutional act. He stated, "It is emphatically, the province and duty of the judicial department, to say what the law is." Fourth, judges take an oath to uphold the Constitution. It would be immoral for them to give effect to an unconstitutional act. Lastly, the phrasing of article VI, paragraph 2, mentions the Constitution first before it mentions laws, and not the other way around. Therefore, the framers of the Constitution must have intended that the basic document be held superior to laws.

Milliken v. Bradley
418 U.S. 717, 94 S. Ct. 3112, 41 L. Ed. 2d 1069 (1974)

A class action suit brought by the local branch of the NAACP alleged that Detroit public schools were segregated on the basis of race, and were in violation of the equal protection clause of the fourteenth amendment. The federal district court ruled in favor of the NAACP and ordered desegregation plans for the Detroit school system, as well as for two or more suburban districts within the metropolitan area. On appeal, the United States Court of Appeals affirmed the district court decision holding that the state had committed de jure acts of segregation in the Detroit area and that the district court had the remedial power to order interdistrict desegregation.

The U.S. Supreme Court reversed the Court of Appeals decision and remanded the case back to the district court for further consideration. Writing for the majority, Chief Justice Burger held that the lower courts had based their decisions on an erroneous standard and was unsupported by evidence that acts of outlying districts affected the discrimination found in the Detroit schools. Unless district lines were deliberately drawn to produce segregation or segregation in one district caused discrimination on the basis of race in another, a federal court does not possess the authority to order busing of students between school districts to remedy de jure segregation that exists in only one of the districts.

Miranda v. Arizona
384 U.S. 436, 86 S. Ct. 1602, 16 L. Ed. 2d 694 (1966)

Together with a group of state and federal cases, this controversy came before the U.S. Supreme Court dealing with the admissibility of statements or confessions made by defendants during custodial interrogations. The Court considered the question of what procedures are necessary to assure that defendants' fifth and sixth amendment rights are protected.

Delivering the majority opinion for the Court, Chief Justice Earl Warren emphasized that the holding is not an innovation in American jurisprudence, but rather an application of long recognized principles of criminal justice. The Court held that in the absence of a clear, intelligent waiver of the constitutional rights involved, a suspect ". . . must be warned prior to any questioning that he has a right to remain silent, that anything he says can be used against him in a court of law, that he has the right to the presence of an attorney, and that if he cannot afford an attorney one will be appointed for him prior to any questioning if he so desires." The Court also noted that if the suspect does not wish to be interrogated, the police must cease the interrogation. Simply because the suspect may have answered questions or volunteered statements does not in any way deprive the suspect of the right to refrain from answering any additional queries until such time as the suspect has had an opportunity to consult with legal counsel and thereafter consents to the questioning.

Missouri v. Holland
252 U.S. 416, 40 S. Ct. 382, 64 L. Ed. 641 (1920)

In 1916, the United States and Great Britain entered into a treaty to protect various species of birds that migrate between the United States and Canada. In 1918, pursuant to the treaty, Congress passed a law authorizing the secretary of agriculture to establish seasons for hunting and other rules concerning the birds named in the treaty. The state of Missouri filed suit in federal district court to enjoin Ray Holland, a U.S. game warden, from enforcement of the act. Following the district court's dismissal of the suit, Missouri appealed to the U.S. Supreme Court. It contended that the subject matter of both the treaty and statute were beyond the enumerated powers of the national government and constituted an invasion of the powers of the state in violation of the tenth amendment.

Speaking for a majority of the Court, Justice Oliver Wendell Holmes held that the tenth amendment does not limit the power of the United States to make treaties. The treaty powers of the federal government are broader than the enumerated powers of Congress. He further stated: "Acts of Congress are the supreme law of the land only when made in pursuance of the Constitution, while treaties are declared to be so when made under the authority of the United States." The treaty making authority cannot be ascertained in the same way as those dictating congressional legislative power. Instead, Holmes maintained the treaty making power must be viewed in light of America's experience as a developing nation. The federal government must act in the national interest to protect the birds and with them our forests and crops. Reliance upon the states is insufficient.

Munn v. Illinois
94 U.S. 113, 24 L. Ed. 77 (1877)

The Granger movement swept across the midwest as a protest against the felt exploitation of farmers by railroads and other business enterprises. In 1871, the Illinois state legislature responded by enacting a law requiring the licensing of grain elevator operators, and established maximum rates elevators could charge for grain storage. Ira Munn refused to comply with the statute, and the state filed suit. A county court ruled against Munn, and on appeal to the Illinois Supreme Court, the lower court judgment was affirmed. On appeal to the U.S. Supreme Court, the judgment was once again affirmed.

Writing for the majority, Chief Justice Morrison Waite rejected Munn's due process and commerce clause arguments. First addressing himself to the fourteenth amendment due process argument, Waite cited a common law principle of property law of at least two hundred years vintage. He wrote: "Property does become clothed with a public interest when used in a manner to make it of public consequence, and affect the community at large. When, therefore, one devotes his property to a use in which the public has an interest, he, in effect, grants to the public an interest in that use, and must submit to be controlled by the public for the common good, to the extent of the interest he has thus created. He may withdraw his grant by discontinuing the use; but, so long as he maintains the use, he must submit to the control." Since the state has not deprived Munn of property but is only controlling it in the public interest, there is no violation of the due process clause of the fourteenth amendment. Munn also argued that he is entitled to a reasonable compensation for use of his property. However, the Supreme Court held that this is a matter of legislative judgment and not the courts. If protection against abuse by the legislature is sought, the proper remedy is at the polls, not the courts. Responding to Munn's interstate commerce clause argument, Waite noted that the state has an interest in regulating business exclusively within the limits of Illinois. Although the regulation of grain elevators may incidentally touch upon interstate commerce, the state may regulate in the absence of congressional regulation.

Murray v. Curlett
(see: School District of Abington Township v. Schempp)

National Labor Relations Board v. Jones & Laughlin Steel Corp.
301 U.S. 1, 57 S. Ct. 615. 81 L. Ed. 893 (1937)

The National Labor Relations Act (Wagner Act) was passed in 1935 to guarantee the right of collective bargaining, and authorizing the National Labor Relations Board to prevent unfair labor relations affecting interstate commerce. The Board found the Jones & Laughlin Steel Corporation had violated provisions of the Wagner Act when it fired ten workers because of their activities on behalf of the union. The NLRB ordered the steel company to reinstate the men. When Jones & Laughlin refused to comply, the NLRB petitioned a U.S. circuit court to enforce its order, but the court agreed with Jones and Laughlin that the Wagner Act is a regulation of labor relations and not commerce within the meaning of the Constitution's commerce clause.

Writing for a 5 to 4 majority, Chief Justice Hughes found that labor relations bears a close and substantial relationship to interstate commerce. Congress cannot be denied the power to protect commerce from burdens and obstructions due to the paralyzing consequences of industrial strife. The decision in this case spelled an end to the judicially created distinction between direct and indirect affects on interstate commerce, and paved the way for extensive congressional legislation in labor management relations.

New York Times Co. v. Sullivan
376 U.S. 254, 84 S. Ct. 710, 11 L. Ed. 2d 686 (1964)

A paid advertisement in the New York Times made certain claims involving the alleged mistreatment of black students and Martin Luther King in Montgomery, Alabama. Though not named directly in this advertisement, Sullivan, an elected county commissioner, contended the word *police* utilized in the ad referred to him as the supervisor of the Montgomery Police Department. Because particulars in the advertisement were not true, Sullivan sued the New York Times under the Alabama libel laws. A state court awarded Sullivan $500,000 damages, and the Alabama Supreme Court affirmed the judgment.

Justice William Brennan announced the constitutional rule which reversed the Alabama courts. To promote expression, robust criticism of government officials and to deter self-censorship, the first and fourteenth amendments offer a conditional shield against libel laws. Public officials may not recover damages for defamation of character unless they can prove actual malice. Defined by the Court, actual malice consists of a false statement made ". . . with knowledge that it was false or with reckless disregard of whether it was false or not."

New York Times Co. v. United States
403 U.S. 713, 91 S. Ct. 2140, 29 L. Ed. 2d 822 (1971)

The United States government sought an injunction to restrain the *New York Times* from publishing the contents of a Pentagon top secret study entitled *History of U.S. Decision-making Process on Vietnam Policy*. The government sought similar injuncture relief in an action against the *Washington Post*. Each district court in which suits were brought denied injunctive relief. The United States Court of Appeals for the District Court of Columbia affirmed the ruling of the district court for the District Court of Columbia, but the U.S. Court of Appeals for the Second Circuit remanded the case to district court for further proceedings.

The Supreme Court affirmed the judgment of the court of appeals for the District of Columbia, and reversed the order of the U.S. Court of Appeals for the Second Circuit with directions to enter a judgment affirming the judgment of the district court. In a *per curiam* decision, the Court held that the government had not overcome the heavy presumption against prior restraint by demonstrating sufficient justification for halting the publications.

Nixon v. Fitzgerald
457 U.S. 731, 102 S. Ct. 2690, 73 L. Ed. 2d 349 (1982)

Mr. A. Ernest Fitzgerald, a civil servant and Pentagon management analyst, appeared before a congressional subcommittee where he testified to waste and mismanagement in the development of a new military transport aircraft. Dismissed from his position, Fitzgerald had reason to believe that the Nixon administration punished him for his whistle-blowing testimony. Fitzgerald named the president and several of his aides in a civil suit for monetary damages. After several administrative and judicial actions, the matter was carried before the U.S. Supreme Court for final adjudication.

The Court concluded that as a former president, Richard Nixon is entitled to absolute immunity from damages predicated on his official acts. Because of his central role in the government, the president must be free from diversions of private lawsuits. While the president has "absolutely immunity" from civil suits for acts within the "outer perimeter" of his official responsibility, his aides are entitled to only "qualified immunity". Thus, in *Harlow v. Fitzgerald* (1982), the Court held that officials performing discretionary functions generally are shielded from civil liability to the extent that their conduct does not violate established rights which a reasonable person would have known.

Palko v. Connecticut
302 U.S. 319, 58 S. Ct. 149, 82 L. Ed. 288 (1937)

Frank Palko was found guilty of second degree murder and was given a life sentence. A Connecticut state statute, however, permitted the state to appeal criminal cases. The Connecticut Supreme Court of Errors ordered a new trial. Palko was tried again, found guilty of first degree murder and sentenced to death. The Connecticut Supreme Court of Errors then affirmed the conviction. Contending that the fourteenth amendment's due process provision makes the double jeopardy provision of the fifth amendment applicable to the states, Palko appealed to the U.S. Supreme Court.

In the decision delivered by Mr. Justice Benjamin Cardozo, the Court affirmed the state court decision. The fourteenth amendment did not serve to incorporate the prohibition against double jeopardy found in the fifth amendment to the states. Cardozo justified the ruling by creating a distinction between those provisions of the Bill of Rights central to "principles implicit in the concept of ordered liberty" and those which are not.

Plessy v. Ferguson
163 U.S. 537, 16 S. Ct. 1138, 41 L. Ed. 256 (1896)

In 1890, the Louisiana state legislature enacted a statute requiring railroads to provide equal but separate accommodations for white and black passengers. The act made it unlawful for a person of one race to occupy a seat in a passenger car designated for passengers of another race. Homer Plessy, seven-eighths Caucasian, refused to give up his seat assigned to a white passenger. During the course of criminal proceedings, Plessy petitioned the Louisiana Supreme Court to enjoin the trial judge, John Ferguson, from continuing the trial against him. After the state supreme court ruled against him, Plessy brought his case to the U.S. Supreme Court.

Writing for the majority, Justice Henry Brown, holding the equal but separate law a reasonable exercise of state power, determined that the state statute did not offend provisions of either the thirteenth or fourteenth amendments. Brown noted that Plessy had not placed much stress upon the thirteenth amendment. He reasoned that the Louisiana law merely implies a legal distinction between the races based on color and possessed no tendency to reestablish slavery—the true purpose of the thirteenth amendment. The fourteenth amendment, Brown argued, was intended to enforce "the absolute equality of the two races before the law, but, in the nature of things, it could not have been intended to abolish distinctions based upon color, or to enforce social, as distinguished from political, equality, or a commingling of the two races upon terms unsatisfactory to either." Brown emphasized that even courts in states where the rights of blacks have been most vigorously enforced, segregation in education and laws against intermarriage have been upheld. Given the customs and traditions of the people, argued Brown, the reasonableness of the statute is within the discretion of the state legislature. This state law does not seem less reasonable than the acts of Congress requiring separate schools for blacks in the District of Columbia. Anticipating the dissent by Justice John Harlan, Brown argued that the enforcement of segregation does not stamp the colored race with a badge of inferiority. "If it be so," Brown stated, "it is not by reason of anything found in the act, but solely because the colored race chooses to put the construction upon it." Finally, Brown stated: "If one race be inferior to the other socially, the constitution of the United States cannot put them upon the same plane."

Pollock v. Farmers' Loan and Trust Co.
158 U.S. 601, 15 S. Ct. 912, 39 L. Ed. 1108 (1895)

In 1894, Congress enacted the Wilson Gorman Tariff Act, establishing a proportional tax on income. Pollock, a shareholder in Farmers' Loan and Trust Co., sued to enjoin the company from paying the tax. A U.S. Circuit Court upheld the tax and Pollock appealed to the Supreme Court. Initially, the Supreme Court, with Justice Howell Jackson absent because of illness, declared the law invalid insofar as it applied to the income from real estate and state and municipal bonds. The Court split on the question of whether stocks, bonds, wages, salaries and professional earnings were subject to taxation. Following Justice Jackson's recovery, however, the Court granted a rehearing.

Writing for the majority, Chief Justice Fuller held the act unconstitutional. Because it was deemed a direct tax and was not apportioned among the states, the tax scheme was viewed as inconsistent with article I, section 8, clause 1. While the Court did not directly invalidate the provisions taxing income derived from wages and professional earnings, under the partial unconstitutionality of statute rule, established in Warren v. Charlestown, 2 Gray, 84, the entire act was held invalid.

Powell v. Alabama
287 U.S. 45, 53 S. Ct. 55, 77 L. Ed. 158 (1932)

Powell and six other black defendants were charged with the capital offense of the rape of two white women. The record indicates that the blacks had been riding in a freight train with seven white boys and two white girls. A fight took place between the black and white boys, during the course of which all but one white was thrown off the train. A message was sent ahead and the blacks were arrested. The two girls testified that they were raped by each black. In a hostile community atmosphere, the defendants were indicted and arraigned. They were not asked whether they had counsel or wished to have counsel appointed or whether friends or relatives might assist them. It was not until the morning of the trial that counsel was appointed. Prior to that time, the trial judge appointed all the members of bar for the limited purpose of arraigning the defendants. Upon conviction, the defendants appealed to the Alabama Supreme Court for review. The trial court judgment was affirmed and the case was appealed to the U.S. Supreme Court.

Writing for the majority, Justice Sutherland held that in light of the circumstances of the case, the defendants were denied the right to legal counsel guaranteed by the due process clause of the fourteenth amendment. Together with its sequel, Norris v. Alabama, 294 U.S. 587 (1935), the cases are popularly known as the "Scottsboro cases."

Regents of the University of California v. Bakke
438 U.S. 265, 98 S. Ct. 2733, 57 L. Ed. 2d 750 (1978)

The medical school of the University of California at Davis established two admission programs. Eighty-four of the one hundred student positions were filled by a regular admissions program. The remaining sixteen positions were set aside for minority applicants considered economically or educationally disadvantaged. These minority applicants were not required to meet the higher scholastic requirements as those admitted under the regular admission program. Allan Bakke, a white, twice denied admission but nonetheless possessing higher academic qualifications than the minority admission applicants, sued alleging that he was denied admission because of his race. A California trial court decided against Bakke, but the California Supreme Court reversed ordering Baake's admission to the medical school. The California Supreme Court based its decision on a finding of a denial of the equal protection of the laws. The University of California appealed to the U.S. Supreme Court.

The U.S. Supreme Court found the Davis medical school admissions program invalid under the fourteenth amendment. However, there was considerable disagreement among the members of the Court about the proper basis for its decision. Justice Lewis Powell, apparently representing a middle position, announced the judgment of the Court. He found that since the special admissions program involved the utilization of an explicit racial classification, it disregards individual rights as guaranteed by the fourteenth amendment. Yet protections afforded individuals are not absolute. Classifications that withstand the strict scrutiny test supercede individual rights. But there must be a demonstration that any classification based on race is "necessary to promote a substantial state interest." Because the Davis medical school failed to show, as claimed, that the preferential classification was likely to have a beneficial impact on better health care delivery to minorities, Powell concluded that it did not meet the test. The California Supreme Court's equal protection holding was therefore affirmed. However, that part of the California decision which enjoined the Davis medical school from any consideration of the race of any applicant was reversed. Limiting the Court's judgment to the particular affirmative action program at Davis, Powell notes that other programs currently in use at other institutions are constitutionally permissible. Programs which consider race as one particular "plus," together with a number of other factors relevant to producing educational pluralism may be weighed without offending the fourteenth amendment. As Powell put it: "The applicant who loses out on the last available seat to another candidate receiving a 'plus' on the basis of ethnic background will not have been foreclosed from all consideration for that seat simply because he was not the right color or had the wrong surname. It would mean only that his combined qualifications, which may have included similar nonobjective factors, did not outweigh those of the other applicant."

Reynolds v. Sims
377 U.S. 533, 84 S. Ct. 1362, 12 L. Ed. 2d 506 (1964)

This case and fourteen companion cases involved the malapportionment of state legislative districts. Challenging the validity of the legislative apportionment for the bicameral state legislature, Sims and other Alabama residents brought suit against Reynolds and other state and party officials.

Despite the requirement in the Alabama Constitution that the legislature be reapportioned on a population basis every ten years, no new apportionment had taken place since 1901. Because the state's population growth had been uneven, Sims asserted that some citizens were victims of serious discrimination. Although the Alabama Supreme Court found that the legislature had failed to comply with the state constitution, it ruled that it could not intervene in legislative apportionment matters. A three judge federal district court, however, found that the state apportionment violated the equal protection clause of the fourteenth amendment. As a result, the Alabama legislature adopted two reapportionment plans, both of which were rejected by the district court. The court then ordered a temporary reapportionment, whereupon Reynolds appealed to the U.S. Supreme Court.

Writing for the majority, Chief Justice Earl Warren held that the equal protection clause of the fourteenth amendment requires that seats in both houses of a bicameral state legislature must be apportioned according to population. Insisting that legislators represent people, not trees or acres, Warren argued that diluting the weight of votes because of place of residence is a form of discrimination as invidious, for example, as race or economic status. In addition, Warren countered the argument that in adopting a bicameral scheme the state had employed the same plans as the federal government by making several points. First, thirty-six original state constitutions provided for representation in both legislative chambers ". . . completely, or predominantly, on population." Second, the Founding Fathers did not intend to establish a model for the states when they established the bicameral system for the national government. Third, unlike the relationship between the federal and state governments, the counties, cities, and other political subdivisions of state government have never been regarded as sovereign entities; rather, they have been regarded as governmental instrumentalities designed to assist the state in carrying out vital governmental functions. Lastly, from a positive viewpoint, bicameralism is in the modern sense highly functional; it provides for mature and deliberate legislative proceedings. Focusing on the implementation of the one man, one vote principle, Warren stated that ". . . the equal protection clause requires that a state make an honest and good faith effort to construct districts, in both houses of its legislature, as nearly of equal population as is practicable. We recognize that it is a practical impossibility to arrange legislative districts so that each one has an identical number of residents, or citizens, or voters. Mathematical exactness or precision is hardly a workable constitutional requirement."

Roe v. Wade
410 U.S. 113, 93 S. Ct. 705, 35 L. Ed. 2d 147 (1973)

An unmarried pregnant woman wishing to terminate her pregnancy by abortion challenged in U.S. District Court Texas statutes prohibiting abortions except with those procured by medical advice for the purpose of saving the life of the mother. The three judge district court heard her cause together with two others and held that an unmarried woman, and a physician who had suffered past prosecutions and was presently facing additional charges, had standing to sue. Moreover, the district court held that the criminal abortion statutes were void because they were unconstitutionally vague and overboard. On appeal to the U.S. Supreme Court, the physician's complaint was dismissed, but the district court judgment with respect to the unmarried pregnant woman was affirmed.

In a decision delivered by Justice Harry Blackmun, the Supreme Court held that a woman's decision to terminate her pregnancy is within her constitutional right to privacy protected under the liberty provision of the due process clause of the fourteenth amendment. The Court acknowledged that while the right to privacy is a fundamental right, such rights may be limited by a compelling state interest. However, a compelling state interest cannot be demonstrated in the first trimester of pregnancy. For the stage beginning with the end of the first trimester, the state in promoting its interest in the health of the mother, may, if it chooses, regulate the abortion procedure in ways that are reasonably related to maternal health. In the last trimester, the state may regulate and even prohibit abortion except where it might be necessary for the preservation of the life or health of the mother.

Schechter Poultry Corp. v. United States
295 U.S. 495, 55 S. Ct. 837, 79 L. Ed. 1570 (1935)

In 1933, in an attempt to stimulate business and reduce unemployment during the Great Depression, the National Industrial Recovery Act (NIRA) was enacted. Among its provisions, the NIRA authorized the president to approve state and local codes establishing standards on wages, hours, trade practices, working conditions, and methods of competition. The Schechter brothers owned slaughterhouses in New York City that received live chickens from other states. They were convicted in a federal district court of violating the Live Poultry Code on counts including filling false sales and price reports and selling diseased poultry. The U.S. Court of Appeals for the Second Circuit affirmed in part the decision of the district court, and both Schechter and the government appealed to the U.S. Supreme Court.

Writing for the Court, Chief Justice Charles Evans Hughes addressed two issues: first, the question of the delegation of legislative power, and, second, the application of the provisions of the Live Poultry Code to intrastate commerce. Because the NIRA supplies no standards for any trade, industry or activity reasoned Hughes, the president is given unfettered discretion in approving or prescribing codes. The NIRA is therefore an unconstitutional delegation of legislative power. Second, the slaughtering and local sale of poultry are transactions in intrastate and not interstate commerce. For Congress to regulate, there must be a direct and not an indirect effect on interstate commerce. Thus, the slaughterhouse and sales activity of the Schechter brothers is not within the power of Congress to regulate.

Schenck v. United States
249 U.S. 47, 39 S. Ct. 247, 63 L. Ed. 470 (1919)

Charles T. Schenck, the general secretary of the Socialist party, and others were charged and indicted under the Espionage Act of 1917 for conspiring to obstruct the recruiting and enlistment service of the United States during the war with Germany. Schenck printed and distributed 15,000 leaflets which urged men to oppose the draft. After conviction in federal district court, Schenck appealed to the U.S. Supreme Court.

Writing for the Court, Justice Oliver Wendell Holmes rejected the claim that the first amendment guarantees absolute free speech. In peacetime, the circulation of the leaflet would be protected. But Holmes argued: ". . . the character of every act depends upon the circumstances in which it is done. . . . The most stringent protection of free speech would not protect a man in falsely shouting fire in a theatre and causing a panic." The test in every case is ". . . whether the words used are used in such circumstances and are of such a nature as to create a clear and present danger that they will bring about the substantive evils that Congress has a right to prevent." Admitting that Schenck and his associates did not bring about the end of conscription, Holmes held that success is not necessary to convict for conspiracy. If the intent and the tendency of the act are the same, ". . . there is no ground for saying that success alone warrants making the act a crime."

School District of Abington Township v. Schempp
Murray v. Curlett
374 U.S. 203, 83 S. Ct. 1560, 10 L. Ed. 2d 844 (1963)

In *School District of Abington Township v. Schempp* the Schempp family, members of the Unitarian church, brought suit to enjoin the enforcement of a Pennsylvania statute requiring bible readings at the beginning of each school day. Student participation, however, was stated as voluntary. The Schempp's contended that the law was violative of the establishment clause of the first amendment. Injunctive relief was granted by a three judge district court panel. In the companion case of *Murray v. Curlett*, the school board, relying on a Maryland state statute, adopted an opening exercise of bible readings similar to those in Abington. Mrs. Murray and her son, a student in a Baltimore school, both of whom were professed atheists, brought suit to compel Curlett, the president of the Maryland Board of School Commissioners, to rescind the bible reading requirement. A Maryland state court ruled against Murray, and the Maryland Court of Appeals affirmed.

Both cases were appealed to the U.S. Supreme Court. The Schempp judgment was affirmed, and the Murray decision was reversed. Writing for the majority, Justice Tom C. Clark expressed the constitutional doctrine with respect to religion. The constitutional test for the establishment clause is ". . . what are the purpose and primary effect of the enactment." If it either advances or inhibits religion then the enactment is unconstitutional. Demonstrating a violation of the free exercise clause of the first amendment requires a showing of a coercive effect as it operates against individuals in the practice of religion. The Court found the Abington and Baltimore practices were religious in character, and that these exercises were violative of the establishment clause of the first amendment.

Shelley v. Kraemer
334 U.S. 1, 68 S. Ct. 836, 92 L. Ed. 1161 (1948)

A majority of the deeds in a St. Louis neighborhood contained restrictive covenant provisions which prohibited property owners from selling their land to Negroes or members of the Mongolian race. Unaware of the restrictive covenant, Shelley, a Negro, purchased property in this neighborhood. When the restrictive covenant provision was discovered, Shelley refused to reconsider the purchase. Kraemer, a neighborhood resident and also a homeowner with a covenant provision on his property, sued to prevent Shelley from taking possession of the property. The trial court, however, found that the restrictive provision was technically faulty. The Missouri Supreme Court reversed the trial court and found that the property restriction was not violative of constitutional rights. Shelley then appealed to the U.S. Supreme Court.

Delivering the unanimous opinion of the Court, Chief Justice Fred Vinson struck down the restrictive covenant as inconsistent with the equal protection provision of the fourteenth amendment. Maintaining the distinction between state and private action, a principle established in the Civil Rights Cases, 109 U.S. 3 (1883), Vinson noted that the fourteenth amendment does not prohibit discrimination by private parties but refers only to official state conduct. The restrictive covenant agreements were, in the first instance, actions of private individuals. However, when as here, the state judiciary is utilized for the enforcement of private contracts, the action of a private citizen is transformed into state action. The chief justice wrote that because the "enjoyment of property rights was among the basic objectives sought to be effectuated by the framers of the fourteenth amendment," state discrimination had occurred.

Slaughterhouse Cases
see: Butchers' Benevolent Association v. Crescent City Livestock Landing and Slaughterhouse Co.

Smith v. Allwright
321 U.S. 649, 64 S. Ct. 757, 88 L. Ed. 987 (1944)

In 1927, the Texas state legislature enacted a law granting political parties the right to establish their own qualifications for party membership. Pursuant to this law, at its 1932 state convention, the Texas Democratic Party adopted a resolution imparting to "all white" citizens of the state membership in the Democratic Party and full entitlement to participate in party deliberations. Because only Democratic Party members were permitted to vote in Democratic Party primary elections, blacks were denied the opportunity to vote in such elections. Smith, a black, brought suit against Allwright, an election judge, for refusing him the opportunity to vote in a primary election. After lower court deliberations, the U.S. Supreme Court granted *certiorari* to hear the case.

Delivering the opinion for the majority, Justice Stanley Reed held the Texas practice a violation of the right to vote guarantee of the fifteenth amendment. Overruling its decision in Grovey v. Townsend, 295 U.S. 45 (1935), the Supreme Court found that the primary elections are "conducted by the party under state statutory authority". Reed further concluded: "The privilege of membership in a party may be, as this Court said in *Grovey v. Townsend* . . . no concern of a state. But when, as here, that privilege is also the essential qualification for voting in a primary to select nominees for a general election, the state makes the action of the party the action of the state."

Stuart v. Laird
5 U.S. (1 Cranch) 299, 2 L. Ed. 115 (1803)

John Laird won a judgment against Hugh Stuart in the Fourth Circuit court of the United States. However, because Congress repealed an 1801 law creating that court with the passage of the Judicial Repeal Act of 1802, Laird applied for and obtained judgment against Stuart. Stuart argued that because the fourth circuit court had decided the case, no other court, to wit, the fifth circuit court, could proceed in the final disposition of the case.

Writing for the Supreme Court, Justice Paterson upheld the constitutionality of the Judicial Repeal Act of 1802. The Court found that the removal of the suit brought by Stuart against Laird from the court of the fourth circuit to the court of the fifth circuit is within the authority of Congress. In addition, the Judicial Repeal Act of 1802 did not deprive judges of good behavior tenure as guaranteed under article III, section 1. Interpreting the statute narrowly, Justice Paterson found that the law did not deprive Stuart of the right to have his case heard by judges serving during good behavior. The law merely transferred his case from a court deriving its authority from a 1801 law to one organized under the Judicial Repeal Act of 1802. Congress has the power to organize the lower federal courts as it wants. The Congress had also compelled Supreme Court justices to sit as circuit judges as John Marshall had done in this cause of action. To this objection Justice Paterson argued that it had become accepted practice for Supreme Court justices to serve as circuit judges without having distinct commissions to do so. This has been true beginning with the commencement of the federal judicial system.

Tinker v. Des Moines Independent Community School District
393 U.S. 503, 89 S. Ct. 733, 21 L. Ed. 2d 731 (1969)

As part of a plan to protest U.S. involvement in the Vietnam conflict, two students, John Tinker and his sister Mary Beth, wore black armbands to school. The school board had previously declared that such action would result in suspension, and when the students refused to remove the armbands they were suspended until they would comply. Represented by their parents, the Tinkers sued in federal district court for injunctive relief. The district court dismissed the complaint. The U.S. Court of Appeals divided evenly. The case was then appealed to the U.S. Supreme Court.

Writing for the majority, Justice Abe Fortas held the suspensions violative of the first and fourteenth amendments and reversed and remanded the case. He maintained that the wearing of armbands in the circumstances of this case was entirely divorced from actual or potential disruptive conduct. Fortas characterized the activity as closely akin to "pure speech." Nor was there any demonstration that engaging in the protest would materially and substantially interfere with the requirements of appropriate student discipline. The Court also noted that other students have worn such political symbols as campaign buttons and even the Iron Cross without penalty. In a vigorous defense of student rights, Fortas wrote: "Students in school as well as out of school are 'persons' under our Constitution. They are possessed of fundamental rights which the State must respect, just as they themselves must respect their obligations to the State. In our system, students may not be regarded as closed-circuit recipients of only that which the State chooses to communicate. They may not be confined to the expression of those sentiments that are officially approved. In the absence of a specific showing of constitutionally valid reasons to regulate their speech, students are entitled to freedom of expression of their views."

Trustees of Dartmouth College v. Woodward
17 U.S. (4 Wheat.) 518, 4 L. Ed. 629 (1819)

Before the Revolutionary War began, Dartmouth College had been granted a charter from King George. The charter authorized the establishment of a Board of Trustees to govern the college and to appointment successors. In 1816, however, the New Hampshire legislature enacted three laws amending the original charter and providing for a new governing body for the college to be appointed by the governor. Refusing to recognize the validity of the legislation, the incumbent trustees brought suit against William Woodward, the secretary treasurer of the new board, to recover the college property. Argued before the New Hampshire Supreme Court, the legislation was upheld and the incumbent trustees brought the case to the U.S. Supreme Court on a writ of error.

Writing for the Court, Chief Justice John Marshall held that the corporate charter, possessing all the characteristics of a contract, was in fact a contract properly understood in article I, section 10 of the Constitution. Because the charter was effectively nullified by the state legislature, the contract was impaired in violation of the constitutional provision.

United States v. Butler
297 U.S. 1, 56 S. Ct. 312, 80 L. Ed. 477 (1936)

Congress enacted the Agricultural Adjustment Act of 1933 (AAA) in an attempt to rescue farmers from the Great Depression. Under terms of the law, farmers who reduced their crop production would receive payments from the government. The revenue for these crop reduction payments was raised by imposing a tax on the commodity processor who prepared farm products for market. The tax was to be equal to the differences between current average farm prices and the price during an earlier base period (1909–1914). Butler, the receiver for a cotton processor, refused to pay the tax. A U.S. District Court ordered the tax paid, but the U.S. circuit court of appeals for the First District reversed the order. The government appealed to the U.S. Supreme Court.

Writing for the majority, Justice Owen Roberts affirmed the circuit court decision and invalidated the Agricultural Adjustment Act. His reasoning turned on the interpretation of three constitutional provisions: taxation, general welfare, and the tenth amendment. He first found that the tax on the processor was not a tax but rather an indispensable part of the regulation of agriculture. Although this does not necessarily render the tax unconstitutional, it does mean that the act cannot be held valid under the congressional taxing power. After discussing the opposing views of Madison and Hamilton, Roberts concluded that Hamilton's broad view of the general welfare clause is the correct one. That is, the Congress does possess the power to appropriate for the general welfare, independent of the other enumerated powers found in article I. Yet after accepting this broad view, Roberts concluded that the AAA is in violation of the reserved powers of the states protected by the tenth amendment. Finding that the act imposed economic coercion to accept benefits and submission to regulation, Congress had misused its power under the general welfare clause. "It is an established principle," Roberts stated, "that the attainment of a prohibited end may not be accomplished under the pretext of the exertion of powers which are granted."

United States v. Curtiss-Wright Export Corp.
299 U.S. 304, 57 S. Ct. 216, 81 L. Ed. 255 (1936)

In 1934, Congress enacted a resolution granting to the president the power to forbid the sale of arms and munitions by American corporations to the hostile states of Paraguay and Bolivia. This power provided for such exceptions or limitations as the president should determine. President Roosevelt then issued a proclamation ordering an embargo on the sale of arms to these countries and charged the secretary of state with its enforcement. Subsequently, the Curtiss-Wright Corporation was charged with violating the proclamation by conspiring to sell fifteen machine guns to Bolivia. Sustaining its demurrer, a federal district court agreed with Curtiss-Wright that the congressional resolution was an unconstitutional delegation of legislative power. The government appealed to the U.S. Supreme Court.

Writing for the majority, Justice George Sutherland, reversed the lower court decision stressing that the power of the federal government when dealing with external affairs is vastly different than those concerning internal affairs. As Sutherland wrote: "The broad statement that the federal government can exercise no powers except those specifically enumerated in the Constitution, and such implied powers as are necessary and proper to carry into effect the enumerated powers, is categorically true only in respect to our internal affairs." Because the national union and not the individual states possess external sovereignty, the federal government alone may exercise power in foreign affairs. Moreover, because of the delicate nature of international relations, the president is the plenary and exclusive authority. Consequently, it is within the broad discretionary authority of the president to determine whether the enforcement of the congressional resolution might have a beneficial effect.

United States v. Darby
312 U.S. 100, 61 S. Ct. 451, 85 L. Ed. 609 (1941)

The Fair Labor Standards Act of 1938 prohibited the interstate shipment of goods produced by employees who worked more than forty-four hours per week, without overtime pay, or who were paid less than the minimum wage. The act also required employers to keep records of employee hours and wages. Fred Darby, the operator of a lumber business in Georgia, was indicted under provisions of this legislation. A federal district court held that the act was an unconstitutional regulation of manufacturing thereby setting aside the indictment. The government appealed directly to the U.S. Supreme Court.

Writing for an unanimous Court, Justice Harlan Stone noted that while manufacturing alone is not itself interstate commerce, "The shipment of manufactured goods interstate is such commerce and the prohibition of such shipment by Congress is indubitably a regulation of commerce." Directly and emphatically overruling the *Child Labor Case*, Hammer v. Dagenhart, 247 U.S. 251 (1918), Stone held that the commerce power is complete and Congress may exclude any good from interstate commerce subject only to the specific limitations found in the Constitution. Rejecting the suggestion that the Court should strike down the legislation because the motive of Congress was to invade the power of the states through the regulation of labor conditions, Stone rejoined, "The motive and purpose of a regulation of interstate commerce are matters for the legislative judgment upon the exercise of which the courts are given no control." Turning to the objection that the wage and hour provisions deal only with intrastate commerce and therefore not subject to congressional regulation, Stone adopted the rule in National Labor Relations Board v. Jones & Laughlin Steel Corp., 301 U.S. 1 (1937). Because Congress could "regulate intrastate activities where they have a substantial effect on interstate commerce," the federal regulation of employee wages was a valid exercise of the commerce power. Finally, the record keeping provisions of the act, even for intrastate transactions, was deemed "an appropriate means to the legitimate end."

United States v. E. C. Knight Co.
156 U.S. 1, 15 S. Ct. 249, 39 L. Ed. 325 (1895)

By purchasing the shares of four Philadelphia refiners with shares of its own stock, the American Sugar Refining Company acquired a monopoly on the manufacture of refined sugar in the United States. The U.S. government brought suit against the company seeking the cancellation of the stock transfer claiming a violation of the 1890 Sherman Antitrust Act. Finding no violation of the Sherman Act, lower federal courts found for American Sugar Refining Company. The United States Supreme Court affirmed the decree.

Writing for an 8-1 majority, Chief Justice Fuller held that the Sherman Act is not applicable to monopolies in manufacturing or production. The regulation of commerce belongs to Congress but manufacturing has only an incidental or indirect relationship to commerce. Consequently, the applicability of the Sherman Act in this case is an intrusion into the reserve power of the states under the tenth amendment. This case is important because it failed to extend Chief Justice Marshall's definition of commerce in Gibbons v. Ogden, 22 U.S. (9 Wheat.) (1824) from the distribution to the production of goods.

Moreover, the Court used similar reasoning to strike down congressional attempts to regulate child labor, mining and agriculture. Though a serious threat to the New Deal, by 1937 the Court changed its interpretation, permitting Congress to enact wide ranging controls over the economic life of the nation.

United States v. Nixon
418 U.S. 683, 94 S. Ct. 3090, 41 L. Ed. 2d 1039 (1974)

After hearing charges concerning the infamous Watergate break-ins, a federal grand jury returned indictments against former Attorney General John Mitchell and others for conspiracy to defraud the government and obstruction of justice in a cover-up. The grand jury also named President Richard Nixon as an unindicted co-conspirator. The special prosecutor sought, and the district court issued, a subpoena duces tecum directing the president to produce tape recordings made in the White House. These recordings contained conversations of the president and his advisors which were claimed by the special prosecutor to be relevant to the prosecution of the criminal cases. The president did release a number of edited transcripts, but he refused to release others requested by the prosecutor and the district court. Arguing that the dispute was nonjusticiable, the president's legal counsel then moved to quash the subpoena. Following legal maneuvers, the Supreme Court granted certiorari and heard oral arguments during a special session.

With Justice Rehnquist not participating, an unanimous Court rejected the president's claim of executive privilege. Chief Justice Warren Burger conceded that the president and his close advisors have need for confidential communication, but he clearly rejected the argument that the doctrine of separation of powers precludes judicial review of the president's claim for executive privilege. Citing John Marshall in Marbury v. Madison, 5 U.S. (1 Cranch) 137 (1803), the Court reaffirmed that "it is 'emphatically the province and the duty' of this Court 'to say what the law is' with respect to the claim of privilege presented in this case." Turning to the president's argument of absolute privilege, Burger noted that "when the privilege is based upon a broad, undifferentiated claim of public interest in the confidentiality of such conversations, a confrontation with other values arises. Absent a claim of need to protect military, diplomatic or sensitive national security secrets, we find it difficult to accept the argument that even the very important interest in confidentiality of presidential communications is significantly diminished by production of such material for in camera inspection with all the protection that a district court will be obliged to provide." Weighing the generalized interest in confidentiality against the fair administration of criminal justice, Burger concludes that the "privilege must yield to the demonstrated, specific need for evidence in a pending criminal trial." The district court acted properly when it treated the subpoenaed material as presumptively privileged and when the special prosecutor overcame the presumption. The order for an in camera inspection, therefore, of the tapes was justified.

United States v. United States District Court
for Eastern District of Michigan
407 U.S. 297, 92 S. Ct. 2125, 32 L. Ed. 2d 752 (1972)

During the course of pretrial proceedings in a case involving the prosecution for conspiracy to destroy government property, the defense moved to compel the government to disclose certain wiretap information which the government had obtained. The purpose of the defense motion was to determine if the information "tainted" the government's evidence against defendants. The government responded by filing a sealed exhibit containing the surveillance logs for the court's in camera inspection. It also produced an affidavit certifying that the attorney general approved the wiretaps and such surveillance was authorized under an interpretation of Title III of the Omnibus Crime Control And Safe Streets Act of 1968. The district court found the surveillance violative of the fourth amendment and ordered full disclosure. The United States Court of Appeals for the Sixth Circuit denied the government's request for a writ of mandamus. The government then appealed to the U.S. Supreme Court.

An unanimous Court, with Justice Rehnquist not participating, upheld the lower courts. First dealing with the government's argument that title III relieves the government from the duty of obtaining a prior judicial warrant, Justice Lewis Powell held that the language of title III, section 2511(3) as well as the legislative history of the statute, refutes such an interpretation. Powell then rejected the government's contention that internal security matters are too complex for judicial evaluation. He wrote: "If the threat is too subtle or complex for our senior law enforcement officers to convey its significance to a court, one may question whether there is probable cause for surveillance." The Court also emphasized that its decision involves only the domestic aspects of national security. It left open the issues involved with respect to activities of foreign powers or their agents.

University of California v. Bakke
(see: Regents of the University of California v. Bakke)

Walz v. Tax Commission of the City of New York
397 U.S. 664, 90 S. Ct. 1409, 25 L. Ed. 697 (1970)

Walz, a real estate owner, brought suit against the New York City Tax Commission for granting tax exemptions on property utilized for religious worship. Walz contended that such exemptions constitute a violation of the first amendment's provision prohibiting government establishment of religion.

The U.S. Supreme Court affirmed the decisions of New York courts in favor of the City of New York. Writing for the majority, Chief Justice Warren Burger reasoned that the legislative purpose of the property tax exemption is neither the advancement nor the inhibition of religion. Rather, the state has determined that certain organizations including not only religious, but also nonprofit hospitals, libraries, scientific and other entities, are beneficial to the community. The state is not attempting to ". . . establish religion; it is simply sparing the exercise of religion from the burden of property taxation levied on private profit institutions." Burger then argued that while the granting of tax exemptions to churches does afford an indirect economic benefit, it also serves to limit church and state entanglements. Taxing church property would involve excessive and continuing official state entanglement with religion. There is less state entanglement with religion by granting tax exemptions than if the state did tax such entities.

West Coast Hotel v. Parrish
300 U.S. 379, 57 S. Ct. 578, 81 L. Ed. 703 (1937)

In 1913, the state of Washington enacted a statute to protect women and minors by establishing a minimum wage and conditions of labor. Elsie Parrish and her husband, employed by the West Coast Hotel Company, brought suit to recover the difference between the wages paid her by the hotel and the minimum wage established by the state. The trial court decided against Parrish, but the Washington State Supreme Court reversed that decision finding the statute constitutionally valid. Relying on the U.S. Supreme Court's decision in Adkins v. Children's Hospital, 261 U.S. 525 (1923), West Coast Hotel appealed to the Supreme Court.

Directly overruling its decision in *Adkins*, the Supreme Court, with Chief Justice Charles Evans Hughes writing for the majority, held that the minimum wage law was not an infringement of the due process clause of the fourteenth amendment. While *Adkins* did involve the due process clause of the fifth amendment, the fundamental issue remained the meaning of freedom of contract. Hughes reasoned that the Constitution does not speak in terms of freedom of contract; rather it ". . . speaks of liberty and prohibits the deprivation of liberty without due process of law." The Constitution does not define liberty in absolute terms. Rather, limitations on liberty are subject to the ". . . restraints of due process, and regulation which is reasonable in relation to its subject and is adopted in the interests of the community. . . ." It is, therefore, within the discretionary authority of the legislature to determine which working conditions are best suited to promote the well being of the community. The abuses of employers may be corrected by the community in the public interest.

West Virginia State Board of Education v. Barnette
319 U.S. 624, 63 S. Ct. 1178, 87 L. Ed. 1628 (1943)

In Minersville School District v. Gobitis, 310 U.S. 586 (1940), the U.S. Supreme Court sustained the constitutionality of an order by a local board of education in Pennsylvania to compel students and teachers to salute the flag. Soon thereafter, the West Virginia legislature passed a law requiring all state schools to conduct classes in civics and history, as well as in the U.S. and West Virginia constitutions. The West Virginia State Board of Education further prescribed that all students and teachers must salute the flag as part of regular daily school activities. Refusal to comply was punishable by student expulsion and parents were subject to both a fine and jail term. Walter Barnette and other Jehovah's Witnesses brought suit after their children were expelled from schools for refusing to salute the flag; they objected to the compulsory flag salute as repugnant to a religious commandment not to worship graven images. A federal district court granted Barnette's petition for injunctive relief. The board of education then appealed directly to the U.S. Supreme Court.

Directly overruling its near unanimous decision just three years earlier in *Gobitis,* Justice Robert Jackson based the Court's majority opinion on the doctrine of clear and present danger. The compulsion of students to declare a belief is made without ". . . any allegation that remaining passive during a flag salute ritual creates a clear and present danger that would justify an effort even to muffle expression," wrote Jackson. "To sustain the compulsory flag salute we are required to say that a Bill of Rights which guards the individual's right to speak his own mind, left it open to public authorities to compel him to utter what is not in his mind." Responding to the argument that applying the first amendment protection to state school boards would convert the Supreme Court into the school board for the country, Jackson held that the fourteenth amendment protects the citizen against all the creatures of the state, including school boards.

Youngstown Sheet and Tube Co. v. Sawyer
343 U.S. 579, 72 S. Ct. 863, 96 L. Ed. 1153 (1952)

During the Korean "police action," a dispute arose between the nation's steel companies and their employees over the terms of a new collective bargaining agreement. After long and bitter negotiations failed, the United Steelworkers of America gave notice of a strike. The Federal Mediation and Conciliation Service then intervened but was unsuccessful in bringing about a settlement. President Truman then referred the dispute to the Federal Wage Stabilization Board, but this attempt also met with failure. Given the repeated failures at a negotiated settlement and the union's strike announcement,

President Truman acted to avert a felt threat to the "police action" in the event of a curtailment of steel production. Just a few hours before the strike was to begin, President Truman issued an executive order directing secretary of commerce Charles Sawyer to seize the steel mills and to keep them running. In a special message to Congress, President Truman reported the seizure inviting legislative action if the Congress deemed it advisable. Congress, however, failed to act. The steel companies immediately attacked the order as unconstitutional, and a district court judge granted a preliminary injunction. After a court of appeals stayed the injunction, the Supreme Court granted certiorari.

In a 6 to 3 decision, marked by five concurring opinions, Justice Hugo Black delivered the opinion of the Court holding the seizure unconstitutional. Avoiding any discussion of executive prerogative in times of national emergency, Black observed that there was no statute expressly authorizing the president's argument that his authority flowed from his powers as chief executive or from his responsibilities as commander-in-chief. Black wrote: "In the framework of our Constitution, the president's power to see that the laws are faithfully executed refutes the idea that he is to be a lawmaker. The Constitution limits his functions in the lawmaking process to the recommending of laws he thinks wise and the vetoing of laws he thinks bad."

Glossary of Terms and Phrases

ABROGATE. The repeal, annulment, or destruction of an order or rule of a lower power by the same or higher authority.

ABSTENTION DOCTRINE. A judicially created policy that federal courts should not exercise jurisdiction in those instances where a federal constitutional question depends on an uncertain interpretation of state law.

ACCUSATORIAL SYSTEM. The legal system which presumes that a person is innocent until proven guilty. The outstanding feature of Anglo-American criminal justice places the burden of proof on the accuser.

AD HOC. For a special or unique purpose; temporary and not permanent.

ADJECTIVE LAW. Generic term referring to rules under which courts or agencies conduct their affairs; procedural as opposed to substantive law.

ADMINISTRATIVE LAW. The branch of public law dealing with the rules and regulations promulgated by government agencies.

ADMIRALTY LAW. The branch of the law concerned with maritime matters.

AD VALOREM. Latin meaning according to value. An *ad valorem* tax is a levy on the value of something rather than a fixed tax regardless of value. For example, an *ad valorem* tax on a diamond ring worth $100 might be $5 while the tax on a $10,000 ring might be $250. The tax varies according to the worth or value of the item rather than a fixed tax of, say, $75 for all diamond rings.

ADVISORY OPINION. A judicial ruling in the absence of an actual case or controversy; a ruling in a hypothetical case without bona fide litigants.

AFFIRMATIVE ACTION. Legislative programs requiring authorities or those benefiting from government programs to positively seek employees or applicants for admission to schools, persons of racial, ethnic or gender minority groups. It is a form of preferential treatment that proponents regard as benign discrimination.

AGENCY. (A) A relationship in which one party acts on behalf of another; the former is authorized by the latter. (B) May refer to an administrative body of government.

ALIEN AND SEDITION ACTS. Passed in 1798 by a Congress controlled by Federalists, the Alien Law lengthened the residence requirement for citizenship from five to fourteen years and gave the president authority to banish aliens. The

Sedition Law declared any libel against the president or any attempt to cause disaffection against the government a crime. These laws were aimed at the Jeffersonian Republican opposition in the country and particularly the Jeffersonian Republican press.

ALL DELIBERATE SPEED. An equity tool in which a court orders others to comply with its command with dispatch and with adequate and careful consideration of the consequences of its action.

AMICUS CURIAE. Latin meaning friend of the court. Normally an outside interest not directly a party to the suit. Usually presents a brief that provides information and argument relevant to a court in its deliberation as to matters of law.

ANALYTICAL JURISPRUDENCE. A school or jurisprudence that attempts to systematize the law utilizing tools of logic. Outstanding proponents include Hans Kelsen, John Austin, and H. L. A. Hart.

ANSWER. Usually a written statement or pleading by the defendant responding to the plaintiff's charges.

APPEAL. A generic term referring to the movement of court proceedings from an inferior to a superior court. Depending on the context, the term may refer to a technical method of moving a case to a superior court.

APPELLANT. The party who takes his or her case from a lower court to a superior court to seek review of the lower court decision.

APPELLATE COURT. A court possessing the authority to review and sustain or reverse the decisions of a lower court.

APPELLEE. The party in a suit against whom the appeal to a superior court is taken; the party with an interest in sustaining the lower court judgment.

ARBITRATION. A third party hearing and settlement of a dispute among contending parties. The decision of the arbitrator(s) may be binding on the participants.

ARGUENTO. Sustaining the assumption that a statement of fact is true, although it may be true or false during the course of an argument. A method of illustrating a line of reasoning found in judicial opinions.

ARRAIGNMENT. The formal court procedure in which a criminal defendant answers an indictment with a plea of guilty, not guilty, or *nolo contendere.*

ASSOCIATE JUSTICE. The title given to judges of an appellate court excluding the chief justice.

ASSUMPSIT. From the law of contracts meaning to undertake the performance of an oral agreement. At common law assumpsit was an action taken to enforce a promise.

BAD TENDENCY DOCTRINE. The now discredited judicial doctrine that limitations on freedom of speech are constitutionally permissible if there is a tendency, no matter how remote, to advance a prohibited activity. Compare, clear and present danger.

BAIL. The security given in the form of cash or a bail bond as a guarantee that a released prisoner will appear at his or her trial. Bail may be forfeited if the released prisoner does not appear at trial.

BAILIFF.   An officer of the court who is in charge of prisoners and who guards the jurors in a court; generally charged with keeping the peace in court.

BANKRUPTCY.   A legal procedure under federal law by which a person is relieved of all debts after placing all property under the court's authority. An organization may be reorganized or terminated by the court in order to pay off creditors.

BAR.   The community of attorneys permitted to practice law in a particular jurisdiction or court.

BARRISTERS.   The English legal profession is divided into two segments, barristers and solicitors. Barristers argue cases in the higher law courts, solicitors do not. Individual barristers are members of one of four Inns of Court. These professional organizations are responsible for certifying educational training and for disciplining its members. Judges are selected from the upper echelons of the barrister class.

BICAMERAL.   Two chambers. Usually refers to a legislative body with two "houses"; for example, a Senate and a House of Representatives.

BILL OF ATTAINDER.   A legislative act declaring a person guilty of a crime and passing sentence without the benefit of a trial. Such legislation is specifically forbidden by the U.S. Constitution.

BLACK LETTER LAW.   Refers to the most basic principle of law accepted by the courts. For example, "obscenity is not protected speech." Generally rejected by political scientists and others as not explanatory of the judicial process.

BLACKSTONE.   Sir William Blackstone, the influential 18th-century jurist and author of *Blackstone's Commentaries on the Common Law.*

BLUE LAW.   Legislative enactment forbidding all or certain business activity on Sundays.

BONA FIDE.   Latin for good faith. A term referring to acting in good faith; without trickery, deceit, fraud, or dishonesty.

BRANDEIS BRIEF.   A written argument presented before an appellate court containing extralegal social science information relevant to the case. Named after Louis Brandeis whose brief in Muller v. Oregon, 208 U.S. 412 (1908) consisted of two pages of formal legal argument and one hundred pages of economic and social data.

BREACH OF CONTRACT.   The nonperformance of the terms of a legally binding oral or written agreement.

BRIEF.   (A) The oral or written argument presented by counsel to a court. (B) A summary of the pertinent elements of a court opinion written by a student as a study guide and aid.

BURDEN OF PROOF.   Although possessing several technical meanings, burden of proof generally refers to the duty of one of the parties to a suit to demonstrate that the weight of evidence or law is on his or her side. Sometimes the burden of proof will shift. In Anglo-American criminal justice the burden of proof is on the prosecution.

CALENDAR.   A list of cases in the order they are to be heard during a court term. Sometimes known as a court docket or trial list.

CANON LAW.   The well-developed body of laws governing ecclesiastical matters of a Christian church; usually thought of in relationship to the Roman Catholic church.

CAPITATION TAX.   A head tax or a tax on persons regardless of such matters as income, assets, status, or personal wealth.

CAROLENE PRODUCTS, FOOTNOTE FOUR.   Mr. Justice Stone in United States v. Carolene Products Co., 304 U.S. 144 (1938) laid down, in footnote four of his opinion, guiding principles for when and how the Supreme Court should treat issues involving fundamental constitutional rights. The summary label for these principles today is the preferred freedoms approach; courts apply strict scrutiny to government regulations that limit fundamental rights.

CASE AND CONTROVERSY.   Legal dispute with *bona fide* adversaries involving live and real issues, and not hypothetical or abstract issues, rights, or claims to be protected.

CASEBOOK.   A law textbook containing leading edited judicial opinions on a particular legal subject. Cases are usually arranged chronologically by subject matter. In 1871, the first casebook was authored and published by the Dean of the Harvard Law School: Langdell, *Selection of Cases on the Law Contracts.*

CASE LAW.   The law as handed down in written judicial opinions.

CASE METHOD.   A rigorous and dominant approach to legal education stressing the reading and in-depth analysis of leading judicial opinions. The growth of the law is traced through the reading of the cases. Professors employ the Socratic questioning method in connection with the cases. Critics of the case method contend that it produces attorneys without appropriate social concern.

CAUSE OF ACTION.   The existence of sufficient facts to warrant a law suit brought by a plaintiff.

CAVEAT EMPTOR.   Latin for let the buyer beware. A warning to a buyer of a product that he or she purchases at his or her own risk.

CERTIFICATION.   A method of appeal by which a lower court requests a higher court to answer certain questions of law so that the lower court may make a correct decision in light of the answer provided.

CERTIORARI, WRIT OF.   An order from a superior to an inferior court to send the entire record of a case to the superior court for review. A discretionary writ employed by the U.S. Supreme Court.

CHAMBERS.   The private office of a judge. Legal activity transacted there is often referred to as "in chambers."

CHANCERY, COURT OF.   An old English court dealing with equity matters. In America most state governments have merged the chancery and law courts into one.

CHARTER.   A document emanating from government granting certain rights, liberties, or powers to an organization, colony, local government, corporation, or people; for example, a city charter, colonial charter, or corporation charter.

CHATTEL.   Personal property excluding land.

CHIEF JUSTICE. The person appointed by the president with the advice and consent of the Senate to head the U.S. Supreme Court.

CIVIL ACTION. A lawsuit typically brought by a private party for the redress of a noncriminal act. Usually the plaintiff seeks money damages for the wrongful conduct of the defendant; for example, suits in negligence, contract, or defamation.

CIVIL LAW. (A) The system of jurisprudence based on Roman law found in most Western European nation-states. It is distinct from the common law. (B) In common law countries, civil law refers to noncriminal legal matters.

CLASS ACTION SUIT. A legal suit brought by one person on behalf of him or herself and all others similarly situated. For example, John Doe, as representative of the class of all persons similarly situated, and for himself, Plaintiff, v. Paul Smith, in his capacity as Chief of Police of the City of XYZ, Defendant.

CLEAR AND PRESENT DANGER DOCTRINE. A judicial rule announced in the case of *Schenck v. United States* (1919). It holds that limitations by government on expressions of speech are constitutionally permissible only if the utterances are likely to result in impending violence or grave harm that the government has a right to prevent.

CLEAR AND PRESENT DANGER TEST. Created by Justice Holmes in Schenck v. United States, 249 U.S. 47 (1919), the clear and present danger test is an alternative to an absolutist interpretation of the first amendment. It indicates that limitations on free speech are permissible if the words are used in "such circumstances and are of such a nature as to create a clear and present danger that they will bring about the substantive evil that Congress has a right to prevent."

COLLUSIVENESS. *See* Feigned Cases.

COMITY. The willingness to extend courtesy and respect to another nation-state or a unit of government within a state motivated by good will and a desire for good relations.

COMMON LAW. The system of law created by the English courts and brought to America by the colonists. Judges are said to find the law in the customs and habits of the people. It is largely judge-made law as distinct from statutory law made by legislators. Its chief competitor is the Roman-founded civil law system of Western Europe.

COMMUTATION OF PUNISHMENT. The reduction of a criminal penalty to a lesser punishment. Differs from a pardon in that it does not require the consent of the convict.

COMPELLING STATE INTEREST. A tool of constitutional interpretation that places the burden of proof on the state to prove that the deprivation of a fundamental right or discrimination of certain classes of people is necessary for the public good. Cp., rational basis test.

COMPLAINT. The plaintiff's initial pleading that frames the issues in a suit.

CONCURRENT JURISDICTION. The authority possessed by two or more courts to hear cases on a given subject.

CONCURRENT POWER. The political authority to exercise independent power by more than one government on the same subject matter; for example, the police and taxing powers in a federal system.

CONFEDERATION. An association or league among sovereign entities in which a central government is given certain limited responsibilities not affecting the basic powers of member entities or states.

CONFLICT OF LAWS. Refers to the field of law dealing with the situation in which a judge must choose among the laws of more than one jurisdiction as to which should apply in a particular case.

CONSPIRACY. Two or more persons acting together to accomplish a criminal objective or to pursue a noncriminal purpose in an unlawful or criminal manner.

CONSTITUTIONAL COURTS. A court named in a constitution or a court given certain protections independent of the other political branches of government. For the U.S. government, a constitutional court is one authorized under article III of the Constitution or designated by the Congress as an article III court. Article III courts are protected as to jurisdiction, appointment, and tenure.

CONSTITUTIONALISM. The principle of the rule of law under which the rulers abide by certain rules limiting their official conduct in return for the right to exercise authority.

CONTEMPT. An act that in some way obstructs or denigrates the dignity of a court, a legislative body, or an administrative agency. Usually a punishable offense.

COOPERATIVE FEDERALISM. A general approach to the American federal system that views the relationship between the national and state governments as a working partnership by which the mutual interests of both may be satisfied. Some take a more extreme view by stressing the "necessity" of national supremacy. Cp. dual Federalism.

CORPUS DELICTI. Latin for the body of the crime. The production of material evidence indicating that the specific charges has in fact been committed and that some individual or group is criminally responsible.

CORPUS JURIS CIVILIS. Latin for the body of civil law. The body of Roman law including the Digests, the Institutes, and the Novelae of Justinian.

CORRUPTION OF BLOOD. Article III, section 3 of the Constitution prohibits the old English practice of preventing the heirs of a person convicted of treason from inheriting property.

COUNT. Separate and independent claims or charges in a civil or criminal matter. A criminal indictment, for example, may contain many counts which if the prosecution should lose on one or more will still have others on which to convict.

COUNTERCLAIM. Constituting a separate cause of action, it is a claim made by the defendant against the plaintiff. Such a practice occurs in civil suits.

COURT OF LAST RESORT. A popular term referring to a court from which there is no appeal.

CRIME. A violation of government's penal laws. The offense is against society and not just a violation of another's individual rights.

CRIMINOLOGY.   A social science concerned with the various causes, prevention, and punishment of crime. Considered a branch of sociology.

CULPABLE.   A term referring to blame-worthy or wrongful conduct. Faultable.

CURIA.   Latin for court.

DAMAGES.   Money awarded by a court to a plaintiff for the wrongful conduct of the defendant.

DECLARATORY JUDGMENT.   A judicial determination of the legal rights of the parties involved in an actual case or controversy, but where the court does not require the parties to abide by the judgment. Differs from an advisory opinion because there is an actual case or controversy.

DECREE.   A court order or sentence specifying the details of a legal settlement; for example, terms of alimony or child custody. A consent decree is an agreement among the parties to conduct their affairs in a certain way. It cannot be amended without the consent of both parties.

DE FACTO.   Refers to the existence of something in fact or reality as distinguished from de jure, by right. Segregation in housing due to custom but not the result of official government action is often termed *de facto* segregation.

DEFAMATION.   The damage to another's reputation by a false statement. *See* Libel; Slander.

DEFENDANT.   In a court case, the person or entity against whom/which a civil or criminal charge is brought.

DE JURE.   Refers to lawful, rightful, or legitimate; opposite of de facto. Segregation in public education mandated by state law was known as *de jure* segregation.

DELIBERATION.   The process of weighing reasons or evidence for or against a course of action. Usually applies to the work of a jury when determining guilt or innocence.

DE MINIMUS NON CURAT LEX.   Latin term meaning that the law is not concerned with trivialities.

DEMURRER.   A legal procedure permitting counsel to object to the sufficiency of a legal cause of action contained in the pleadings of the other side. Even if the act complained of did in fact occur, the law as presented by the other side does not cover that situation.

DE NOVO.   Latin for anew, once more, again. Usually applies to a case being retried on order of an appellate court. Some court systems permit *de novo* appeals.

DEPOSITION.   A legal process to take the sworn testimony of a witness out of court. Usually both plaintiff and defendant attorneys are present and participate.

DICTA.   *See* Obiter dicta.

DISCOVERY.   The stage of litigation in which the parties to the suit learn what evidence is in the possession of the other side. Discovery procedures exist to take the surprise out of litigation and to facilitate adequate case preparation. Discovery tools include pretrial depositions, interrogatories, physical and mental examinations, and the admission and inspection of books and records.

DIVERSITY JURISDICTION. Refers to the authority of federal courts to hear cases involving citizens of different states.

DOCKET. A listing of cases to be heard by a court.

DOUBLE JEOPARDY. Tried twice for the same crime. Prohibited by U.S. Constitution.

DUAL FEDERALISM. The general approach to the American federal system that views the relationship between the national and state governments as adversarial. Best represented by the position of states' rights that views the powers of the central government as strictly limited by the enumerated provisions in the Constitution; all other powers are reserved to the states by way of the tenth amendment. Cp. cooperative Federalism.

ECCLESIASTICAL COURTS. In England, those courts dealing with spiritual matters presided over by members of the clergy; not part of the judicial system of the United States.

EMINENT DOMAIN. The right and ability of government to take private property for a public use.

EMOLUMENTS CLAUSE. Article I, section 6 of the Constitution prohibits the appointment of any member of Congress to a position in government during his or her elected term if during that term Congress created the office or increased the pay or benefits arising from the office.

EN BANC. Sometimes appearing as *En Banke*, meaning all the judges of a court or all jury members sitting together to hear a case.

EQUITY. The administration of justice based on principles of fairness rather than strictly applied rules found in the common law. Because the common law courts of England became too rigid, equity courts were created; in the United States, courts of law and courts of equity have largely been merged.

ERIE DOCTRINE. In Erie R. Co. v. Tompkins, 304 U.S. 64 (1938), the Supreme Court held that except for matters covered by the U.S. Constitution or by congressional enactment, a federal court is bound by the statutes and case precedents of the state in which it sits. Therefore, there is no federal common law about state matters. This doctrine prevents conflicts between federal and state courts by reaching different results on the same issues.

ERROR, WRIT OF. A method of appeal by which an appellate court orders a lower court to send a case to the higher court for review of alleged mistakes (errors) made by the lower court. Matters of law and not of fact are reviewed. The U.S. Supreme Court no longer employs this appeal method.

ESCHEAT. If the rightful owner or heir of property cannot be located, the property goes to the state.

ESTABLISHMENT CLAUSE. The First Amendment clause prohibiting Congress from making any laws respecting the establishment of religion.

EXCLUSIONARY RULE. The policy created by the U.S. Supreme Court that evidence illegally obtained in violation of constitutional principles is inadmissible in a court of law to convict a criminal defendant.

EXCLUSIVE JURISDICTION.   The sole authority vested in one court to hear a case on a given subject-matter; for example, for the U.S. Supreme Court, suits between and among the states, foreign ambassadors, bankruptcy, and prosecutions of federal criminal law.

EXCLUSIVE POWER.   The sole exercise of authority by one governmental body; for example, only the federal government possesses the authority to make war.

EXECUTIVE AGREEMENT.   An international agreement made by the president under his constitutional authority as commander-in-chief and in his capacity as the nation's spokesperson in foreign affairs. These agreements do not require senatorial approval as is the case for a treaty.

EXECUTIVE ORDERS.   A directive from the president requiring the implementation of policy. The source of this authority stems from congressional authorization with the president as chief executive delineating the details of policy implementation.

EXECUTIVE PRIVILEGE.   The claim that executive officials including the President have the constitutional right to refuse to appear and give testimony before the Congress or courts. A fundamental premise is that communication between the president and subordinates must be protected from inspection by officials of other branches of government because of the separation of powers principle.

EX PARTE.   A judicial hearing when only one party is present, such as when the appellant is in prison.

EXPATRIATION.   Either a voluntary or involuntary act resulting in the abandonment, repudiation, or renouncement of citizenship.

EX POST FACTO LAW.   Latin for a law after the fact. An *ex post facto* law attempts to make an act a crime that was not a crime when it was done. Specifically prohibited by the U.S. Constitution.

EX. REL.   An abbreviation for *Ex Relatione* meaning on relation or information. A designation appearing in case titles indicating that the suit is instituted by a state but at the instigation or insistence of an individual; for example, *Missouri ex. rel. Gaines* v. *S.W. Canada.* The state of Missouri is bringing the suit at the instigation of Lloyd Gaines against S.W. Canada.

EXTRADITION.   The surrender of a fugitive by one jurisdiction to another.

FEDERAL QUESTION DOCTRINE.   Those cases which directly involve the U.S. Constitution, the laws of the U.S. or treaties of the U.S. The U.S. Supreme Court has often maintained that its jurisdiction is limited to federal questions; it is one method of exercising judicial self-restraint.

FEDERATION.   A structure of government dividing powers between the central and state governments; both the state and national governments operate directly on the people.

FEIGNED CASE.   A law suit in which there is no real controversy between the parties. The parties pretend there is a controversy to accomplish some other goal such as a wager.

FELONY.   A crime designated by statute as serious. More serious than a misdemeanor, a felony may involve capital punishment or imprisonment for a long duration.

FIDUCIARY.   A relationship in which one person acts in a position of trust for another. Sometimes involves management of money or property.

FIGHTING WORDS DOCTRINE.   This doctrine is a limitation on the exercise of free speech because the utterance of such words convey an emotional message intended to incite a rapid and unthinking violent response by listeners.

FULL FAITH AND CREDIT CLAUSE.   Article IV, section 1 of the Constitution provides that the public acts, records, and proceedings of each state are to be honored by every other state; for example, a divorce granted in one state is upheld in every other state.

FUNDAMENTAL RIGHTS.   Although a matter of controversy, Justice Cardozo defined fundamental rights in *Palko v. Conn.* (1937) as those "so rooted in the traditions and collective conscience of our people as to be ranked as fundamental." These rights are those found in the Bill of Rights, and those that justices may determine.

GERRYMANDERING.   The drawing of legislative or other political district boundaries in such a manner as to give advantage to one political party or interest.

GRAND JURY.   A jury of inquiry designed to determine whether there is sufficient evidence to justify a criminal trial.

GUARANTEE CLAUSE.   Under article IV, section 4 of the Constitution, the federal government owes a duty to every state to guarantee a "republican form of government." The Supreme Court has consistently held that this clause is nonjusticiable.

GUARANTY CLAUSE.   See Guarantee Clause.

HABEAS CORPUS, WRIT OF.   A writ directing that a person held in custody be brought before the court to determine if he or she is being lawfully held.

HISTORICAL JURISPRUDENCE.   The application of the method of historical criticism to the study of law. Historical jurists study the customs and historical development of a people and their law. In the United States, the employment of the case method is its greatest manifestation. The writings of Karl Von Savigny, Sir Henry Maine, and Christopher Columbus Langdell are preeminent in this area.

HUNG JURY.   A jury that cannot agree upon a verdict. May result in a new trial.

IGNORAMUS.   Latin for we are ignorant or we ignore it. A formal designation employed by a grand jury when it finds insufficient evidence to warrant an indictment.

IMMUNITY.   An exemption from performing a duty. The grant of immunity in a criminal prosecution exempts a person from prosecution on the condition that he or she provides desired information.

IMPLIED POWERS.   Those powers not specifically delegated to the national government but may be inferred because they are necessary and proper for carrying out the delegated powers.

IN CAMERA.   Latin for vaulted chamber. A device by which a judge hears a case or part of a case in his or her chambers with spectators excluded.

INDICTMENT.   A written accusation presented by a grand jury to a court charging one or more individuals with having committed a public offense.

IN FORMA PAUPERIS.   Latin for in the manner of a pauper. It is a device for indigents to sue without liability for costs. Provided for by U.S. statutory law permitting any citizen upon the execution of an oath to enter proceedings in any federal court. The most celebrated case reaching the U.S. Supreme Court in this manner is *Gideon v. Wainwright.*

INFORMATION.   A device replacing indictment by grand jury in which the prosecutor submits his or her charges supported by evidence and sworn testimony to a trial court. Employed in England and many jurisdictions in the United States.

INJUNCTION.   A court order directing someone to do something or refrain from doing something.

IN PERSONAM.   Latin meaning toward a person or individual. It is a legal action taken against an individual and not against the whole world.

INQUISITORIAL SYSTEM.   A criminal justice system which assumes implicitly the guilt of the defendant, as opposed to common law systems. Civil law systems are said to employ this procedure; however, this characterization is not entirely correct because the highly professional magistrates take great care in reaching truth.

IN RE.   Latin referring to the matter of. Employed in entitling judicial proceedings where there are no adversary parties; for example, *In re: Jones.*

IN REM.   A legal action to enforce property rights against the whole world and not one brought to enforce a legal right against individuals (In personam).

INTEGRATED BAR.   A system of bar organization requiring all practicing attorneys within a state to belong to one organization (bar association). The integrated bar plan came from Canada, and North Dakota was the first state to adopt it. In labor terms, it is a closed shop.

INTEREST BALANCING TEST.   When a court weighs the interest of the community in a certain value against the community's interest in a competing value.

INTERGOVERNMENTAL TAX IMMUNITY.   The Supreme Court doctrine that because the power to tax is the power to destroy one division of government may not tax another.

INTERNATIONAL LAW.   The law governing relations among nation-states. It is a body of general principles and rules accepted by the international community as binding. Because there is no sovereign authority, some do not consider international law as law properly so-called.

INTERPRETIVISM.   Contemporary conservatives on and off the Supreme Court argue that judges must focus on the words and substantive intentions of the Framers of the Constitution when interpreting the basic document. In so doing, conservative proponents claim judicial decisions are objective or principled and not a matter of subjective value and moral judgments. Cp., noninterpretivism.

INTERSTATE COMPACT.   An agreement between two or more states, ratified by law of each state and approved by Congress.

INTESTATE.   Dying without a will.

IPSE DIXIT.   Latin for he himself said it. An arbitrary statement depending on the authority of the one who said it.

IPSO FACTO.   Latin for by the fact itself. The fact speaks for itself.

JUDICIAL REVIEW.   The power of a court to examine legislative enactments and acts of executive officials to determine their validity with respect to a written constitution; for example, *Marbury v. Madison*.

JUDICIAL SELF-RESTRAINT.   The position accepted by many that judges should refrain from substituting their values for those of political decisionmakers closer to the sentiments of the people. Operationally, the U.S. Supreme Court has devised various techniques of restraint so as to defer to other decisionmakers.

JURISPRUDENCE.   (A) The philosophy or science of law. (B) Sometimes refers to a body of law.

JURISPRUDENCE OF ORIGINAL INTENTION.   This is a view of constitutional interpretation popularized by Attorney General Edwin Meese. It is the attempt to ascertain what the Framers of the Constitution really meant when they wrote the Constitution, and to remain true to those principles when interpreting the basic document.

JURY.   A group of persons charged by a law court with the duty to examine facts and determine the truth.

JUS SANGUINIS.   Latin for right of blood. Refers to gaining citizenship by virtue of being born of parents who are citizens.

JUS SOLI.   Latin for the right of land. Refers to gaining citizenship by virtue of place or country in which a person is born.

JUSTICE OF THE PEACE.   Usually an elected official in rural areas with jurisdiction over minor civil or criminal matters.

LARCENY.   The theft of the personal property of another. Stealing.

LEGAL REALIST SCHOOL OF JURISPRUDENCE.   A heterodox group of scholars sharing a cynical attitude toward the law. They are concerned with the actual as opposed to an idealized notion of the operation of law. They apply the social scientific approach to the study of law as defined by such figures as Karl Llewellyn and Jerome Frank.

LEGISLATIVE COURTS.   Courts established by the legislature. For the U.S. government, legislative courts are not protected by article III. *See* Constitutional courts.

LEGISLATIVE INTENT.   Refers to the motives of legislators when enacting a law. Usually involves a reading and interpreting by a court of the legislative history of a statute.

LEGISLATIVE VETO.   A device invented in this century by Congress to gain control over the expansion of executive power. It is part of some legislation that allows the rejection of an administrative or executive action by either the House or the Senate, singularly or together, without the consent of the president. This procedure was declared unconstitutional in *Immigration and Naturalization Service v. Chadha* (1983).

LIABILITY.   Responsible for performing a legally enforceable duty or obligation resulting from the commission of a wrongful act.

LIBEL.   The written expression of a falsehood about another resulting or tending to result in damage to reputation. The written form of defamation of character, the other being slander, or spoken defamation.

LIEN.   The legal right to possess property of another as security against a debt. If the debt is not paid or discharged, the property may be sold to satisfy the debt obligation.

LITIGANT.   An active participant in a lawsuit; for example, *Smith v. Jones.* Both Smith and Jones are litigants.

MALPRACTICE.   Refers to professional misconduct or the below-standard performance of professional skills. Usually applies to suits against physicians and lawyers.

MANDAMUS, WRIT OF.   Latin for we command. It is a court order commanding a public official or government agency to perform a certain act. It may apply to all branches of government.

MANSLAUGHTER.   The crime of taking the life of another without malice.

MARTIAL LAW.   The displacement of civilian law and government by the military. Rules usually depend solely on the commands of the military ruler in charge and often tend to be arbitrary. Martial law is often imposed in time of war, insurrection, or *coup d'etat.*

MAXIM.   A certain precept or axiom of law applied to all cases covered by its usage.

MECHANICAL JURISPRUDENCE.   The widespread belief, held by many judges but discounted by political scientists, that judges only discover the law, they do not make it.

MEMORANDUM DECISION.   A court ruling giving only what has been decided and what should be done but without the reasons for the decision.

MENS REA.   Latin referring to the mind or guilt of the defendant. A chief function of juries in criminal trials is to ascertain the criminal intent *(mens rea)* of defendants.

MINISTERIAL.   The execution of orders without making policy choices. No exercise of judgment or discretion.

MISCELLANEOUS DOCKET.   The listing of *in forma pauperis* cases to be heard by the U.S. Supreme Court.

MISDEMEANOR.   A criminal offense designated by statute to be of a lesser nature than a felony. Penalties are relatively minor.

MOOT.   A discussion or argument of a hypothetical situation.

MOOT QUESTION.   In a lawsuit, when the situation changes so that the relief sought is no longer applicable. For example, if during the course of a lengthy lawsuit for admission to a professional school, the student petitioner in fact graduates from the school then the question of admission becomes moot.

MOTION.   A request by an attorney to the judge to take some action; for example, dismiss the case.

NATURAL LAW.   A higher law transcending positive law; coming from God, nature, the universe, or reason; it lacks the ability to enforce commands.

NATURAL LAW SCHOOL OF JURISPRUDENCE.   A school of law that posits the existence of universal principles of justice. It is concerned with what the law ought to be and thus is an ideal perspective for criticizing what the law is. Although ancient in origin, this school is enjoying renewed interest.

NECESSARY AND PROPER CLAUSE.   Contained in the last paragraph of article 1, section 8 of the Constitution, this clause authorizes the passage of laws which may be "necessary and proper" for carrying out enumerated powers. This clause is also called the "elastic clause." It is the constitutional provision used by Chief Justice John Marshall in *McCulloch v. Maryland* (1819) to establish the concept of implied powers.

NEGLIGENCE.   A subfield of tort law dealing with cases in which it is alleged that the defendant failed to exercise reasonable care, thereby resulting in injury or harm to another, some object, or thing.

NISI PRIUS.   Latin meaning if not, unless before. Usually employed when referring to jury trial before a single judge as distinguished from an appellate court.

NOLO CONTENDERE.   Latin meaning no contest. Without directly admitting guilt, it is a plea in a criminal proceeding in which the defendant does not offer a defense. A sentence is then handed down with the assumption of guilt.

NONINTERPRETIVISM.   This is the view of constitutional interpretation that openly acknowledges the imprecise nature of constitutional provisions and maintains that many important constitutional provisions of contemporary interest require that judges give meaning beyond the literal words or specific intentions of the constitutional framers. Cp., interpretivism.

NOVUS HOMO.   Latin meaning a new man. Applied in reference to a person pardoned of a crime.

OBITER DICTA.   That part of the reasoning of a judicial opinion which is not necessary or pertinent to the result reached by the court. It is extra and unnecessary verbiage included for a variety of reasons. Often simply referred to as *dicta* or *obiter*.

ORDINANCE.   Usually refers to a local law.

ORIGINAL JURISDICTION.   The court where legal proceedings begin. It is the power of a court to hear a case in the first instance. The U.S. Supreme Court possesses both original and appellate jurisdiction.

OVERBROAD STATUTE.   A legislative enactment controlling activities not limited to constitutionally protected subjects or activities. The statute goes beyond what is permissible, usually invading First Amendment rights of protected persons or activities.

PARDON.   An act by an executive exempting a person guilty of a crime from punishment under the law.

PER CURIAM OPINION.   A judicial opinion by the whole court expressing the views of the justice collectively.

PETITIONER.   The party to a lawsuit who brings the case to a court by way of a petition; for example, the petition for a writ of *certiorari*. The party the petition is brought against is called the respondent.

PETIT JURY.   A trial jury.

PLAIN MEANING RULE.   When the language of a statute is clear and may be interpreted in only one way, a court employing this rule considers only the language and not other sources for assigning meaning.

PLAINTIFF.   The party to a conflict who brings a lawsuit against another (defendant).

PLEA.   The first pleading made by a defendant; a formal response to a criminal charge; for example, guilty, not guilty, or *nolo contendere*.

PLEA BARGAIN.   The result of negotiation and compromise between the prosecution and defense by which the prosecution agrees to reduce the charges or counts in return for the defendant's guilty plea. The defendant, in these cases, is said to "cop a plea."

PLEADINGS.   The formal and technical written statements made by the litigants framing the issues brought before a court.

POLITICAL QUESTION DOCTRINE.   A principle of judicial self-restraint holding that certain issues are best left to the other coordinate branches of government; such issues are said to be nonjusticiable.

POLL TAX.   Any fee attached to voting is outlawed in federal elections by the passage of the twenty-fourth amendment in 1964. In 1966, the Supreme Court found the poll tax unconstitutional in state elections because of the equal protection clause of the fourteenth amendment.

POSITIVE LAW.   Man-made laws enacted by a ruler, judge, or a legislature of some kind. Cp. natural law.

PRECEDENT.   A previously decided judicial opinion which serves as a guide for the decision in a present case. The facts of the past and present cases must be deemed sufficiently similar to serve as a precedent.

PRESENTMENT.   A device by which a grand jury acting on its own, without the consent or participation of a public prosecutor, formally accuses persons of criminal offenses. It differs from an indictment because the grand jury acts without the prosecutor.

PRESENTMENT CLAUSE.   Article I, section 7, clause 2 of the Constitution provides that bills passed by the House of Representatives and the Senate, shall, before becoming law, be presented to the president for action.

PRIMA FACIE.   Latin for at first sight, on first view. Prima facie evidence is such evidence that, if not later contradicted or in some way explained, is sufficient to sustain one's claim. A *prima facie* case is one that has proceeded to the point where it will support the charge if not later contradicted.

PRIOR RESTRAINT.   A limitation or prohibition against expression before actual publication is regarded as an attack on freedom of the press.

PRIVATE LAW.   (A) A statute enacted dealing with one person or a group; for example, a law passed to compensate Mr. Smith for damage to his property because of Army exercises. (B) A generic term referring to the law governing conflicts among private parties; for example, contracts, property, torts, or divorce.

PROCEDURAL LAW. The various and often complex rules governing the conduct of court cases.

PROPERTY. Ownership divided into two major parts. Real property, ownership in land, and personal property, ownership in movable objects or chattels.

PUBLIC LAW. (A) A statute enacted dealing with the society as a whole; for example, minimum wage laws, energy legislation, reorganization of governmental agencies. In Congress, such laws are given a number, for example, "Public Law No. 35." (B) A generic term referring to law governing operations of government and the government's relationships with persons; for example, constitutional law, criminal law, administrative law.

PUNITIVE DAMAGES. Sometimes called "exemplary damages," it is awarded for malicious or willful harm inflicted by the defendant in a civil case. It is money damages awarded by a court over and beyond actual and compensatory damages for the harm suffered and is intended to act as a warning and deterrent against future wrongful conduct.

QUAERE. A question or query involving a matter in doubt.

QUID PRO QUO. That which is given in return for something else, something for something. In contract law it constitutes legal consideration.

QUORUM. The number of members in an organization or body required to conduct business. Often a quorum is set at a majority of the entire membership.

RATIO DECIDENDI. Latin for the ground or reason for the decision. The very essence or central core of a judicial opinion, the principle of the case. To find the *ratio decidendi* the reader must establish which facts are treated by the judge as material and immaterial and his or her decision based on them.

RATIONAL BASIS TEST. A tool of constitutional interpretation that places the burden of proof on the individual challenging a state deprivation of a nonfundamental right or discrimination of nonsuspect classes of people. The court discerns only if the state action is reasonable. The Supreme Court has employed this test in cases involving indigency, age, mental retardation, certain instances involving alienage, international travel, education, welfare, and housing.

REAL PROPERTY. Ownership of land.

RECESS APPOINTMENT. The constitutional provision of article II, section 2, clause 3, providing that the president shall have the authority to fill all vacancies that may occur during the recess of the Senate. The presidential commission ends at the end of the Senate's next session.

RECUSATION. Because of possible prejudice, a judge is disqualified from hearing a case. Recusation may be requested through motion of litigants or may be voluntary.

REMEDY. The legal means through a court order to enforce a right or to redress or compensate for a harm.

RES JUDICATA. Sometimes *res a judicata*. Latin for a thing decided. It is a fundamental principle in civil proceedings that once a conflict has been decided by the court the decision is conclusive and the parties may not bring the same case before the court again.

RES NOVA.   Latin for a new thing or matter. Refers to a new legal question which has not been decided before.

RESPONDENT.   The party to a lawsuit against whom a petition is brought. Also called an appellee.

RESTITUTION.   To restore or to make good on something for example, to return or pay for a stolen item.

RIGHT.   The legal ability to perform or refrain from the performance of actions or the ability to control objects in one's possession. It also entails the ability to control the actions of others. In a legal sense, a right is enforceable as law as distinguished from a moral right.

RULE OF FOUR.   To grant the petition for a writ of certiorari four justices must vote do so.

SCIENTER.   With knowledge; prior knowledge that the act was wrong.

SCINTILLA.   A particle, the least bit. Usually refers to the least particle of evidence in a case.

SELF-EXECUTING.   Legislative enactments, judicial decisions, agreements, or documents requiring no further official action to be implemented.

SEQUESTER.   To isolate. For example, when during a trial the jury is kept from having contacts with the outside world.

SERIATIM.   Latin meaning individually, one by one, in order, point by point. The practice of each judge writing and recording his or her own views of a case. *Seriatim* is opposed to a collective opinion of the court representing the views of the majority, minority, or the whole court. Before the accession of John Marshall to the U.S. Supreme Court, the *seriatim* practice was generally employed.

SHOW CAUSE ORDER.   A command to a person to appear in court to explain why the court should not take a proposed course of action or accept a point of law before it.

SLANDER.   The oral expression of a falsehood about another resulting or tending to result in damage to reputation. One form of defamation of character, the other being libel.

SOCIOLOGICAL JURISPRUDENCE.   A school of jurisprudence that attempts to make the study of law a social science by substituting social psychological conceptions for legal notions such as the origins of law and the impact of law on human society. It is also prescriptive. Roscoe Pound is generally viewed as the intellectual father of this school.

SOLICITORS.   One segment of the legal profession in England. Solicitors do the routine office work dealing with clients directly and prepare cases for the barristers who argue before the bench in the higher courts.

SPEECH AND DEBATE CLAUSE.   Article I, section 6 of the Constitution makes the conduct of members of Congress, when in the course of their official duties, immune from civil or criminal liability.

STANDING TO SUE.   Sometimes referred to as simply, standing. The necessity of a plaintiff to demonstrate that he or she has a personal and vital interest in the outcome of the legal case or controversy brought before the court.

STARE DECISIS. Latin for the decision to stand, abide by or adhere to decided cases. A deeply-rooted common law tradition that once a court has determined a legal principle for a given set of facts, all future cases with similar facts should be decided in the same way.

STATUTE. A law enacted by a legislative body.

STATUTE OF LIMITATIONS. A legislative enactment prescribing a limited time period within which a legal suit may be started for a given offense.

STRICT SCRUTINY TEST. This approach to constitutional interpretation is applicable when government uses a suspect class such as race or alienage to classify persons or when it is alleged that government abridges a fundamental right. When either condition is present the government has the burden to demonstrate a compelling interest or a clear and present danger. The legislation or otherwise official action must be tailored narrowly to advance the legitimate government interest so as not to unduly burden the exercise of constitutional rights.

SUBPOENA. An order by a court or other duly authorized body to appear and testify before it.

SUBPOENA DUCES TECUM. An order directed toward a person by a court or other duly authorized body to appear before it with certain papers, documents, or other things.

SUBSTANTIVE DUE PROCESS. A widely discredited practice of courts to look at the basis of legislation to determine whether it comports with principles of fairness or nature. Jurists using this conception of due process substitute their judgments of good public policy for those of legislators.

SUBSTANTIVE LAW. The basic law governing relationships; for example, criminal law, constitutional law, property law, family law, torts. Substantive law is to be contrasted with procedural law; for example, law of evidence.

SUFFRAGE. The right to vote.

SUMMARY PROCEEDING. Any judicial business conducted before a court which is disposed of in a quick and simplified manner. Sometimes without a jury or indictment. For the U.S. Supreme Court it entails a judgment without the benefit of hearing oral arguments.

SUMMONS. A legal notice to a named defendant that he or she is being sued and must appear in court at a given time and place.

SUSPECT CLASS. Government classifications that reflect prejudice against discrete and insular minorities. As of 1988, the Supreme Court has included race and alienage in general as suspect classes.

SYMBOLIC SPEECH. The communication of ideas or beliefs without the use of words. Wearing armbands, displaying flags, conducting sit-in demonstrations are examples of symbolic speech protected by the First Amendment.

TEST CASE. A lawsuit brought to clarify, overturn, or establish a legal principle. Usually sponsored by an interest group, but nevertheless there is a *bona fide* litigant.

TORT. A civil wrong or injury inflicted upon another. It does not include contract matters. Examples include negligence, defamation of character, and wrongful death.

TRANSCRIPT OF RECORD. A printed copy (sometimes typed) of the proceedings of a court case. The transcript is used by an appellate court in reviewing the proceedings below.

TREATY. A formal agreement between or among sovereign states creating rights and obligations under international law. In the United States all treaties must be ratified by two-thirds vote of the Senate.

TRIAL DE NOVO. *See* De novo.

ULTRA VIRES. Latin meaning outside or beyond authority or power. A term indicating an action taken outside the legal authority of the person or body performing it.

VAGUENESS DOCTRINE. A criminal statute which does not give fair notice about what activity is proscribed and so fails to inform the population and interpreting authorities about what conduct is criminal.

VENUE. The location within a jurisdiction where a legal dispute is tried by a court.

VOIR DIRE EXAMINATION. The examination by legal counsel and the judge of a potential jury member as to his or her competency to serve.

WAIVER. The relinquishing or giving up of a legally enforceable right, privilege, or benefit voluntarily, with full knowledge; for example, when a criminal defendant gives up his or her right to remain silent by taking the witness stand on his or her own behalf.

WARRANT. A legal instrument issued by a judicial magistrate to arrest someone or to search premises.

WRIT. An order in the form of a letter from a court commanding that something be done.

WRIT OF CERTIORARI. *See* Certiorari, Writ of.

WRIT OF ERROR. *See* Error, Writ of.

WRIT OF MANDAMUS. *See* Mandamus, Writ of.

Bibliography

The Judicial System

Abraham, Henry J. *Justices and Presidents: A Political History of Appointments to the Supreme Court.* 2d ed. New York: Oxford University, 1985.
————. *The Judicial Process.* 5th ed. New York: Oxford University Press, 1986.
Agresto, John. *The Supreme Court and Constitutional Democracy.* Ithaca, NY: Cornell University, 1986.
Antieau, Chester J. *Adjudicating Constitutional Issues.* Dobbs Ferry, NY: Oceana Publications, Inc., 1985.
Ball, Howard. *Courts and Politics: The Federal Judicial System.* Englewood Cliffs, NJ: Prentice-Hall, 1980.
Bartee, Alice F. *Cases Lost, Causes Won: The Supreme Court and the Judicial Process.* New York: St. Martin's Press, 1984.
Baum, Lawrence. *The Supreme Court.* 3d ed. Washington, D.C.: Congressional Quarterly Press, 1988.
Beckstrom, John H. *Sociobiology and the Law: The Biology of Altruism in the Court of the Future.* Champaign: University of Illinois Press, 1985.
Berger, Raoul. *Government by Judiciary: The Transformation of the Fourteenth Amendment.* Cambridge: Harvard University Press, 1977.
Bobbitt, Philip. *Constitutional Fate: Theory of the Constitution.* New York: Oxford University, 1982.
Cannon, Mark, and O'Brien, David, eds. *Views from the Bench: The Judiciary and Constitutional Politics.* Chatham, NJ: Chatham House, 1985.
Carp, Robert A., and Rowland, C. Y. *Policymaking and Politics in the Federal District Courts.* Knoxville, TN: University of Tennessee Press, 1983.
Carp, Robert A., and Stidham, Ronald. *Federal Courts.* Washington, DC: Congressional Quarterly Press, 1985.
Carter, Lief H. *Contemporary Constitutional Lawmaking: The Supreme*

Court and the Art of Politics. Elmsford, NY: Pergamon Press, Inc., 1985.

Chinn, Nancy, and Berkson, Larry. *Literature on Judicial Selection*. Chicago: American Judicature Society, 1980.

Choper, Jesse H. *Judicial Review and the National Political Process: A Functional Reconsideration of the Role of the Supreme Court*. Chicago: University of Chicago Press, 1980.

Clinton, Robert L. *From Precedent to Myth: Marbury v. Madison and the History of Judicial Review in America*. Lawrence: University Press of Kansas, 1989.

Congressional Quarterly. *Guide to the U.S. Supreme Court*. 2d ed. Washington, D.C.: Congressional Quarterly, Inc., 1989.

————. *The Supreme Court*. Washington, DC: Congressional Quarterly Press, 1984.

DuBois, Philip, ed. *An Analysis of Judicial Reform*. Lexington: Lexington Books, 1982.

Ducat, Craig R. *Modes of Constitutional Interpretation*. St. Paul, MN: West Publishing Co., 1978.

Ely, John Hart. *Democracy and Distrust: A Theory of Judicial Review*. Cambridge: Harvard University Press, 1980.

Fairchild, Erika S., and Webb, Vincent J., eds. *The Politics of Crime and Criminal Justice*. Beverly Hills: Sage Publications, 1985.

Federalist Society. *The Great Debate: Interpreting Our Written Constitution*. Washington, DC: The Federalist Society, 1986.

Fish, Peter. *The Office of Chief Justice*. Charlottesville: University of Virginia Press, 1984.

Gabin, Sanford Byron. *Judicial Review and the Reasonable Doubt Test*. Port Washington, NY: Kennikat Press, 1980.

Garranty, John A. *Quarrels That Have Shaped the Constitution*. rev. ed. New York: Harper and Row, 1987.

Glick, Henry Robert. *Courts, Politics, and Justice*. New York: McGraw-Hill Book Co., 1983.

Goldman, Sheldon, and Jahnige, Thomas P. *The Federal Courts as a Political System*. 3d ed. New York: Harper & Row Publishers, 1985.

————, and Lamb, Charles M., eds. *Judicial Conflict and Consensus: Behavioral Studies of American Appellate Courts*. Lexington: University Press of Kentucky, 1986.

————, and Sarat, Austin. *American Court Systems: Readings in Judicial Process and Behavior*. 2d ed. New York: Longman, Inc., 1989.

Goulden, Joseph C. *The Benchwarmers: The Private World of the Powerful Federal Judges*. New York: Weybright and Talley, 1974.

Hall, Kermit L., ed. *The Judiciary in American Life*. New York: Garland Publishing Inc., 1987.

Halpern, Stephen C., and Lamb, Charles M. *Supreme Court Activism and Restraint*. Lexington, MA: Lexington Books, 1983.

Harrington, Christine. *Shadow Justice: The Ideology and Institutionalization of Alternatives to Court*. Westport, CT: Greenwood Press, 1985.

Higgins, Thomas J. *Judicial Review Unmasked*. Norwell, MA: Christopher Publications House, 1981.

Horowitz, Donald L. *The Courts and Social Policy*. Washington, DC: Brookings Institution, 1977.

Howard, Woodford. *Courts of Appeal in the Federal Judicial System: A Study of the Second, Fifth, and District of Columbia Circuits*. Princeton: Princeton University Press, 1982.

Jackson, Robert H. *The Supreme Court in the American System of Government*. Cambridge: Harvard University Press, 1955.

Jacob, Herbert. *Justice in America: Courts, Lawyers, and the Judicial Process*. 4th ed. Boston: Little, Brown, 1984.

Jacobsohn, Gary J. *The Supreme Court and the Decline of Constitutional Aspiration*. Totowa, NJ: Rowman and Littlefield, 1986.

Johnson, Charles A., and Canon, Bradley C. *Judicial Policies: Implementation & Impact*. Washington, DC: Congressional Quarterly, Inc., 1984.

Levin, A. Leo, and Wheller, Russell R. *The American Judiciary*. San Mateo, CA: Sage Publications, 1982.

McCann, Michael W., and Houseman, Gerald L., eds. *Judging the Constitution: Critical Essays on Judicial Lawmaking*. Glenview, IL: Scott, Foresman and Company, 1989.

McDowell, Gary L. *Taking the Constitution Seriously: Essays on the Constitution and the Constitutional Law*. Dubuque, IA: Kendall/Hunt Publishing Co., 1981.

————. *Equity and the Constitution: The Supreme Court, Equitable Relief and Public Policy*. Chicago: University of Chicago Press, 1982.

McLauchlan, William P. *American Legal Processes*. New York: John Wiley & Sons, 1977.

Melone, Albert P., and Mace, George. *Judicial Review and American Democracy*. Ames, IA: Iowa State University Press, 1988.

Mendelson, Wallace. *Supreme Court Statecraft: The Rule of Law and Men*. Ames, IA: Iowa State University Press, 1985.

Miller, Arthur Selwyn. *Toward Judicial Activism: The Political Role of the Supreme Court*. Westport, CT: Greenwood Press, 1982.

————. *Politics, Democracy and the Supreme Court: Essays on the Frontier of Constitutional Theory*. Westport, CT: Greenwood Press, Inc., 1985.

Murphy, Bruce. *The Brandeis/Frankfurter Connection: The Secret Political Activities of Two Supreme Court Justices*. New York: Oxford University Press, 1982.

Murphy, Walter F., and Pritchett, C. Herman. *Courts, Judges, and Politics.* 4th ed. New York: Random House, 1986.

Nagel, Stuart, Fairfield, Erika, and Champagne, Anthony, eds. *The Political Science of Criminal Justice.* Springfield, IL: Charles C Thomas Publishers, 1981.

Neely, Richard. *How Courts Govern America.* New Haven: Yale University, 1981.

————. *Judicial Jeopardy: When Business Collides with the Courts.* New York: Addison-Wesley, 1986.

Neubauer, David W. *America's Courts and the Criminal Justice System.* North Scituate, MA: Duxbury Press, 1979.

Oakley, John Bilyeu, and Thompson, Robert S. *Law Clerks and the Judicial Process: Perceptions of the Qualities and Functions of Law Clerks in American Courts.* Berkeley: University of California Press, 1980.

O'Brien, David M. *Storm Center: The Supreme Court in American Politics.* New York: W. W. Norton, 1986.

Peltason, Jack W. *Federal Courts in the Political Process.* New York: Random House, 1955.

Perry, Michael J. *The Constitution, the Court, and Human Right: An Inquiry into the Legitimacy of Constitutional Policy-Making by the Judiciary.* New Haven: Yale University Press, 1982.

Pinkele, Carl, and Louthan, William, eds. *Discretion, Justice, and Democracy: A Public Policy Perspective.* Ames, IA: Iowa State University Press, 1985.

Posner, Richard A. *The Federal Courts: Crisis and Reform.* Cambridge: Harvard University, 1985.

Provine, Doris Marie. *Case Selection in the United States Supreme Court.* Chicago: University of Chicago Press, 1980.

————. *Judging Credentials: Nonlawyer Judges and the Politics of Professionalism.* Chicago: University of Chicago Press, 1986.

Pugh, J. Donna, et al. *Judicial Rulemaking: A Compendium.* Lanham, MD: University Publications of America, 1985.

Radcliffe, James E. *The Case or Controversy Provision.* University Park: Pennsylvania State University Press, 1978.

Rehnquist, William. *The Supreme Court: How It Was, How It Is.* New York: William Morrow, 1987.

Rohde, David W., and Spaeth, Harold J. *Supreme Court Decision Making.* San Francisco: Freeman, 1976.

Schmidhauser, John R. *Judges and Justices: The Federal Appellate Judiciary.* Boston: Little, Brown, 1979.

Schwartz, Bernard. *Super Chief: Earl Warren and His Supreme Court—A Judicial Biography.* New York: New York University Press, 1983.

Shetreet, Shimon, and Deschenes, Jules. *Judicial Independence: The Contemporary Debate.* Norwell, MA: Kluwer Academic Publishers, 1985.

Spaeth, Harold J. *Supreme Court Policy Making: Explanation and Prediction*. San Francisco: W. H. Freeman, 1979.

Stern, Robert L., and Gressman, Eugene. *Supreme Court Practice*. 6th ed. Washington, DC: The Bureau of National Affairs, Inc., 1986.

Storme, M. *Effectiveness of Judicial Protection and the Constitutional Order*. Norwell: Kluwer Academic Publishers, 1983.

Stumpf, Harry P. *American Judicial Politics*. New York: Harcourt Brace Jovanovich, 1988.

Tribe, Laurence. *God Save This Honorable Court*. New York: Random House, 1985.

————. *Constitutional Choices*. Cambridge: Harvard University Press, 1985.

Ulmer, S. Sidney, ed. *Courts, Law, and Judicial Processes*. New York: The Free Press, 1981.

Wasby, Stephen L. *The Supreme Court in the Federal Judicial System*. 3d ed. Chicago: Nelson-Hall Publishers, 1989.

Wolfe, Christopher. *The Rise of Modern Judicial Review: From Constitutional Interpretation to Judge-Made Law*. New York: Basic Books, 1986.

Woodward, Bob, and Armstrong, Scott. *The Brethren: Inside the Supreme Court*. New York: Simon & Schuster, 1979.

Jurisprudence

Ackerman, Bruce A. *Social Justice in the Liberal State*. New Haven: Yale University Press, 1980.

Austin, John. *Lectures on Jurisprudence*. 2 vols. New York: James Crockcraft, 1875.

Bishin, William R., and Stone, Christopher D. *Law, Language, Ethics: An Introduction to Law and Legal Method*. Mineola, NY: The Foundation Press, Inc. 1972.

Bodenheimer, Edgar. *Jurisprudence: The Philosophy and Method of the Law*. Rev. ed. Cambridge: Harvard University Press, 1974.

Brkić, Jovan. *Norm and Order: An Investigation into Logic, Semantics, and the Theory of Law and Morals*. New York: Humanities Press, 1970.

————. *Legal Reasoning: Semantic and Logical Analysis*. New York: Peter Lang, 1985.

Bronaugh, Richard. *Readings in the Philosophy of Constitutional Law*. 2d ed. Dubuque, IA: Kendall/Hunt Publishing Co., 1985.

Cardozo, Benjamin. *The Nature of the Judicial Process*. New Haven: Yale University Press, 1921.

Carter, Lief H. *Reason in Law*. 3d ed. Boston: Little, Brown, 1988.

Cohen, Morris. *Reason and Law*. New York: The Free Press, 1950.

d'Entreves, A. P. *Natural Law: An Introduction to Legal Philosophy*. 2d ed. London: Hutchinson, 1970, 1977.

Dworkin, Ronald. *Law's Empire*. Cambridge: Harvard University Press, 1986.

Edelman, Martin. *Democratic Theories and the Constitution*. Albany, NY: State University of New York Press, 1985.

Fine, Bob. *Democracy and the Rule of Law: Liberal Ideals and Marxist Critiques*. Wolfeboro, NH: Longwood Publishing Group, Inc., 1984.

Firth, Brian W. *The Constitution of Consensus: Democracy as an Ethical Imperative*. New York: Peter Lang Publishing, Inc., 1987.

Frank, Jerome. *Courts on Trial: Myth and Reality in American Justice*. Princeton: Princeton University Press, 1949.

Friedrich, Carl Joachim. *The Philosophy of Law in Historical Perspectives*. 2d ed. Chicago: University of Chicago Press, 1963.

Fuller, Lon. *The Morality of Law*. New Haven: Yale University Press, 1964.

Glennon, Robert J. *The Iconoclast as Reformer: Jerome Frank's Impact on American Law*. Ithaca, NY: Cornell University, 1985.

Hall, Jerome. *Foundations of Jurisprudence*. Indianapolis: Bobbs-Merrill, 1973.

———. *Readings in Jurisprudence*. Indianapolis: Bobbs-Merrill, 1973.

Levi, Edward. *An Introduction to Legal Reasoning*. Chicago: University of Chicago Press, 1949.

Llewellyn, Karl. *The Bramble Bush*. New York: Oceana Publications, 1930.

———. *The Common Law Tradition: Deciding Appeals*. Boston: Little, Brown, 1962.

Morris, Clarence, ed. *The Great Legal Philosophers: Selected Readings in Jurisprudence*. Philadelphia: University of Pennsylvania Press, 1971.

Murphy, G. Jeffrie, and Coleman, L. Jules. *The Philosophy of Law: An Introduction to Jurisprudence*. Totowa, NJ: Rowman and Littlefield Publishers, 1984.

Patterson, Edwin W. *Jurisprudence: Men and Ideas of the Law*. Brooklyn: The Foundation Press, 1953.

Pound, Roscoe. *An Introduction to the Philosophy of Law*. Revised edition. New Haven: Yale University Press, 1954.

Rawls, John. *A Theory of Justice*. Cambridge: Belknap Press of Harvard University Press, 1971.

Savigny, Friedrick K. *Of the Vocation of Our Age for Legislation and Jurisprudence*. Translated by A. Hayward. London: Littlewood, 1831.

Schauer, Frederick. *Free Speech: A Philosophical Inquiry*. New York: Cambridge University Press, 1982.

Shklar, Judith N. *Legalism*. Cambridge: Harvard University Press, 1964.

Smith, Roger M. *Liberalism and American Constitutional Law*. Cambridge: Harvard University Press, 1985.

Twining, William, ed. *Legal Theory and Common Law*. Oxford: Basil Blackwell, 1986.

Zelermyer, William. *The Process of Legal Reasoning*. Englewood Cliffs: Prentice-Hall, 1963.

Constitutional Law—General

Bartholomew, Paul C., and Menez, Joseph F. *Summaries of Leading Cases on the Constitution*. 12th edition. Totowa, NJ: Rowman Littlefield, Helix Books, 1983.

Congressional Quarterly. *The Supreme Court: Justice and the Law*. 2d ed. Washington, DC: Congressional Quarterly, 1985.

Congressional Research Service, Library of Congress. *The Constitution of the United States of America: Analysis and Interpretation*. Washington, DC: U.S. Government Printing Office, 1987.

Corwin, Edward S. *The Constitution and What It Means Today*. 14th ed. Revised by Harold W. Chase and Craig R. Ducat. Princeton: Princeton University Press, 1978.

Crews, Kenneth D. *Edward S. Corwin and the American Constitution: A Bibliographical Analysis*. Westport, CT: Greenwood Press, 1985.

Curry, James A., Riley, Richard B., and Battistoni, Richard M. *Constitutional Government: The American Experience*. St. Paul: West Publishing Company, 1989.

Goldman, Sheldon. *Constitutional Law: Cases and Essays*. New York: Harper and Row, 1987.

Kurland, Philip B. and Lerner, Ralph. *The Founders' Constitution*, 5 Vols. Chicago: University of Chicago Press, 1987.

Padover, Saul K. *The Living U.S. Constitution*. Second Revised Edition by Landynski, Jacob W. New York: New American Library, 1983.

Peltason, J. W. *Understanding the Constitution*. 8th ed. New York: Holt, Rinehart and Winston, 1979.

———. *Corwin and Peltason's Understanding the Constitution*. 11th ed. Holt, Rinehart and Winston, 1988.

Pritchett, C. Herman. *The American Constitution*. 3d ed. New York: McGraw-Hill, 1977.

———. *The American Constitutional System*. 5th ed. New York: McGraw-Hill, 1981.

Rotunda, Ronald D., Nowark, John E. and Young, J. Nelson. *Constitutional Law: Treatise on Substance and Procedure*. St. Paul: West Publishing Co., 1986.

Schwartz, Bernard. *Constitutional Law: A Textbook*. 2d ed. New York: Macmillan, 1979.

Smith, Edward C. and Spaeth, Harold J. *The Constitution of the United States—With Case Summaries*. Bicentennial edition. New York: Barnes and Noble, 1987.

Tribe, Laurence H. *American Constitutional Law*. 2d ed. Mineola, N.Y.: The Foundation Press, 1988.

Williams, Jerre S. *Constitutional Analysis in a Nutshell*. St. Paul, MN.: West, 1979.

Constitutional History

Adams, Willi Paul. *The First American Constitutions: Republican Ideology and the Making of the State Constitutions in the Revolutionary Era*. Translated by Rita and Robert Kimberg. Chapel-Hill: University of North Carolina Press, 1980.

Allen, W. B., and Lloyd, Gordon, eds. *The Essential Antifederalist*. Lanham, MD: University Press of America, 1985.

Amlund, Curtis Arthur. *Federalism in the Southern Confederacy*. Washington: Public Affairs Press, 1966.

Beard, Charles Austin. *The Federalist*. New York: F. Ungar, 1959.

———. *The Supreme Court and the Constitution*. Englewood Cliffs: Prentice-Hall, 1962.

———. *An Economic Interpretation of the United States*. New York: Free Press, 1986.

Beth, Loren P. *The Development of the American Constitution, 1877–1917*. New York: Harper & Row, 1971.

Biasi, Vincent. *The Burger Court: The Counter-Revolution that Wasn't*. New Haven: Yale University, 1983.

Boles, Donald E. *Mr. Justice Rehnquist, Justice Activist: The Early Years*. Ames, IA: Iowa State University Press, 1987.

Boorstin, Daniel J. *The Americans: The Colonial Experience*. New York: Random House, 1958.

Bowen, Catherine Drinker. *Miracle at Philadelphia: The Story of the Constitutional Convention May to September 1787*. Boston: Atlantic-Little Brown, 1986.

Boyd, Steven R. *The Politics of Opposition: Antifederalists and the Acceptance of the Constitution*. Millwood, NY: KTO Press, 1979.

Burgess, John William. *Recent Changes in American Constitutional Theory*. New York: Arno Press, 1972.

Burns, Edward McNall. *James Madison: Philosopher of the Constitution*. New York: Octagon Books, 1968.

Collier, Christopher, and Collier, James Lincoln. *Decision in Philadelphia: The Constitutional Convention of 1787.* New York: Random House, Ballantine Books, 1987.

Cope, Alfred Haines. *Franklin D. Roosevelt and the Supreme Court.* Lexington, MA: Heath, 1969.

Corwin, Edward S. *The Doctrine of Judicial Review.* Princeton: Princeton University Press, 1914.

Cox, Archibald. *The Warren Court.* Cambridge: Harvard University Press, 1968.

Cripps, Louise L. *Human Rights in a United States Colony.* Cambridge: Schenkman Books Inc., 1982.

Crosskey, William W. *Politics and the Constitution in the History of the United States.* 2 vols. Chicago: University of Chicago Press, 1953.

Currie, David P. *The Constitution in the Supreme Court: The First Hundred Years.* Chicago: University of Chicago Press, 1985.

Dewey, Donald O. *Union and Liberty: A Documentary History of American Constitutionalism.* New York: McGraw-Hill, 1969.

————. *Marshall Versus Jefferson: The Political Background of Marbury v. Madison.* New York: Knopf, 1970.

Donovan, Frank Robert. *Mr. Madison's Constitution: the Story Behind the Constitutional Convention.* New York: Dodd, Mead, 1965.

Douglas, William O. *The Court Years, 1935–1975.* New York: Random House, 1980.

Dunning, William Archibald. *Essays on the Civil War and Reconstruction.* New York: Harper & Row, 1965.

Duram, James C. *Justice William O. Douglas.* Boston: K. G. Hall, 1981.

Elliot, Jonathan. *The Debates in the Several State Conventions on the Adoption of the Federal Constitution as Recommended by the General Convention at Philadelphia in 1787.* New York: B. Franklin, 1968.

Faber, Doris, and Faber, Harold. *We the People: The Story of the United States Constitution Since 1787.* New York: Charles Scribner's Sons, 1987.

Farrand, Max. *The Framing of the Constitution of the United States.* New Haven: Yale University Press, 1913.

————, ed. *The Records of the Federal Convention of 1787.* 4 vols. New Haven: Yale University Press, 1937, 1966, 1986.

Ford, Saul Leicester, ed. *The Federalist.* New York: H. Holt, 1898.

Friedman, Leon, and Israel, Fred L., eds. *The Justices of the United States Supreme Court 1789–1978: Their Lives and Major Opinions,* 5 Vols. New York and London: Chelsea House Publishers, 1980.

Funston, Richard Y. *Constitutional Counterrevolution? The Warren and the Burger Courts: Judicial Policy Making in Modern America.* New York: Halsted Press, 1977.

Graham, George J. and Graham, Scarlett G., eds. *Founding Principles of American Government*. Chatham, NJ: Chatham House Publishers Inc., 1984.

Green, Fletcher M. *Constitutional Development in the South Atlantic States*. New York: W. W. Norton, 1966.

Grier, Stephenson D. Jr. *The Supreme Court and the American Republic: An Annotated Bibliography*. New York: Garland Publishing Inc., 1981.

Haines, Charles G. *The Role of the Supreme Court in American Government and Politics, 1789–1835*. Berkeley: University of California Press, 1944.

———, and Sherwood, Foster H. *The Role of the Supreme Court in American Government and Politics, 1835–1864*. Berkeley: University of California Press, 1957.

———. *The American Doctrine of Judicial Supremacy*. 2d ed. Berkeley: University of California Press, 1959.

Hall, Kermit L., ed. *A Comprehensive Bibliography of Constitutional and Legal History, 1896–1979*. White Plains: Kraus International Publications, 1982.

———. *Liberties in American History*. New York: Garland Publishing, Inc., 1987.

Harmon, M. Judd, ed. *Essays on the Constitution of the United States*. Port Washington, NY: Kennikat Press, 1978.

Hentoff, Nat. *The First Freedom: The Tumultuous History of Free Speech in America*. New York: Delacorte Press, 1980.

Higginbotham, A. Leon, Jr. *In the Matter of Color: Race and the American Legal Process, The Colonial Period*. New York: Oxford University Press, 1978.

Hirsch, H. N. *The Enigma of Felix Frankfurter*. New York: Basic Books, 1981.

Hockett, Homer Carey. *The Constitutional History of the United States*. New York: Macmillan, 1939.

Hoffer, Peter C., and Hull, N. E. *Impeachment in America, 1635–1805*. New Haven: Yale University, 1985.

Horwitz, Morton J. *The Transformation of American Law, 1780–1860*. Cambridge: Harvard University Press, 1977.

Howard, A. *The Road From Runnymede: Magna Carta and Constitutionalism in America*. Charlottesville: University of Virginia Press, 1968.

Hurst, Willard. *The Growth of American Law, The Law Makers*. Boston: Little, Brown, 1950.

Hyman, Harold Melvin. *A More Perfect Union: The Impact of the Civil War and Reconstruction on the Constitution*. Boston: Houghton Mifflin, 1975.

Jaffa, Harry V. *American Conservatism and the American Founding*. Durham, NC: Carolina Academic Press, 1983.

Jellinek, George. *The Declaration of the Rights of Man and of Citizens: A*

Contribution to Modern Constitutional History. Westport, CT: Hyperion Press, Inc., 1985.

Jenson, Carol E. *Agrarian Pioneer in Civil Liberties: The Nonpartisan League in Minnesota During World War I*. New York: Garland Publishing, Inc., 1987.

Kelly, Alfred H., Harbison, Winfred A., and Belz, Herman. *The American Constitution: Its Origins and Development*. 6th ed. New York: W. W. Norton and Co., Inc., 1983.

Kenyon, Cecelia M., ed. *The Antifederalists*. Boston, MA: Northeastern University Press, 1985.

Ketcham, Ralph, ed. *The Antifederalist Papers and the Constitutional Convention Debates*. New York: New American Library, 1986.

Kurland, Philip B. *Supreme Court Review*. Chicago: University of Chicago Press. Annual since 1960.

―――. *Politics, The Constitution, and the Warren Court*. Chicago: University of Chicago Press, 1970.

Kutler, I. Stanley. *Judicial Power and Reconstruction Politics*. Chicago: University of Chicago, 1968.

Lash, Joseph P., ed. *From the Diaries of Felix Frankfurter*. New York: W. W. Norton, 1975.

Levy, Leonard Williams. *Essays on the Making of the Constitution*. New York: Oxford University Press, 1969.

Lofgren, Charles. *The Plessy Case: A Legal-Historical Interpretation*. New York: Oxford University Press, 1987.

Magee, James J. *Mr. Justice Black: Absolutist on the Court*. Charlottesville: University of Virginia Press, 1980.

Main, Jackson Turner. *The Antifederalists: Critics of the Constitution*. New York: W. W. Norton, 1974.

Manley, John F., and Dolbeare, Kenneth, eds. *The Case Against the Constitution: From the Antifederalists to the Present*. Armonk, NY: M. E. Sharpe, Inc., 1987.

Marks, Federick W. *Independence on Trial: Foreign Affairs and the Making of the Constitution*. Baton Rouge: Louisiana State University Press, 1973.

Mason, Alpheus Thomas. *The Supreme Court from Taft to Warren*. Baton Rouge: Louisiana State University Press, 1958.

―――. *The States Rights Debate: Antifederalism and the Constitution*. 2d ed. New York: Oxford University Press, 1972.

―――. *The Supreme Court from Taft to Burger*. 3d ed. Baton Rouge: Louisiana State University Press, 1979.

McCloskey, Robert G. *The American Supreme Court*. Chicago: University of Chicago Press, 1960.

―――. *The Modern Supreme Court*. Martin Shapiro, ed. Cambridge: Harvard University Press, 1972.

McDonald, Forrest. *A Constitutional History of the United States*. New York: Watts Franklin, Inc., 1982.

———. *Novus Ordo Seclorum: The Intellectual Origins of the Constitution*. Lawrence: University Press of Kansas, 1985.

McLaughlin, Andrew Cunningham. *A Constitutional History of the United States*. New York: Appleton-Century-Crofts, 1963.

———. *The Confederation and the Constitution*. New York: Collier Books, 1971.

———. *The Courts, the Constitution, and Parties: Studies in Constitutional History and Politics*. New York: Da Capo Press, 1972.

———. *The Foundations of American Constitutionalism*. Gloucester, MA: P. Smith, 1972.

Millett, Stephen M. *A Selected Bibliography of American Constitutional History*. Santa Barbara, CA: Clio Books, 1975.

Mitchell, Broadus. *A Biography of the Constitution of the United States: Its Origin, Formation, Adoption, Interpretation*. 2d ed. New York: Oxford University Press, 1975.

Morris, Richard B. *Witnesses at the Creation: Hamilton, Madison, Jay, and the Constitution*. New York: New American Library, 1985.

Murphy, Bruce Allen. *The Brandeis-Frankfurter Connection*. New York: Oxford University Press, 1982.

Murphy, Paul L. *The Constitution in Crisis Times, 1918–1969*. New York: Harper & Row, 1972.

———. *World War I and the Origin of Civil Liberties in the United States*. New York: W. W. Norton, 1979.

Newmyer, Kent R. *Supreme Court Justice Story: Statesman of the Old Republic*. Chapel Hill: University of North Carolina Press, 1985.

Nieman, Donald G. *To Set the Law in Motion: The Freedmen's Bureau and the Legal Rights of Blacks, 1865–1868*. Millwood, NY: KTO Press, 1979.

Paludan, Phillip S. *A Covenant with Death: The Constitution, Law and Equality in the Civil War Era*. Urbana: University of Illinois Press, 1975.

Parrish, Michael. *Felix Frankfurter and His Times: The Reform Years*. New York: Free Press, 1982.

Patterson, James T. *The New Deal and the States: Federalism in Transition*. Westport, CT: Greenwood Press Inc., 1981.

Pfeffer, Leo. *This Honorable Court: A History of the Supreme Court of the United States*. Boston: Beacon Press, 1965.

Pohlman, H. L. *Justice Oliver Wendell Holmes and Utilitarian Jurisprudence*. Cambridge: Harvard University Press, 1984.

Pollack, Louis. *The Constitution and the Supreme Court: A Documentary History*. 2 vols. Cleveland: World Publishing Co., 1966.

Pritchett, C. Herman. *The Roosevelt Court: A Study of Judicial Votes and Values, 1937–1947*. New York: Macmillan, 1948.

————. *Civil Liberties and the Vinson Court*. Chicago: University of Chicago Press, 1954.

Rodell, Fred. *Nine Men: A Political History of the Supreme Court from 1790–1955*. New York: Random House, 1955.

————. *55 Men: The Story of the Constitution*. 1987 edition. Washington, DC: Liberty Lobby, 1987.

Rossiter, Clinton. *1787: The Grand Convention*. New York: Macmillan, 1966.

Rutland, Robert A. *The Birth of the Bill of Rights, 1776–1791*. New York: Macmillan, 1962.

Schmidhauser, John R. *Constitutional Law in American Politics*. Monterey, CA: Brooks/Cole Publishing Company, 1984.

Schwartz, Bernard. *From Confederation to Nation: The American Constitution, 1835–1877*. Baltimore: Johns Hopkins University Press, 1973.

————. *Super Chief: Earl Warren and His Court*. New York: New York University Press, 1983.

Schwartz, Herman, ed. *The Burger Years: Rights and Wrongs in the Supreme Court, 1969–1986*. New York: Viking-Penguin, 1987.

Scott, Eben G. *Development of Constitutional Liberty in the English Colonies of America*. 3d ed. Littleton, CO: Fred B. Rothman & Co., 1982.

Silverstein, Mark. *Constitutional Faiths: Felix Frankfurter, Hugo Black, and the Process of Judicial Decisionmaking*. Ithaca, NY: Cornell University Press, 1984.

Simon, James F. *In His Own Image: The Supreme Court in Richard Nixon's America*. New York: David McKay, 1973.

————. *Independent Journey: The Life of William O. Douglas*. New York: Harper and Row, 1980.

Smith, David G. *The Convention and the Constitution: The Political Ideas of the Founding Fathers*. New York: St. Martin's Press, 1965.

Solberg, Winston U., ed. *The Federal Convention and the Formation of the Union of the American States*. Indianapolis: Bobbs-Merrill, 1958.

Steamer, Robert J. *The Supreme Court in Crisis: A History of Conflict*. Amherst: University of Massachusetts Press, 1971.

————. *Chief Justice: Leadership and the Supreme Court*. University of South Carolina Press, 1986.

Storing, Herbert J., ed. *The Abridged Anti-Federalist*. Chicago: University of Chicago Press, 1985.

Strum, Philippa. *Louis Brandeis: Justice for the People*. Cambridge: Harvard University Press, 1984.

Sutherland, Arthur E. *Constitutionalism in America: Origin and Evolution of its Fundamental Ideas*. New York: Blaisdell Publishing, 1965.

Swisher, Carl Brent. *American Constitutional Development*. Boston: Houghton Mifflin, 1954.

————. *The Growth of Constitutional Power in the United States*. Chicago: University of Chicago Press, 1963.

U.S. Congress. The Debates and Proceedings in the Congress of the United States. *A Second Federalist: Congress Creates a Government.* New York: Appleton-Century-Crofts, 1967.

U.S. Constitutional Convention, 1787. *Notes of Debates in the Federal Convention of 1787, reported by James Madison.* Ohio University Press, 1966.

U.S. Constitution Sesquicentennial Commission. *History of the Formation of the Union Under the Constitution with Liberty Documents and Report of the Commission.* New York: Greenwood Press, 1968.

Virginia Commission on Constitutional Government. *The Constitution of the United States of America, with a Summary of the Actions by the States in Ratification of the Provisions thereof.* Richmond: Virginia Commission on Constitutional Government, 1965.

Vose, Clement E. *Constitutional Change: Amendment Politics and Supreme Court Litigation Since 1900.* Lexington, MA: Lexington Books, 1972.

Warren, Charles. *The Supreme Court in United States History.* 2 vols. Boston: Little, Brown, 1947, 1987.

————. *The Making of the Constitution.* New York: Barnes & Noble, 1967.

————. *Congress, the Constitution and the Supreme Court.* New York: Johnson Reprint Corp., 1968.

Wasby, Stephen L. *Continuity and Change: From the Warren Court to the Burger Court.* Pacific Palisades, CA: Goodyear Publishing, 1976.

Westin, Alan F. *An Autobiography of the Supreme Court.* New York: Macmillan, 1963.

Wiecek, William M. *Constitutional Development in a Modernizing Society.* Washington: American Historical Association, 1985.

Wood, S. B. *Constitutional Politics in the Progressive Era.* Chicago: University of Chicago Press, 1968.

Woodward, C. Vann. *The Strange Career of Jim Crow.* 3d ed. New York: Oxford University Press, 1974.

Wright, Benjamin Fletcher. *The Growth of American Constitutional Law.* Chicago: University of Chicago Press, 1967.

Federalism

Ackerman, B. A. *Private Property and the Constitution.* New Haven: Yale University Press, 1977.

Baxter, Maurice G. *The Steamboat Monopoly: Gibbons v. Ogden, 1824.* New York: Knopf, 1972.

Benson, Paul R., Jr. *The Supreme Court and the Commerce Clause.* New York: Dunellen, 1970.

Cooley, Thomas M. *Constitutional Limitations.* New York: Da Capo Press, 1972.

Cortner, Richard C. *The Jones and Laughlin Case*. New York: Knopf, 1970.

Corwin, Edward Samuel. *The Commerce Power Versus States Rights*. Magnolia, MA: Peter Smith, 1962.

Davis, S. Rufus. *The Federal Principle*. Berkeley: University of California Press, 1978.

Duchacek, I. D. *Comparative Federalism: The Territorial Dimension of Politics*. Lanham, MA: University Press of America, 1987.

Elazar, Daniel J. *American Federalism: A View From the States*. 2d ed. New York: Harper and Row, 1972.

————, ed. *Federalism & Political Integration*. Lanham, MA: University Press of America, 1985.

————. *Exploring Federalism*. Tuscaloosa, AL: University of Alabama Press, 1987.

Engdahl, D. E. *Constitutional Power: Federal and State*. St. Paul: West Publishing, 1974.

————. *Constitutional Federalism in a Nutshell*. St. Paul, MN: West Publishing Co., 1987.

Flack, Horace, *The Adoption of the Fourteenth Amendment*. Baltimore: Johns Hopkins Press, 1908.

Folgelson, R. M., and Susskind, L. E. *American Federalism*. New York: Arno Press, 1977.

Frankfurter, Felix. *The Commerce Clause Under Marshall, Taney and Waite*. Chicago: Quadrangle Books, 1964.

Freilich, Robert H., and Carlisle, Richard G. *Section 1983, Sword and Shield: Civil Rights Violation and the Liability of Urban, State, and Local Government*. Chicago: American Bar Association, 1983.

Gelfand, M. David. *Federal Constitutional Law and American Local Government*. Charlottesville, VA: Michie Co., 1984.

Glendening, Parris N., and Reeves, Mavis M. *Pragmatic Federalism: An Intergovernmental View of American Government*. 2d ed. Pacific Palisades, CA: Palisades Publishers, 1984.

Grodzins, Morton. *The American System*. Chicago: Rand McNally, 1966.

————. *The American System: A New View of Government in the United States*. New Brunswick, NJ: Transaction Books, 1983.

Hall, Kermit L., ed. *Federalism: A Nation of States*. New York: Garland Publishing Inc., 1987.

Hallman, Howard W. *Emergency Employment: A Study of Federalism*. Alabama: University of Alabama Press, 1977.

Hawkins, Robert B., Jr., ed. *American Federalism: A New Partnership for the Republic*. San Francisco: ICS Press, 1982.

Hay, Peter, and Rotunda, Ronald D. *The United States Federal System: Legal Integration in the American Experience*. Dobbs Ferry, NY: Oceana Publications, Inc., 1982.

Hening, Jeffrey R. *Public Policy and Federalism: Issues in State and Local Politics*. New York: St. Martin's Press, Inc., 1985.

Hodgkinson, Virginia A., ed. *Impact and Challenges of a Changing Federal Role*. San Francisco: Jossey-Bass Inc., 1985.

Hoose, Bernard. *Proportionalism: The American Debate and Its European Roots*. Washington, DC: Georgetown University Press, 1987.

Howitt, Arnold M. *Managing Federalism: Studies in Intergovernmental Relations*. Washington, DC: Congressional Quarterly, Inc., 1984.

Kenyon, Cecelia M., ed. *The Antifederalists*. New York: Bobbs Merrill, 1964.

Kettl, Donald F. *The Regulation of American Federalism*. Baton Rouge, LA: Louisiana State University Press, 1983.

———. *The Regulation of American Federalism*. Baltimore, MD: Johns Hopkins University Press, 1987.

King, Preston. *Federalism and Federation*. Baltimore, MD: Johns Hopkins University Press, 1983.

Leach, Richard. *American Federalism*. New York: Oxford University Press, 1972.

Lee, Mark R. *Antitrust Law and Local Government*. Westport, CT: Greenwood Press, Inc., 1985.

Lewis, Frederick P. *The Dilemma in the Congressional Power to Enforce the Fourteenth Amendment*. Washington: University Press of America, 1980.

Low, Peter W. and Jeffries, John C., Jr. *Federal Courts and the Law of Federal-State Relations*. Mineola, NY: Foundation Press, Inc., 1987.

Magrath, C. Peter. *Yazoo: The Case of Fletcher v. Peck*. New York: W. W. Norton, 1966.

Mason, Alpheus Thomas. *The States Rights Debate: Antifederalism and the Constitution*. New York: Oxford University Press, 1972.

Melnick, Shep. *Regulation and the Courts: The Case of the Clean Air Act*. Washington, DC: Brookings Institution, 1983.

Ostrom, Vincent. *The Political Theory of a Compound Republic: Designing the American Experiment*. Lincoln, NE: University of Nebraska Press, 1987.

Peterson, Paul E., et al. *When Federalism Works*. Washington, DC: Brookings Institution, 1986.

Porter, Marty Cornelia, and Tarr, Allan G., eds. *State Supreme Courts: Policymakers in the Federal System*. Westport, CT: Greenwood Press, 1982.

Press, Charles, and Verburg, Kenneth. *State and Community Governments in the Federal System*. New York: Macmillan, 1983.

Reagan, Michael D. and John Sanzone. *The New Federalism*. 2d ed. New York: Oxford University Press, 1980.

Ridgeway, Marian E. *Interstate Compacts: A Question of Federalism*. Carbondale: Southern Illinois University Press, 1971.

Riker, William. *Federalism: Origin, Operation, Significance*. Boston: Little, Brown, 1964.

———. *The Development of American Federalism*. Norwell, MA: Kluwer Academic Publishers, 1987.

Schmidhauser, John R. *The Supreme Court as Final Arbiter in Federal/State Relations, 1789–1957*. Westport, CT: Greenwood Press, 1973.

Shepard's Citation, Inc. *Civil Actions Against State Government, Its Divisions, Agencies and Officers*. Colorado Springs, CO: Shepard's McGraw-Hill, 1982.

Smith, Michael. *Qualified Immunity from Liability for Violations of Federal Rights: A Modification*. Chapel Hill: University of North Carolina, Institute of Government, 1983.

Sprague, John D. *Voting Patterns of the United States Supreme Court: Cases in Federalism, 1889–1959*. Indianapolis: Bobbs-Merrill, 1968.

Stewart, William H. *Concepts of Federalism*. Lanham, MA: University Press of America, 1984.

Sunquist, James L. *Making Federalism Work*. Washington, DC: Brookings Institution, 1969.

Tarr, George Alan. *Judicial Impact and State Supreme Courts*. Lexington, MA: Lexington Books, 1977.

Wheare, K. C. *Federal Government*, 4th ed. New York: Oxford University Press, 1963.

Wildavsky, Aaron. *American Federalism in Perspective*. Boston: Little, Brown, 1967.

Wright, Benjamin Fletcher. *The Contract Clause of the Constitution*. Cambridge: Harvard University Press, 1938.

Wright, Deil S. and White, Harvey L., eds. *Federalism and Intergovernmental Relations: PAR Classics V*. Washington, DC: American Society for Public Administration, 1984.

Congress

American Bar Association Staff and Cox, Henry B. *War, Foreign Affairs, and Constitutional Power, 1829–1901*. Cambridge, MA: Ballinger Publishing Co., 1984.

Barber, S. A. *The Constitution and the Delegation of Congressional Power*. Chicago: University of Chicago Press, 1975.

Baxter, M. G. *Daniel Webster and the Supreme Court*. Amherst: University of Massachusetts Press, 1967.

Berger, Raoul. *Congress Versus the Supreme Court*. Cambridge: Harvard University Press, 1969.

Breckenridge, A. C. *Congress Against the Court*. Lincoln: University of Nebraska Press, 1970.

Claude, Richard. *The Supreme Court and the Electoral Process*. Baltimore: Johns Hopkins Press, 1970.

Congressional Quarterly. *Guide to the Congress of the United States: Origins, History, and Procedure*. Washington, DC: Congressional Quarterly Service, 1971.

————. *Impeachment and the United States Congress*. Washington, DC: Congressional Quarterly, 1974.

Cortner, Richard C. *The Jones and Laughlin Case*. New York: Knopf, 1970.

Craig, Barbara H. *Chadha: The Story of an Epic Constitutional Struggle*. New York: Oxford University Press, Inc., 1987.

Craig, Barbara H. *The Legislative Veto: Congressional Control of Regulation*. Boulder, CO: Westview Press, 1984.

Elliott, Ward E. Y. *The Rise of Guardian Democracy: The Supreme Court's Role in Voting Rights Disputes, 1845–1969*. Cambridge: Harvard University Press, 1974.

Ethridge, Marcus E. *Legislative Participation in Implementation: Policy Through Politics*. New York: Praeger Press, 1985.

Field, O. P. *Effect of an Unconstitutional Statute*. New York: Da Capo Press, 1971.

Fisher, Louis. *President and Congress: Power and Policy*. New York: Free Press, 1972.

————. *The Constitution Between Friends: Congress, the President, and the Law*. New York: St. Martin's Press, 1978.

Flynn, John J. *Federalism and State Antitrust Regulation*. Ann Arbor: University of Michigan Law School, 1964.

Frankfurter, Felix. *The Commerce Clause under Marshall, Taney, and Waite*. Chicago: Quadrangle Books, 1964.

Gallagher, Hugh Gregory. *Advise and Obstruct: The Role of United States Senate in Foreign Policy Decisions*. New York: Delacarte Press, 1969.

Goldwin, Robert A., and Kaufman, Art, eds. *Separation of Powers: Does It Still Work?* Washington, DC: American Enterprise Institute for Public Policy Research, 1986.

Goodman, Walter. *The Committee: The Extraordinary Career of the House Committee on Un-American Activities*. New York: Farrar, Straus and Giroux, 1968.

Hamilton, James. *The Power to Probe*. New York: Vintage Books, 1977.

Harrell, Karen F. *The Constitutional and Political Aspects of the Legislative Veto*. Monticello, IL: Vance Bibliographies, 1985.

Lakeman, Enid. *Power to Elect: The Case for Proportional Representation*. New York: Holmes and Meier Publishers, Inc., 1982.

Lee, R. Alton. *A History of Regulatory Taxation*. Lexington: University Press of Kentucky, 1973.

Letwin, William. *Law and Economic Policy in America: the Evolution of the Sherman Antitrust Act*. Edinburgh: Edinburgh University Press, 1967.

Lucie, Patricia A. *Freedom and Federalism, Congress and Courts, 1861–1866*. New York: Garland Publishing Inc., 1987.

Mansfield, Harvey C., Sr. *Congress Against the President.* New York: Praeger, 1975.

McGeary, M. Nelson. *The Development of Congressional Investigating Power.* New York: Octagon Books, 1966.

Mendelson, Wallace. *Capitalism, Democracy, and the Supreme Court.* New York: Appleton-Century-Crofts, 1960.

Merry, Henry J. *The Constitutional System: The Group Character of the Elected Institutions.* New York: Praeger Publishers, 1986.

Miller, Arthur S. *The Supreme Court and American Capitalism.* New York: Free Press, 1968.

Morgan, Donald Grant. *Congress and the Constitution: A Study of Responsibility.* Cambridge: Belknap Press of Harvard University Press, 1966.

Murphy, Walter F. *Congress and the Court: A Case Study in the American Political Process.* Chicago: University of Chicago Press, 1964.

Polsby, Nelson W. *Congress and the Presidency.* Englewood Cliffs, NJ: Prentice Hall, 1986.

Pritchett, C. Herman. *Congress Versus the Supreme Court.* Minneapolis: University of Minnesota Press, 1961.

Reams, Bernard D., Jr., and Haworth, Charles H. *Congress and the Courts: A Legislative History: 1787–1977, 1978–1984.* Buffalo, NY: William S. Hein and Company, 1978, 1985.

Roche, John P., and Levy, Leonard. *The Congress.* New York: Harcourt, 1964.

Rothman, David J. *Politics and Power: The United States Senate, 1869–1901.* New York: Atheneum, 1969.

Rush, Kenneth, et al. *The President, the Congress, and Foreign Policy: A Joint Project of the Association of Former Members of Congress and the Atlantic Council of the United States.* Lanham, MA: University Press of America, 1986.

Schmidhauser, John R., and Berg, Larry L. *The Supreme Court and Congress: Conflict and Interaction, 1945–1968.* New York: Free Press, 1972.

Shuman, Howard E. *Politics and the Budget: The Struggle Between the President and the Congress.* Englewood Cliffs, NJ: Prentice Hall, 1984.

Vieira, Edwin, Jr. *Pieces of Eight: Monetary Powers and Disabilities of the United States Constitution.* Greenwich, CT: Devin-Adair Publishers, Inc., 1983.

Warren, Charles. *Congress, the Constitution and the Supreme Court.* New York: Johnsson Reprint Corp., 1968.

Weeks, K. M. *Adam Clayton Powell and the Supreme Court.* New York: Dunellen, 1971.

Whalen, Charles W., Jr. *The House & Foreign Policy: The Irony of Con-*

gressional Reform. Chapel Hill: University of North Carolina Press, 1982.

Wilson, Woodrow. *Congressional Government.* Cleveland: Meridian Books, 1885, 1967.

Wormuth, Francis D., and Firmage, Edwin B. *Proposals for Line-Item Veto Authority: Legislative Analysis.* Washington, DC: American Enterprise Institute for Public Policy Research, 1984.

————. *To Chain the Dog of War: The War Power of Congress in History and Law.* Dallas, TX: Southern Methodist University Press, 1986.

Presidency

Abraham, Henry. *Justices and Presidents: A Political History of Appointments to the Supreme Court.* 2d ed. New York: Oxford University Press, 1985.

Adler, David G. *The Constitution and the Termination of Treaties.* New York: Garland Publishing Inc., 1986.

American Bar Association Staff, and Cox, Henry B. *War, Foreign Affairs, and Constitutional Power, 1829–1901.* Cambridge: Ballinger Publishing Co., 1984.

American Civil Liberties Union. *Why President Richard Nixon Should be Impeached.* Washington, DC: Public Affairs Press, 1973.

Amlund, Curtis Arthur. *New Perspectives on the Presidency.* New York: Philosophical Library, 1969.

Anderson, Donald F. *William Howard Taft: A Conservative's Conception of the Presidency.* Ithaca, NY: Cornell University Press, 1973.

Barber, James D. *The Presidential Character.* 2d ed. Englewood Cliffs, NJ: Prentice-Hall, 1977.

Barger, Harold M. *The Impossible Presidency: Illusions and Realities of Executive Power.* Glenview, IL: Scott, Foresman, 1984.

Benedict, Michael Les. *The Impeachment and Trial of Andrew Johnson.* New York: W. W. Norton, 1973.

Berger, Raoul. *Executive Privilege: A Constitutional Myth.* Cambridge: Harvard University Press, 1974.

————. *Impeachment: The Constitutional Problems.* Cambridge: Harvard University Press, 1974.

Bessett, Joseph M., and Tulis, Jeffrey, eds. *The Presidency in the Constitutional Order.* Baton Rouge: Louisiana State University Press, 1981.

Bickel, Alexander M. *Reform and Continuity: The Electoral College, the Convention and the Party System.* New York: Harper and Row, 1971.

Blackman, John L., Jr. *Presidential Seizure and Labor Disputes.* Cambridge: Harvard University Press, 1967.

Brandy, Gene F., and Helmich, Donald L. *Executive Succession: Toward*

Excellence in Corporate Leadership. Englewood Cliffs, NJ: Prentice-Hall, 1984.

Brant, Irving. *Impeachment: Trials and Errors*. New York: Knopf, 1972.

Breckenridge, Adam Carlyle. *The Executive Privilege: Presidential Control over Information*. Lincoln: University of Nebraska Press, 1974.

Burns, James M. *Presidential Government: The Crucible of Leadership*. Boston: Houghton Mifflin, 1973.

Chase, Harold W. *Federal Judges: The Appointing Process*. Minneapolis: University of Minnesota Press, 1972.

Cheney, Dick, et al. *War Powers and the Constitution*. Washington, DC: American Enterprise Institute for Public Policy Research, 1984.

Corwin, Edward S. *The President: Office and Powers. 1787–1984*. 5th ed. New York: New York University Press, 1984.

Cronin, Thomas E., ed. *The Presidential Advisory System*. New York: Harper & Row, 1969.

De Chambrum, Adolphe. *The Executive Power in the United States: A Study of Constitutional Law*. Holmes Beach, FL: William W. Gaunt and Sons, Inc., 1974.

Denton, Robert E., Jr., and Hahn, Dan F. *Presidential Communication: Description and Analysis*. New York: Praeger Publishers, 1986.

Donovan, Robert J. *Conflict and Crisis: The Presidency of Harry S. Truman, 1945–1948*. New York: W. W. Norton, 1977.

Edwards, George C. III. *Presidential Influence in Congress*. San Francisco: Freeman, 1980.

Feerick, John D. *From Failing Hands: The Story of Presidential Succession*. New York: Fordham University Press, 1965.

Fisher, Louis. *President and Congress: Power and Policy*. New York: Free Press, 1973.

———. *Presidential Spending Power*. Princeton: Princeton University Press, 1975.

———. *The Constitution Between Friends: Congress, The President, and The Law*. New York: St. Martin's Press, 1978.

Fowler, Michael R. *Thinking About Human Rights: Contending Approaches to Human Rights in U.S. Foreign Policy*. Lanham, MD: University Press of America, 1987.

Friedland, Robert A. *Struggle for Supremacy: Presidential War Power & Foreign Policy*. Ardsley-on-Hudson, NY: Transnational Publications, Inc., 1987.

Funderburk, Charles. *Presidents and Politics: The Limits of Power*. Pacific Grove, CA: Brooks/Cole Publishing Co., 1982.

Genovese, Michael A. *The Supreme Court, the Constitution, and Presidential Power*. Washington, DC: University Press of America, 1980.

Goldsmith, William M., ed. *Growth of Presidential Power: A Documentary History*. New York: Chelsea House Publishers.

Haight, David, and Johnston, L., eds. *The President: Roles and Powers.* Chicago: Rand McNally, 1965.

Hardin, Charles M. *Presidential Power and Accountability.* Chicago: University of Chicago Press, 1974.

Hart, James. *The Ordinance-Making Powers of the President of the United States.* New York: Da Capo Press, 1970.

Hart, John. *The Presidential Branch.* Elmsford, NY: Pergamon Press Inc., 1987.

Henkin, Louis. *Foreign Affairs and the Constitution.* New York: Foundation Press, 1972.

Hirschfield, Robert S. *The Power of the Presidency.* 2d ed. Chicago: Aldine Publishing, 1973.

Jackson, Carlton. *Presidential Vetos, 1792–1945.* Athens: University of Georgia Press, 1967.

Javits, Jacob Koppell. *Who Makes War: The President Versus Congress.* New York: Morrow, 1973.

Johnson, Loch K. *The Making of International Agreements: Congress Confronts the Executive.* New York: New York University Press, 1984.

Johnstone, Robert M. *Jefferson and the Presidency: Leadership in the Young Republic.* Ithaca, NY: Cornell University Press, 1978.

Kallenbach, Joseph E. *The American Chief Executive.* New York: Harper and Row, 1966.

Kessler, Francis P. *The Dilemmas of Presidential Leadership: of Caretakers and Kings.* Englewood Cliffs, NJ: Prentice Hall, 1982.

Keynes, Edward. *Undeclared War: Twilight Zone of Constitutional Power.* University Park, PA: Pennsylvania State University Press, 1982.

Koenig, Louis W. *The Chief Executive.* New York: Harcourt, Brace and World, 1968.

——— et al. *Congress, the Presidency, and the Taiwan Relation Act.* New York: Praeger Publishers, 1985.

Labovitz, John R. *Presidential Impeachment.* New Haven: Yale University Press, 1978.

Latham, Earl. *Kennedy and Presidential Power.* Lexington, MA: Heath, 1972.

Lofgren, Charles. *Government from Reflection and Choice: Constitutional Essays on War, Foreign Relations and Federalism.* New York: Oxford University Press, 1986.

Longley, Lawrence D., and Braun, Alan G. *The Politics of Electoral College Reform.* 2d ed. New Haven: Yale University Press, 1975.

Lowi, Theodore J. *The Personal President: Power Invested, Promise Unfulfilled.* Ithaca, NY: Cornell University Press, 1986.

Lynn, Naomi B., and McClure, Arthur F. *The Fulbright Premise: Senator J. William Fulbright's Views on Presidential Power.* Cranbury, NJ: Bucknell University Press, 1973.

Mackenzie, G. Galvin. *The Politics of Presidential Appointment*. New York: Free Press, 1980.

Meltsner, Arnold J., ed. *Politics and the Oval Office: Toward Presidential Governance*. San Francisco: ICS Press, 1981.

Merry, Henry J. *Constitutional Function of Presidential-Administrative Separation*. Washington, DC: University Press of America, 1978.

————. *Five-Branch Government: The Full Measure of Constitutional Checks and Balances*. Urbana: University of Illinois Press, 1980.

Miller, Arthur S. *Presidential Power in a Nutshell*. St. Paul: West Publishing, 1977.

Milton, George Fort. *The Use of Presidential Power, 1789–1943*. New York: Octagon Book, 1965.

Moore, John N. *Law and the Indo-China War*. Princeton: Princeton University Press, 1972.

Nathan, Richard P. *The Plot That Failed: Nixon and the Administrative Presidency*. New York: John Wiley and Sons, Inc., 1975.

Navasky, Victor. *Kennedy Justice*. New York: Atheneum, 1971.

Neustadt, Richard E. *Presidential Power: The Politics of Leadership from FDR to Carter*. New York: John Wiley & Sons, 1980.

Orman, John M. *Presidential Secrecy and Deception: Beyond the Power to Persuade*. Westport, CT: Greenwood Press, 1980.

Polsby, Nelson W. *Congress and the Presidency*. 2d ed. Englewood Cliffs, NJ: Prentice-Hall, 1971.

Pusey, Merlo J. *The Way We Go to War*. Boston: Houghton Mifflin, 1969.

Raven-Hansen, Peter. *First Use of Nuclear Weapons: Under the Constitution, Who Decides?* Westport, CT: Greenwood Press, Inc., 1987.

Reveley, W. Taylor. *War Powers of the President and Congress: Who Holds the Arrow and Olive Branch?* Charlottesville, VA: University Press of Virginia, 1981.

Roche, John, and Levy, Leonard. *The Presidency*. New York: Harcourt, Brace and World, 1964.

Rossiter, Clinton. *The Supreme Court and the Commander-in-Chief*. Ithaca, NY: Cornell University Press, 1976.

Rush, Kenneth, et al. *The President, the Congress, and Foreign Policy: A Joint Project of the Association of Former Members of Congress and the Atlantic Council of the United States*. Lanham, MA: University Press of America, 1986.

Schlesinger, Arthur M., Jr. *The Imperial Presidency*. Houghton Mifflin, 1973.

Scigliano, Robert. *The Supreme Court and the Presidency*. New York: The Free Press, 1972.

Silva, Ruth C. *Presidential Succession*. Westport, CT: Greenwood, 1968.

Smith, John Malcolm. *Powers of the President During Crises*. New York: Da Capo Press, 1972.

Tatalovich, Raymond, and Daynes, Byron W. *Presidential Power in the United States.* Pacific Grove, CA: Brooks/Cole Publishing Co., 1983.

Tugwell, Rexford G., and Cronin, T. E. *The Presidency Reappraised.* 2d ed. New York: Praeger, 1977.

Westin, Alan F. *The Anatomy of a Constitutional Law Case.* New York: Macmillan, 1958.

Young, Donald. *American Roulette: The History and Dilemma of the Vice-Presidency.* New York: Holt, Rinehart and Winston, 1965.

Civil Rights and Liberties

Abernathy, Glenn. *The Right of Assembly and Association.* Columbia: South Carolina University Press, 1961.

Abraham, Henry J. *Freedom & the Court: Civil Rights & Liberties in the United States.* 5th ed. New York: Oxford University Press, 1988.

Anastapolo, George. *The Constitutionalist: Notes on the First Amendment.* Dallas: Southern Methodist University Press, 1971.

Auerbach, Jerold S. *Justice Without Law?* New York: Oxford University Press, 1983.

Baer, Judith A. *Equality Under the Constitution: Reclaiming the Fourteenth Amendment.* Ithaca, NY: Cornell University, 1984.

Baker, Gordon E. *The Reapportionment Revolution.* New York: Random House, 1966.

Baker, Liva Miranda. *Crime, Law and Politics.* New York: Atheneam, Publishers, 1983.

Barsh, Lawrence, and Henderson, James Youngblood. *The Road: Indian Tribes and Political Liberty.* Berkeley: University of California Press, 1980.

Beardslee, William R. *The Way Out Must Lead In: Life Histories in the Civil Right Movement.* Rev. ed. Westport, CT: Hill, Lawrence, and Co., Inc., 1983.

Becker, Carl L. *Freedom and Responsibility in the American Way of Life.* New York: Knopf, 1945.

Benokraitis, Nijole V., and Feagin, Joe R. *Affirmative Action and Equal Opportunity: Action, Inaction, Reaction.* Boulder, CO: Westview Press, 1978.

Berger, Raoul. *Death Penalties: The Supreme Court's Obstacle Course.* Cambridge: Harvard University Press, 1982.

Berlowitz, Marvin J., and Edari, Ronald S., eds. *Racism and the Denial of Human Rights: Beyond Ethnicity.* Minneapolis, MN: MEP Publications, 1984.

Bernner, Philip. *The Limits and Possibilities of Congress.* New York: St. Martin's Press, 1983.

Berns, Walter. *Freedom, Virtue, and the First Amendment*. Baton Rouge: Louisiana State University Press, 1957.

———. *Religion and the Constitution*. Washington, DC: American Enterprise Institute for Public Policy Research, 1984.

Berry, Mary Frances. *Military Necessity and Civil Rights Policy: Black Citizenship and the Constitution, 1861–1868*. Port Washington, NY: Kennikat Press, 1977.

Bigel, Alan I. *The Supreme Court on Emergency Powers, Foreign Affairs, and Protection of Civil Liberties*. Lanham, MD: University Press of America, 1986.

Black, Charles L. Jr. *The Humane Imagination*. Woodbridge, CT: Ox Bow Press, 1987.

Blaustein, Albert P., and Ferguson, Clarence C. Jr. *Desegregation and the Law*. New Brunswick, NJ: Rutgers University Press, 1957.

Boles, Janet K. *The Politics of the Equal Rights Amendment: Conflict and the Decision Process*. New York: Longman Inc., 1979.

Boozhie, E. X. *The Outlaw's Bible: How to Evade the System Using Constitutional Strategy*. Scottsdale, AZ: Circle-A Publishers, 1985.

Bosmajian, Haig A., ed. *The Freedom to Read*. New York: Neal-Schuman Publishers, Inc., 1987.

Bowles, Samuel, and Gintis, Herbert. *Democracy and Capitalism: Property, Community, and the Contradiction of Modern Social Thought*. New York: Basic Books Inc., 1987.

Brant, Irving. *The Bill of Rights: Its Origin and Meaning*. Indianapolis: Bobbs-Merrill, 1965.

Breckenridge, Adam Carlyle. *The Right to Privacy*. Lincoln: University of Nebraska Press, 1970.

Brenton, Myron. *The Privacy Invaders*. New York: Coward-McCann, 1964.

Brown, Everett Somerville. *Ratification of the Twenty-first Amendment to the Constitution of the United States: State Convention Records and Laws*. New York: Da Capo Press, 1970.

Bullock, Charles, and Lamb, Charles M. *Implementation of Civil Rights Policy*. Monterey, CA: Brooks/Cole, 1983.

Bumiller, Kristin. *The Civil Rights Society: The Social Construction of Victim*. Baltimore: Johns Hopkins University Press, 1988.

Cahn, Edmond, ed. *The Great Rights*. New York: Macmillan, 1963.

Carr, Robert K. *Federal Protection of Civil Rights: Quest for a Sword*. Ithaca, NY: Cornell University Press, 1949.

Carter, T. Barton, et al. *The First Amendment and the Fourth Estate*. Atlanta, GA: Foundation Press, 1985.

Chaffee, Zechariah, Jr. *Free Speech in the United States*. Cambridge: Harvard University Press, 1942.

———. *Documents on Fundamental Human Rights*. 3 vols. Cambridge: Harvard University Press, 1951.

————. *How Human Rights Got into the Constitution*. Boston: Boston University Press, 1952.

————. *The Blessings of Liberty*. Philadelphia: J. B. Lippincott, 1956.

Chandler, Ralph. *The Constitutional Law Dictionary: Individual Rights Supplement*. Santa Barbara, CA: ABC-Clio, Inc., 1985.

Chase, Harold W. *Security and Liberty, the Problem of Native Communists, 1947–1955*. Garden City, NY: Doubleday, 1955.

Commager, Henry S. *Freedom, Loyalty, Dissent*. New York: Oxford University Press, 1954.

Congressional Quarterly, and Witt, Elder, ed. *The Supreme Court and Individual Rights*. Washington, DC: Congressional Quarterly, Inc., 1988.

Conwey, Flo, and Siegelman, Jim. *Holy Terror: The Fundamentalist War on America's Freedoms in Religion, Politics, and Our Private Lives*. New York: Dell Publishing Co., Inc., 1984.

Cook, Constance Ewing. *Nuclear Power and Legal Advocacy: The Environmentalists and the Courts*. Lexington, MA: Lexington Books, D. C. Heath, 1980.

Cook, Joseph G. *Constitutional Rights of the Accused*. 2d ed. New York: Lawyers Co-operative Publishing Co., 1985.

Cook, Joseph G., and Sobieski, John L. *Civil Rights Actions*. New York: Bender, Matthew, & Co., Inc., 1986.

Cook, Thomas I. *Democratic Rights Versus Communist Activity*. Garden City, NY: Doubleday, 1954.

Corbin, Carole L. *The Right to Vote*. New York: Watts, Franklin, Inc., 1985.

Cortner, Richard. *The Supreme Court and the Second Bill of Rights: The Fourteenth Amendment and the Nationalization of Civil Liberties*. Madison: University of Wisconsin Press, 1981.

Corwin, Edward S. *Liberty Against Government*. Baton Rouge: Louisiana State University Press, 1948.

Cover, Robert. *Justice Accused: Antislavery*. New Haven: Yale University Press, 1984.

Cowles, Willard Bunce. *Treaties and Constitutional Law: Property Interferences and Due Process of Law*. Westport, CT: Greenwood Press, 1975.

Dahl, Robert A. *Democracy, Liberty & Equality*. Philadelphia: Coronet Books, 1986.

De Gvazia, E., and Newan, R. K. *Banned Films: Movies' Censors, and the First Amendment*. New York: R. R. Bowker Co., 1983.

Dilliard, Irving, ed. *The Spirit of Liberty: Papers and Addresses of Learned Hand*. 3d ed. New York: Knopf, 1960.

Dimond, Paul R. *Beyond Busing: Inside the Challenge to Urban Segregation*. Ann Arbor: University of Michigan Press, 1985.

Dixon, Robert G. *Democratic Representation: Reapportionment in Law and Politics.* New York: Oxford University Press, 1968.

Donner, Frank J. *The Age of Surveillance: The Aims and Methods of America's Political Intelligence System.* New York: Knopf, 1980.

Dorn, Edwin. *Rules and Racial Equality.* New Haven: Yale University Press, 1979.

Dorsen, Norman, ed. *The Rights of Americans: What They Are—What They Should Be.* New York: Vintage Books, 1971.

———, and Gillers, Stephen, eds. *None of Your Business: Government Secrecy in America.* New York: Penguin Books, 1975.

Dorsen, Norman, ed. *Our Endangered Rights: The ACLU Reports on Civil Liberties Today.* New York: Pantheon Books, 1984.

Douglas, William Orville. *Freedom of the Mind.* Garden City, NJ: Doubleday, 1964.

Eagles, Charles W., ed. *The Civil Rights Movement in America.* Jackson: University Press at Mississippi, 1986.

Edds, Margart. *Free at Last.* Bethesda, MD: Adler & Adler, Publishers, 1987.

Eisenberg, Theodore. *Civil Rights Legislation.* Charlottesville, VA: The Michie Co., 1986.

Elam, Stanley M., ed. *Public Schools and the First Amendment.* Bloomington, IN: Phi Delta Kappa Educational Foundation, 1983.

Elliff, John T. *The Reform of FBI Intelligence Operations.* Princeton: Princeton University Press, 1979.

Emerson, Thomas I. *The System of Freedom of Expression.* New York: Random House, 1970.

Engberg, Edward. *The Spy in the Corporate Structure and the Right to Privacy.* Cleveland: World Publishing Co., 1967.

Ennis, Bruce, and Siegel, Loren. *The Rights of Mental Patients.* New York: Avon Books, 1973.

Epstein, Richard A. *Takings: Private Property and the Power of Eminent Domain.* Cambridge: Harvard University Press, 1985.

Fager, Charles. *Selma, Nineteen Sixty-Five: The March That Changed the South.* New York: Beacon Press Inc., 1985.

Fairman, Charles, and Morrison, Stanley. *The Fourteenth Amendment and the Bill of Rights: The Incorporation Theory.* New York: Da Capo Press, 1970.

Farley, Reynolds. *Black and White.* Cambridge: Harvard University Press, 1986.

Farmer, James. *Lay Bare the Heart: An Autobiography of the Civil Rights Movement.* New York: Arbor House Publishing Co., 1985.

Felkenes, George T. *Constitutional Law for Criminal Justice.* 2d ed. Englewood Cliffs, NJ: Prentice Hall, 1988.

Fellman, David. *The Constitutional Right of Association*. Chicago: University of Chicago Press, 1963.

———. *The Defendant's Rights Today*. Madison: The University of Wisconsin Press, 1976.

Finkelman, Paul. *The Law of Freedom and Bondage: A Casebook*. New York: Oceana Publications, Inc., 1986.

Fisher, Louis. *Constitutional Conflicts Between Congress and the President*. Princeton: Princeton University Press, 1985.

Flack, Horace Edgar. *The Adoption of the Fourteenth Amendment*. Gloucester, MA: P. Smith, 1965.

Franklin, Bob, ed. *The Rights of Children*. Oxford: Blackwell, 1986.

Frederickson, George H., and Chandler, Ralph Clark, eds. *Citizenship and Public Administration*. Washington, DC: American Society for Public Administration, 1984.

Freund, Paul. *Religion and the Public Schools*. Cambridge: Harvard University Press, 1965.

Friedland, Martin L. *Double Jeopardy*. Oxford: Clarendon Press, 1969.

Friedrich, Carl J. *Transcendent Justice: The Religious Dimensions of Constitutionalism*. Durham: Duke University Press, 1964.

Friendly, Alfred. *Crime and Publicity: The Impact of News and the Administration of Justice*. Millwood, NY: Kraus Reprint Co., 1975.

Gelin, Jacques B., and Miller, David W. *The Federal Law of Eminent Domain*. Charlottesville, VA: The Michie Co., 1982.

Gellhorn, Walter. *Individual Freedom and Governmental Restraints*. Baton Rouge: Louisiana State University Press, 1956.

Gillette, William. *The Right to Vote: Politics and the Passage of the Fifteenth Amendment*. Baltimore: Johns Hopkins Press, 1965.

Gora, Joel M. *The Rights of Reporters*. New York: Avon Books, 1974.

Green, Philip. *Retrieving Democracy: In Search of Civic Equality*. Totowa, NJ: Rowman & Littlefield, Publishers, 1985.

Grimes, Alan P. *Democracy and the Amendments to the Constitution*. Lexington, MA: Lexington Books, 1978.

Grimes, William A. *Criminal Law Outline*. Reno, NV: National Judicial College, 1985.

Griswold, Erwin N. *Search and Seizure: A Dilemma of the Supreme Court*. Lincoln: University of Nebraska Press, 1975.

Grofman, Bernard, et al. *Representation & Redistricting Issues*. Lexington, MA: Lexington Books, 1982.

Guthrie, William Cameron. *Lectures on the Fourteenth Article of Amendment to the Constitution of the United States*. New York: Da Capo Press, 1970.

Hachten, William A. *The Supreme Court on Freedom of the Press: Decisions and Dissents*. Ames, IA: Iowa State University Press, 1968.

Halpern, Stephen, ed. *The Future of Our Liberties: Perspectives on the Bill of Rights*. Westport, CT: Greenwood Press, 1982.

Hand, Learned. *The Bill of Rights*. New York: Atheneum, 1964.

Handlin, Oscar, and Handlin, Mary. *The Dimensions of Liberty*. Cambridge: Harvard University Press, 1961.

Hanson, Royce. *The Political Thicket: Reapportionment and Constitutional Democracy*. Englewood Cliffs, NJ: Prentice-Hall, 1966.

Hardy, David T. *Origins and Development of the Second Amendment*. Southpost, CT: Blacksmith Corp., 1986.

Harris, Robert J. *The Quest for Equality: The Constitution, Congress, and the Supreme Court*. Baton Rouge: Louisiana State University Press, 1960.

Hayden, Trudy. *Your Rights to Privacy: The Basic ACLU Guide for Your Rights to Privacy*. New York: Avon Books, 1980.

Heller, Francis Howard. *The Sixth Amendment to the Constitution of the United States: A Study in Constitutional Development*. New York: Greenwood Press, 1969.

Hemmer, Joseph J. *Free Speech*. Millbrae, CA: Scarecrow, 1979.

Hentoff, Nat. *The First Freedom: The Tumultuous History of Free Speech in America*. New York: Delacorte, 1980.

Heumann, Milton. *Plea Bargaining: The Experiences of Prosecutors, Judges, and Defense Attorneys*. Chicago: University of Chicago Press, 1978.

Hill, S. Samuel, and Owen, Dennis E. *The New Religious-Political Right in America*. Nashville, TN: Abingdon Press, 1982.

Holzer, Henry M. *Sweet Land of Liberty? The Supreme Court & Individual Rights*. Medfield, MA: Common Sense Alternatives, 1983.

Howe, Mark De Wolfe. *Garden and the Wilderness: Religion and Government in American Constitutional History*. Chicago: University of Chicago Press, 1965.

Hudson, Edward. *Freedom of Speech and Press in America*. Washington, DC: Public Affairs Press, 1963.

Huey, Gary L. *Rebel with a Cause: P. D. East, Southern Liberation and the Civil Rights Movement, 1953–71*. Wilmington, DE: Scholarly Research Inc., 1985.

Humphrey, Hubert H., ed. *School Desegregation: Documents and Commentaries*. New York: Thomas Crowell, 1964.

Hyman, Harold M., and Wiecek, William M. *Equal Justice under Law: Constitutional Development 1835–1875*. New York: Harper & Row Publishers, Inc., 1982.

Institute of Early American History and Culture Service. *The Development of American Citizenship*. Chapel Hill: University of North Carolina Press, 1984.

Jackson, Michael W. *Matter of Justice*. New York: Methuen, Inc., 1986.

Kaczorowski, Robert J. *The Nationalization of Civil Rights: Constitutional Theory and Practice in a Racist Society, 1866–1883*. New York: Garland Publishing, Inc., 1987.

Kalven, Harry. *The Negro and the First Amendment*. Columbus: Ohio State University Press, 1965.

Karnig, Albert K., and Welch, Susan. *Black Representation and Urban Policy*. Chicago: University of Chicago Press, 1981.

Kauper, Paul G. *Religion and the Constitution*. Baton Rouge: Louisiana State University Press, 1964.

Kendrigan, Mary Lou. *Political Equality in a Democratic Society: Women in the United States*. Westport, CT: Greenwood Press, Inc., 1984.

King, Mary. *Freedom Song: A Personal Story of the Nineteen Sixty's Civil Rights Movement*. New York: William Morrow & Co., Inc., 1986.

Klein, Irving J. *Constitutional Law for Criminal Justice Professionals*. 2d ed. Miami: Coral Gables Publishing Co., 1986.

Konvitz, Milton R. *Fundamental Liberties of a Free People: Religion, Speech, Press, Assembly*. Ithaca, NY: Cornell University Press, 1957.

———. *A Century of Civil Rights*. New York: Columbia University Press, 1967.

———. *Religious Liberty and Conscience: A Constitutional Inquiry*. New York: Viking Press, 1968.

Kramer, Daniel C. *Comparative Civil Rights and Liberties*. Washington, DC: University Press of America, 1982.

Kurland, Philip B. *Religion and the Law*. Chicago: Aldine Publishing Company, 1962.

Ladenson, Robert F. *A Philosophy of Free Expression and Its Constitutional Applications*. Totowa, NJ: Rowman & Littlefield, Publishers, 1983.

LaFave, Wayne R. *Search and Seizure: A Treatise on the Fourth Amendment*, 2d ed. St. Paul: West Publishing Company, 1987.

Landynski, Jacob W. *Searches and Seizures and the Supreme Court*. Baltimore: Johns Hopkins University Press, 1966.

Lasson, Nelson Bernard. *The History and Development of the Fourth Amendment to the United States Constitution*. New York: Da Capo Press, 1970.

Lasswell, Harold D. *National Security and Individual Freedom*. New York: McGraw-Hill, 1950.

Law, Sylvia. *The Rights of the Poor*. New York: Avon Books, 1974.

Lee, Francis G. *Neither Conservative nor Liberal: The Burger Court on Civil Rights & Civil Liberties*. Melbourne, FL: Robert E. Krieger Publishing Co., Inc., 1983.

Lester, Richard A. *Reasoning About Discrimination: The Analysis of Professional and Executive Work in Federal Antibias Programs*. Princeton: Princeton University Press, 1980.

Levine, Alan H., Carey, Eve, and Divoky, Diane. *The Rights of Students*. New York: Avon Books, 1973.

Levitan, Sar A.; Johnston, William B.; and Taggart, Robert. *Minorities in the United States*. Washington, DC: Public Affairs Press, 1976.

Levy, Leonard. *Legacy of Suppression, Freedom of Speech and Press in Early American History.* Cambridge: Harvard University Press, 1960.

————. *Jefferson and Civil Liberties: The Darker Side.* Cambridge: Harvard University Press, 1963.

————, ed. *Freedom of the Press from Zenger to Jefferson: Early American Libertarian Theories.* Indianapolis: Bobbs-Merrill Co., 1966.

————. *Origins of the Fifth Amendment: The Right Against Self-Incrimination.* New York: Oxford University Press, 1968.

Lewis, Anthony. *Gideon's Trumpet.* New York: Random House, 1960.

Lien, Arnold Johnson. *Concurring Opinion: the Privileges or Immunities Clause of the Fourteenth Amendment.* Westport, CT: Greenwood Press, 1975.

Loeb, Ben F. *Eminent Domain Procedure Under General Statues.* Chapel Hill: University of North Carolina, Institute of Government, 1984.

Lofton, John. *The Press as Guardian of the First Amendment.* Colombia: University of South Carolina Press, 1980.

Longaker, Richard P. *The Presidency and Civil Liberties.* Ithaca, NY: Cornell University Press, 1962.

Longnecker, Stephen. *Selma's Peacemaker: Ralph Smeltzer & Civil Rights Mediation.* Philadelphia: Temple University Press, 1987.

Maguire, Daniel C. *The New Subversives: Anti-Americanism of the Religious Right.* Freedom, CA: Crossroads Press, 1982.

Manwaring, David P. *Render unto Caesar: the Flag-Salute Controversy.* Chicago: University of Chicago Press, 1962.

Martin, John Frederick. *Civil Rights and the Crisis of Liberalism: The Democratic Party 1945–1976.* Boulder, CO: Westview Press, 1979.

Masaoka, Mike, and Hosokawa, Bill. *They Call Me Moses Masaoka.* New York: William Morrow & Co., Inc., 1987.

Mashaw, Jerry L. *Due Process in the Administrative State.* New Haven: Yale University Press, 1985.

Matthews, John Mabry. *Legislative and Judicial History of the Fifteenth Amendment.* New York: Da Capo Press, 1971.

McClosky, Herbert, and Brill, Alida. *Dimensions of Tolerance: What Americans Believe about Civil Liberties.* New York: Russell Sage Foundation, 1986.

McKay, Robert. *Reapportionment: The Law and Politics of Equal Representation.* New York: Twentieth Century Fund, 1965.

McNeil, Genna R. *Groundwork: Charles Hamilton Houston & the Struggle for Civil Rights.* Philadelphia: University of Pennsylvania Press, 1983.

Meiklejohn, Alexander. *Political Freedom: The Constitutional Powers of the People.* New York: Harper and Row, 1960.

————. *Free Speech in Relation to Self-Government.* Port Washington, NY: Kennikat Press, 1971.

Meltsner, M. *Cruel and Unusual: The Supreme Court and Capital Punishment*. New York: Morrown, 1973.

Mendelson, Wallace. *Discrimination, Based on the Report of the United States Commission on Civil Rights*. Englewood Cliffs, NJ: Prentice-Hall, 1962.

Meyer, Hermine Herta. *The History and Meaning of the Fourteenth Amendment: Judicial Erosion of the Constitution Through the Misuse of the Fourteenth Amendment*. New York: Vantage Press, 1977.

Mian, Badshah K. *American Habeas Corpus: Law, History, and Politics*. San Francisco: Cosmos of Humanists Press, 1984.

Miller, Leonard G. *Double Jeopardy and The Federal System*. Chicago: University of Chicago Press, 1968.

Miller, Robert D. *Involuntary Civil Commitment of the Mentally Ill in the Post-Reform Era*. Springfield, IL: Charles C. Thomas Publishers, 1987.

Milner, Neal A. *The Court and Local Law Enforcement: the Impact of Miranda*. Beverly Hills: Sage Publications, 1971.

Mills, Henry E. *A Treatise Upon the Law of Eminent Domain*. Littleton, CO: Fred B. Rothman and Co., 1982.

Morgan, Richard E. *The Supreme Court and Religion*. New York: Free Press, 1972.

————. *The Politics of Religious Conflict: Church and State in America*. Lanham, MD: University Press of America, 1980.

————. *The Politics of Religious Conflict: Church and State in America*. 2nd ed. Washington, DC: University Press of America, 1980.

————. *Disabling America: The "Rights Industry" in Our Time*. New York: Basic Books Inc., 1986.

Morris, Aldon D. *The Origins of the Civil Rights Movement: Black Communities Organizing for Change*. New York: Free Press, 1986.

Murphy, Paul L. *The Meaning of Freedom of Speech: First Amendment Freedoms from Wilson to FDR*. Westport, CT: Greenwood, 1973.

Murphy, Walter F. *Wiretapping on Trial: A Case Study in the Judicial Process*. New York: Random House, 1965.

Mykkeltvedt, Ronald Y. *The Nationalization of the Bill of Rights: Fourteenth Amendment Due Process and Procedural Rights*. New York: Associated Faculty Press, 1983.

Nelson, Harold L., ed. *Freedom of the Press from Hamilton to the Warren Court*. Indianapolis: Bobbs-Merrill, 1967.

Newfield, J. *Cruel and Unusual Justice*. New York: Holt, Rinehart and Winston, 1974.

Norrell, Robert J. *Reaping the Whirlwind: The Civil Rights Movement in Tuskegee*. New York: Random House Inc., 1986.

Novak, Michael. *Human Rights and the New Realism: Strategic Thinking in a New Age*. New York: Associated Faculty Press, Inc., 1983.

Nuter, Harold F. *American Servicemembers' Supreme Court*. Lanham, MD: University Press of America, 1982.

O'Brien, Dan. *Eminent Domain*. Iowa City: University of Iowa Press, 1987.

O'Brien, David M. *Privacy, Law, and Public Policy*. New York: Praeger Publishers, 1979.

O'Brien, John L. *National Security and Individual Freedom*. Cambridge: Harvard University Press, 1955.

O'Connor, Karen. *Women's Organizations' Use of the Courts*. Lexington, MA: Lexington Books, 1980.

Orfield, Gary. *Must We Bus? Segregated Schools and National Policy*. Washington, DC: The Brookings Institution, 1978.

O'Rourke, Timothy G. *The Impact of Reapportionment*. New Brunswick, NJ: Transaction Books, 1980.

Palmer, John W. *Constitutional Rights of Prisoners*. 3d ed. Cincinnati: Anderson Publishing Co., 1986.

Paterson, Judith, et al. *Civil Rights Held Hostage: The United States Catholic Conference and the Civil Rights Restoration Act*. Washington, DC: Catholics for a Free Choice, 1987.

Paul, Ellen F. *Property Rights and Eminent Domain*. New Brunswick, NJ: Transaction Books, 1986.

Peltason, Jack W. *Fifty-Eight Lonely Men, Southern Federal Judges and School Desegregation*. New York: Harcourt, Brace and World, 1961.

Perry, Richard L. *Sources of Our Liberties*. Chicago: American Bar Foundation, 1959.

Pfeffer, Leo. *The Liberties of an American*. Boston: Beacon Press, 1956.

―――. *Church and State in the United States*. New York: Harper & Row, 1964.

―――. *Church, State, and Freedom*. Boston: Beacon Press, 1967.

Phillips, Michael J. *The Dilemmas of Individualism: Status, Liberty & American Constitutional Law*. Westport, CT: Greenwood Press, Inc., 1983.

Pipel, Harriet E. *Obscenity and the Constitution*. New York: R. R. Bowker, 1973.

Pound, Roscoe. *The Development of Constitutional Guarantees of Liberty*. New Haven: Yale University Press, 1957.

Prettyman, Barrett, Jr. *Death and the Supreme Court*. New York: Harcourt, Brace and World, 1961.

Price, Don K. *America's Unwritten Constitution: Science, Religion, and Political Responsibility*. Baton Rouge: Louisiana State University Press, 1983.

Pritchett, C. Herman. *Civil Liberties and the Vinson Court*. Chicago: University of Chicago Press, 1954.

―――. *The Political Offender and the Warren Court*. Boston: Boston University Press, 1958.

―――. *Constitutional Civil Liberties*. Englewood Cliffs, NJ: Prentice-Hall, 1984.

Provenzano, Johanna Z. *Guide to Title XII*. Wheaton, MD: National Clearinghouse for Bilingual Education, 1984.

Pyle, Christopher H. *Military Surveillance of Civilian Politics, 1967–1970*. New York: Garland Publishing, Inc., 1986.

Rankin, Robert S., and Dallmayr, Winifred R. *Freedom and Emergency Powers in the Cold War*. New York: Appleton-Century-Crofts, 1964.

Richey, Charles R. *Manual on Employment Discrimination and Civil Rights Actions in the Federal Courts: Attorney's Edition*. New York: Kluwer Law Book Publishers, Inc., 1987.

Ringer, Benjamin B. *We The People and Others: Duality and America's Treatment of Its Racial Minorities*. New York: Methuen Inc., 1986.

Rivkin, Robert S. *The Rights of Servicemen*. New York: Avon Books, 1972.

Roche, John T. *Courts and Rights, The American Judiciary in Action*. New York: Random House, 1961.

Roettger, Garry J. *Condemnation Practice (1982)*. 2d ed. Newark, NJ: New Jersey Institute for Continuing Legal Education, 1985.

Roettinger, Ruth L. *The Supreme Court and State Police Power*. Washington, DC: Public Affairs Press, 1957.

Rosengart, Oliver. *The Rights of Suspects*. New York: Avon Books, 1974.

Ross, Susan C. *The Rights of Women*. New York: Avon Books, 1973.

Rudovsky, David. *The Rights of Prisoners*. New York: Avon Books, 1973.

Rutland, Robert A. *The Birth of the Bill of Rights, 1776–1791*. Chapel Hill: University of North Carolina Press, 1955.

Sackman, Julius, and Van Brunt, Russell. *Nichols on Eminent Domain*. New York: Matthew Bender & Co., Inc., 1986.

Samet, Andrew J., ed. *Human Rights Law and the Reagan Administration: 1981–1983*. Washington, DC: International Law Institute, 1984.

Scheingold, Stuart A. *The Politics of Law and Order*. White Plains, NY: Longman, 1984.

Schlesinger, Steven R. *Exclusionary Injustice: The Problem of Illegally Obtained Evidence*. New York: Marcel Dekker, 1977.

Schreibman, Vigdor. *The Doctrines on Race, Economics and Sex*. Mclear, VA: Americas Publications, 1987.

Schuck, Peter H. *Suing Government: Citizen Remedies for Official Wrongs*. New Haven: Yale University Press, 1986.

Schwartz, Bernard. *Statutory History of the United States: Civil Rights*. 2 vols. New York: Chelsea House, 1970.

———, ed. *The Fourteenth Amendment: Centennial Volume*. New York: New York University Press, 1970.

———. *The Great Rights of Mankind: A History of the American Bill of Rights*. New York: Oxford University Press, 1977.

———. *Swann's Way: The School Busing Case and the Supreme Court*. Oxford: Oxford University Press, 1986.

Scorer, Catherine, and Sedley, Ann. *Amending the Equality Laws*. New York: State Mutual Book and Periodical Service, 1983.

Scotch, Richard K. *From Good Will to Civil Rights: Transforming Federal Disability Policy*. Philadelphia: Temple University Press, 1985.

Shapiro, Martin. *Freedom of Speech: the Supreme Court and Judicial Review*. Englewood Cliffs, NJ: Prentice-Hall, 1966.

————. *The Pentagon Papers and the Courts: A Study in Foreign Policy Making and Freedom of the Press*. San Francisco: Chandler Publishing Co., 1972.

Shuck, Peter H., and Smith, Rogers M. *Citizenship Without Consent: Illegal Aliens in the American Polity*. New Haven: Yale University Press, 1985.

Sigler, Jay A. *Double Jeopardy: The Development of a Legal and Social Policy*. Ithaca, NY: Cornell University Press, 1969.

Sindler, Allan P. *Bakke, Deffunis, and Minority Admissions: The Quest for Equal Opportunity*. New York: Longman Inc., 1978.

Slavin, Sarah, ed. *The Equal Rights Amendment: The Policy and Process of Ratification of the 27th Amendment to the U.S. Constitution*. New York: The Harworth Press, Inc., 1982.

Smith, Michael. *Qualified Immunity from Liability for Violations of Federal Rights: A Modification*. Chapel Hill: University of North Carolina, Institute of Government, 1983.

Smith, Rodney K. *Public Prayer and the Constitution*. Delaware: Scholarly Resources, Inc., 1987.

Sornarajah, M., ed. *The Pursuit of Nationalized Property*. Norwell, MA: Kluwer Academic Publishers, 1986.

Southwestern Legal Foundation. *Annual Institute on Planning and Zoning and Eminent Domain: Sixteenth Annual Institute*. New York: Matthew Bender & Co. Inc., 1987.

Spurrier, Robert L., Jr. *Rights, Wrongs and Remedies: Section Nineteen 1983 and Constitutional Rights Vindication*. New York: Associated Faculty Press, Inc., 1986.

Stephens, Otis H. *The Supreme Court and Confessions of Guilt*. Nashville: University of Tennessee Press, 1973.

Stouffer, Samuel A. *Communism, Conformity, and Civil Liberties*. Garden City, NY: Doubleday, 1955.

Taper, Bernard. *Gomillion v. Lightfoot, the Tuskegee Gerrymander Case*. New York: McGraw-Hill, 1962.

Taylor, Telford. *Two Studies in Constitutional Interpretations: Search, Seizure, and Surveillance, and Fair Trial and Free Press*. Columbus: Ohio State University Press, 1969.

Tedford, Thomas. *Freedom of Speech*. New York: Random House, 1985.

Ten Broek, Jacobus. *Equal Under Law [Anti-Slavery Origins of the Fourteenth Amendment]*. New York: Collier Books, 1965.

Theoharis, Athan. *Spying on Americans: Political Surveillance from Hoover to the Huston Plan*. Philadelphia: Temple University Press, 1978.

Thomas, Robert J. *Citizenship, Gender, and Work: The Social Organization of Industrial Agriculture*. Berkeley: University of California Press, 1985.

Van Alstyne, William. *Interpretations of the First Amendment*. Durham, NC: Duke University Press, 1984.

Van Gerpen, Maurice. *Privileged Communication and the Press: The Citizen's Right to Know versus the Law's Right to Confidential News Source Evidence*. Westport, CT: Greenwood Press, 1979.

Vance, Mary A. *Civil Rights in the U.S. Material Published 1980–1984*. Monticello, IL: Vance Bibliographies, 1985.

Von Hirsch, Andrew. *Past or Future Crimes: Deservedness and Dangerousness in the Sentencing of Criminals*. Manchester, U.K.: Manchester University Press, 1985.

Vose, Clement E. *Caucasians Only: The Supreme Court, the NAACP, and the Restrictive Covenant Cases*. Berkeley: University of California Press, 1959.

Walentyrowicz, Len. *How to Stay in America Legally*. Bethesda, MD: National Press Inc., 1988.

Walton, Hanes, Jr. *When the Marching Stopped: The Politics of Civil Rights Regulatory Agencies*. Albany, NY: State University of New York Press, 1988.

Walzer, Michael. *Obligations: Essays on Disobedience, War, and Citizenship*. Cambridge: Harvard University Press, 1982.

Warren, Earl. *The Bill of Rights and the Military*. New York: University Law Center, 1962.

Warsoff, Louis A. *Equality and the Law*. Westport, CT: Greenwood, 1975.

Wasby, Stephen L., D'Amato, Anthony A., and Metrailer, Rosemary. *Desegregation from Brown to Alexander: An Exploration of Supreme Court Strategies*. Carbondale: Southern Illinois University Press, 1977.

Way, H. Frank. *Liberty in Balance: Current Issues in Civil Liberties*. 5th ed. New York: McGraw-Hill, 1981.

Westin, Alan. *Privacy and Freedom*. New York: Atheneum, 1967.

Whalen, Charles, and Whalen, Barbara. *The Longest Debate: A Legislative History of the 1964 Civil Rights Act*. Bethesda, MD: Seven Locks Press, 1985.

Whitney, Sharon. *The Equal Rights Amendments: The History and the Movements*. New York: Watts, Franklin, Inc., 1984.

Wiener, Solomon. *Questions and Answers on American Citizenship*. New York: Regents Publishing Co., Inc., 1982.

Williams, Jerre, et al. *Our Freedoms: Rights and Responsibilities*. Austin: University of Texas Press, 1985.

Williams, Juan. *Eyes on the Prize: America's Civil Rights Year, 1954–1965*. New York: Viking Penguin Inc., 1986.

Williamson, Joe. *A Rage for Order: Black-White Relations in the American South Since Emancipation*. New York: Oxford University Press, 1986.

Wise, David. *The American Police State*. New York: Random House, 1976.

Witt, Elder, ed. *The Supreme Court and Individual Rights*. Washington, DC.: Congressional Quarterly, Inc., 1988.

Yarbrough, Tinsley E. *Judge Frank Johnson and Human Rights in Alabama*. Tuscaloosa, AL: University of Alabama, 1981.

————. *A Passion for Justice: J. Waties Waring and Civil Rights*. New York: Oxford University Press, 1987.

Zagel, James. *Confessions and Interrogations After Miranda: A Comprehensive Guideline of the Law*. Alexandria, VA: National District Attorneys Association, 1982.

Zangrando, Robert L. *The NAACP Crusade Against Lynching, 1909–1950*. Philadelphia: Temple University Press, 1980.

Zinn, Howard. *SNCC: The New Abolitionists*. Westport, CT: Greenwood Press Inc., 1985.

Law and Society

Alcock, Anthony E.; Taylor, Brian K.; and Welton, John M. *The Future of Cultural Minorities*. New York: St. Martin's Press, 1979.

Alix, Ernest Kahlar. *Ransom Kidnapping in America, 1874–1974*. Carbondale: Southern Illinois University Press, 1978.

Ball, Milner S. *Lying Down Together: Law, Metaphor, and Theology*. Madison: University of Wisconsin Press, 1985.

Bayley, David. *Forces of Order: Police Behavior in Japan and in the United States*. Berkeley: University of California Press, 1976.

Belknap, Michael, ed. *American Political Trials*. Westport, CT: Greenwood Press, 1981.

Berkman, Ronald. *Opening the Gates: The Rise of the Prisoners' Movement*. Lexington, MA: Lexington Books, 1979.

Berry, Mary Frances. *Why ERA Failed: Politics, Women's Rights and the Amending Process of the Constitution*. Bloomington, IN: Indiana University Press, 1986.

Berry, Robert C.; Gould, William B.; and Standohar, Paul D. *Labor Relations in Professional Sports*. Dover, MA: Auburn House, 1986.

Bohannan, Paul, ed. *Law and Warfare*. Garden City, NY: Natural History Press, 1967.

Bonsignore, John J., Katsh, Ethan, d'Errico, Peter, Pipkin, Ronald M., Arons, Stephen, and Rifkin, Janet. *Before the Law: An Introduction to the Legal Process*. 4th ed. Boston: Houghton Mifflin, 1989.

Braithwaite, John. *Inequality, Crime and Public Policy*. Boston: Routledge and Kegan Paul, 1979.

————. *Corporate Crime in the Pharmaceutical Industry*. London: Routledge and Kegan Paul, 1984.

Bromberg, Walter. *The Uses of Psychiatry in the Law: A Clinical View of Forensic Psychiatry*. Westport, CN: Greenwood, 1979.

Burkhardt, Kathryn. *Women in Prison*. Garden City, NY: Doubleday, 1973.

Burt, Robert A. *Taking Care of Strangers: The Rule of Law in Doctor-Patient Relations*. New York: The Free Press, 1979.

Cain, Maureen, and Hunt, Alan. *Marx and Engels on Law*. New York: Academic Press, 1979.

Chambliss, William, and Seidman, Robert. *Law, Order and Power*. Reading, MA: Addison-Wesley, 1971.

Channels, Noreen L. *Social Science Methods in the Legal Process*. Totowa, NJ: Rowman & Littlefield Publishers, 1985.

Cleaver, Eldridge. *Soul On Ice*. New York: McGraw-Hill, 1968.

Cohen, Morris L., Ronen, Naomi, and Stepan, Jan, comps. *Law and Science*. Cambridge: The MIT Press, 1980.

Cohen, Stanley. *Visions of Social Control: Crime, Punishment and Classification*. Oxford: Polity Press, 1985.

Coser, Lewis. *The Functions of Social Conflict*. New York: The Free Press, 1956.

Dahl, Tove Stang. *Child Welfare and Social Defence*. Oslo: Norwegian University Press, 1985.

Davis, Karl. *Discretionary Justice*. Baton Rouge: Louisiana State University Press, 1969.

Dominguez, Virginia R. *White by Definition: Social Classification in Creole Louisiana*. New Brunswick, NJ: Rutgers University Press, 1986.

Eckelaar, John, and Maclean, Mavis. *Maintenance After Divorce*. Oxford: Clarendon Press, Oxford Socio-Legal Studies, 1986.

Ehrlich, Eugen. *Fundamental Principles of the Sociology of Law*. Translated by W. Moll. New York: Russell and Russell, 1962.

Erikson, Kai T. *Wayward Puritans: A Study in the Sociology of Deviance*. New York: John Wiley and Sons, 1966.

Faden, Ruth R., Beauchamp, Tom L., and King, Nancy M. P. *A History and Theory of Informed Consent*. Oxford: Oxford University Press, 1986.

Fairchild, Erika S., and Webb, Vencent J., eds. *The Politics of Crime and Criminal Justice*. Beverly Hills: Sage Publications, 1985.

Feild, Hubert S., and Bienen, Leigh B. *Jurors and Rape: A Study in Psychology and Law*. Lexington, MA: Lexington Books, 1980.

Finkelman, Paul. *The Law of Freedom and Bondage: A Casebook*. New York: Oceana Publications, New York University School of Law: Ingram Documents in American Legal History, 1986.

Fitzmaurice, Catherine, and Pease, Ken. *The Psychology of Judicial Sentencing*. Manchester: Manchester University Press, 1986.

Forsyth, Walter. *History of Trial by Jury*. New York: Burt Franklin, 1971.

Foucault, Michel. *The Birth of the Prison*. New York: Pantheon, 1978.

Foust, Cleon H., and Webster, Robert D. *An Anatomy of Criminal Justice*. Lexington, MA: Lexington Books, 1980.

Friedlander, Judith, Cook, Blance Wiesen, Kessler-Harris, Alice, and Smith-Rosenberg, Carroll, eds. *Women in Culture and Politics: A Century of Change*. Bloomington, IN: Indiana University Press, 1986.

Freidson, Eliot. *Professional Powers: A Study of the Institutionalization of Formal Knowledge*. Chicago: University of Chicago Press, 1986.

Gardiner, John A., ed. *Public Law and Public Policy*. New York: Praeger Publishers, 1977.

Geis, Gilbert, and Stotland, Ezra. *White-Collar Crime: Theory and Research*. Beverly Hills: Sage Publications, 1980.

Goldberg, Stephen B., Green, Eric D., and Sander, Frank E. A., eds. *Dispute Resolution*. Boston: Little, Brown, 1985.

Goldstein, Paul J. *Prostitution and Drugs*. Lexington, MA: Lexington Books, 1979.

Gould, David J. *Law and the Administrative Process: Analytic Frameworks for Understanding Public Policymaking*. Washington, DC: University Press of America, 1979.

Gregory, Charles O., and Katz, Harold A. *Labor and the Law*. 3d ed. New York: W. W. Norton, 1979.

Grilliot, Harold J. *Introduction to Law and the Legal System*. 3d ed. Boston: Houghton Mifflin, 1983.

Grossman, Joel B., and Grossman, Mary H., eds. *Law and Change in Modern America*. Pacific Palisades, CA: Goodyear Publishing, 1971.

Gulliver, P. H., ed. *Cross-Examinations: Essays in Memory of Max Gluckman*. Leiden, The Netherlands: E. J. Brill, 1978.

Gulliver, P. H. *Disputes and Negotiations: A Cross-Cultural Perspective*. New York: Academic Press, Inc. 1979.

Gurr, Ted Robert. *Violence in America: Historical and Comparative Perspectives*. New York: Bantam Books, 1970.

Hall, N. E. H. *Female Felons: Women and Serious Crime in Colonial Massachusetts*. Urbana: University of Illinois Press, 1987.

Hans, Valerie P., and Vidmar, Neil. *Judging the Jury*. New York: Plenum, 1986.

Harris, Donald, Maclean, Mavis, Genn, Hazel, Lloyd-Bostock, Sally, Fenn, Paul, Corfied, Peter, and Brittan, Yvonne. *Compensation and Support for Illness and Injury*. Oxford: Clarendon Press, 1984.

Harris, John. *Violence and Responsibility*. Boston: Routledge and Kegan Paul, 1980.

Hartzler, H. Richard, and Allan, Harry. *An Introduction to Law*. Glenview, IL: Scott, Foresman, 1969.

Hirsch, Werner Z. *Law and Economics: An Introductory Analysis*. New York: Academic Press, 1979.

Hoff-Wilson, Joan, ed. *Rights of Passage: The Past and Future of the ERA*. Bloomington, IN: Indiana University Press, 1986.

Hudson, Joe, and Galaway, Burt, eds. *Victims, Offenders, and Alternative Sanctions*. Lexington, MA: Lexington Books, 1980.

Kalven, Harry, Jr., and Zeisel, Hans. *The American Jury*. Boston: Little, Brown, 1966.

Karlen, Delmar. *The Citizen in Court*. New York: Holt, Rinehart and Winston, 1964.

Katz, Michael B. *In the Shadow of the Poorhouse: A Social History of Welfare in America*. New York: Basic Books, 1986.

Kirchheimer, Otto. *Political Justice*. Princeton: Princeton University Press, 1961.

Kittrie, Nicholas N., and Wedlock, Eldon D. Jr., eds. *The Tree of Liberty: A Documentary History of Rebellion and Political Crime in America*. Baltimore: Johns Hopkins University Press, 1986.

Kolasa, Blair J., and Meyer, Bernadine. *Legal Systems*. Englewood Cliffs, NJ: Prentice-Hall, 1978.

Levine, James P., Musheno, Michael C., and Palumbo, Dennis J. *Criminal Justice: A Public Policy Approach*. New York: Harcourt, Brace and Jovanovich, 1980.

Lidz, Charles W., Meisel, Alan, Zerubavel, Eviatar, Carter, Mary, Sestak, Regina M., and Roth, Loren H. *Informed Consent: A Study of Decisionmaking in Psychiatry*. New York: Guilford Press, 1984.

Lieberman, Jethro K. *The Litigious Society*. New York: Basic Books Inc., 1980.

Llewellyn, Karl, and Hoebel, E. Adamson. *The Cheyenne Way*. Norman: University of Oklahoma Press, 1941.

Loewen, James W. *Social Science in the Courtroom: Statistical Techniques and Research Methods for Winning Class-Action Suits*. Lexington, MA: D.C. Heath Co., 1982.

LoPuck, Lynn M. *Player's Manual for the Debtor-Creditor Game*. St. Paul, MN: West, 1985.

————. *Strategies for Creditors in Bankruptcy Proceedings*. Boston: Little, Brown, 1985.

Macneil, Iran R. *The New Social Contract: An Inquiry into Modern Contractual Relations*. New Haven: Yale University Press, 1980.

Maine, Henry. *Ancient Law*. London: Oxford University Press, 1931.

Malinchak, Alan A. *Crime and Gerontology*. Englewood Cliffs, NJ: Prentice-Hall, Inc., 1980.

Matasar, Ann B. *Corporate PACs and Federal Campaign Financing Laws*. Westport, CT: Quorum Books, 1986.

McDonald, Douglas Carry. *Punishment without Walls: Community Service Sentences in New York City*. New Brunswick, NJ: Rutgers University Press, 1986.

Menninger, Kar. *The Crime of Punishment*. New York: Viking Press, 1968.

Merryman, John Henry, Clark, David S., and Friedman, Lawrence M. *Law and Social Change in Mediterranean Europe and Latin America: A Handbook of Legal and Social Indicators for Comparative Study*. Dobbs Ferry, NY: Oceana Publications, Inc., 1980.

Morris, Norville. *The Future of Imprisonment*. Chicago: University of Chicago Press, 1977.

Nader, Laura, ed. *Law in Culture and Society*. Chicago: Aldine, 1969.

Neier, Aryeh. *Only Judgement: The Limits of Litigation in Social Change*. Middletown, CT: Wesleyan University, 1982.

Parry, Ruth S., Broder, Elsa A., Schmitt, Elizabeth A. G., Saunders, Elizabeth B., and Hood, Eric, eds. *Custody Disputes: Evaluation and Intervention*. Lexington, MA: Lexington Books, D.C. Heath, 1986.

Pound, Roscoe. *Social Control Through Law*. New Haven: Yale University Press, 1942.

Provine, Doris Marie. *Judging Credentials: Nonlawyer Judges and the Politics of Professionalism*. Chicago: University of Chicago Press, 1986.

Quinney, Richard. *Critique of Legal Order*. Boston: Little, Brown, 1974.

———. *Class, State and Crime*. New York: McKay, 1977.

Reiss, Albert. *The Police and the Public*. New Haven: Yale University Press, 1971.

Robbins, Ira P. *Comparative Postconviction Remedies*. Lexington, MA: Lexington Books, 1980.

Rubin, Eva R. *The Supreme Court and the American Family: Ideology and Issues*. Westport, CT: Greenwood Press, Contributions in American Studies 85, 1986.

Saks, Michael. *Jury Verdict: The Role of Group Size and Social Decision-Rule*. Lexington, MA: Lexington Books, 1977.

Schichor, David, and Kelly, Delos H., eds. *Critical Issues in Juvenile Delinquency*. Lexington, MA: Lexington Books, 1980.

Schur, Edwin. *Law and Society*. New York: Random House, 1968.

Schwitzgebel, Robert L., and Schwitzgebel, R. Kirland. *Law and Psychological Practice*. New York: John Wiley & Sons, 1980.

Shapiro, Susan P. *Wayward Capitalists: Target of the Securities and Exchange Commission*. New Haven: Yale University Press, Yale Studies on White-Collar Crime, 1984.

Siegan, Bernard H. *Regulation, Economics, and the Law*. Lexington, MA: Lexington Books, 1979.

Simon, Rita James, ed. *The Sociology of Law: Interdisciplinary Readings*. San Francisco: Chandler Publishing, 1968.

Skolnick, Jerome. *Justice Without Trial: Law Enforcement in a Democratic Society*. New York: John Wiley, 1966.

Spence, Gerry. *Of Murder and Madness: A True Story of Insanity and the Law*. New York: NY: Doubleday & Co., Inc., 1983.

Steiner, Y. Gilbert. *The Abortion Dispute and the American System*. Washington, DC: Brookings Institution, 1983.

Summers, Robert. *Law: Its Nature, Functions and Limits*. Englewood Cliffs, NJ: Prentice-Hall, 1972.

Szasz, Thomas. *Law, Liberty and Psychiatry*. New York: Macmillan, 1963.

———. *Psychiatric Justice*. New York: Collier Books, 1965.

Thornes, Barbara, and Collard, Jean. *Who Divorces?* Boston: Routledge and Kegan Paul, 1979.

Tonry, Michael, Zimring, Franklin E., eds. *Reform and Punishment: Essays on Criminal Sentencing*. Chicago: University of Chicago Press, Studies in Crime and Justice, 1983.

Tonnies, Ferdinand. *Community and Society*. Edited and translated by Charles P. Loomis. New York: Harper and Row, 1963.

Walker, Samuel. *Popular Justice: A History of American Criminal Justice*. New York: Oxford University Press, 1980.

———. *Sense and Nonsense About Crime: A Policy Guide*. Monterey, CA: Brooks/Cole, Contemporary Issues in Crime and Justice, 1985.

Walsh, Dermot. *Heavy Business: Commercial Burglary and Robbery*. London: Routledge and Kegan Paul, 1986.

Weber, Max. *On Law in Economy and Society*. Translated with introduction by Max Rheinstein et al. Cambridge: Harvard University Press, 1954.

Wechsler, Henry, ed. *Minimum Drinking Age Laws: An Evaluation*. Lexington, MA: Lexington Books, 1980.

Weinberg, Lee S., and Weinberg, Judith W. *Law and Society: An Interdisciplinary Introduction*. Washington, DC: University Press of America, 1980.

Westley, William A. *Violence and the Police*. Cambridge: MIT Press, 1971.

Wilburn, James R., ed. *Freedom, Order, and the University*. Los Angeles: Pepperdine Press University, 1982.

Wilson, James Q. *Varieties of Police Behavior*. Cambridge: Harvard University Press, 1968.

Winslade, William J., and Ross, Judith W. *The Insanity Plea: Uses and Abuse*. New York: Charles Scribner's Sons, 1983.

Wood, James E., Jr., ed. *Religion, the State, and Education*. Waco, TX: Baylor University, 1984.

Wright, Eric Olin. *The Politics of Punishment*. New York: Harper Colophon Books, Harper and Row, 1973.

Yarmey, A. Daniel. *The Psychology of Eyewitness Testimony*. New York: The Free Press, 1979.

Zelizer, Viviana A. *Pricing the Priceless Child: The Changing Social Value of Children*. New York: Basic Books, 1985.

Zimmer, Lynn E. *Women Guarding Men*. Chicago: University of Chicago Press, Studies in Crime and Justice, 1986.

Legal Profession

Auerbach, Jerome. *Unequal Justice*. New York: Oxford University Press, 1976.

Black, Jonathan, ed. *Radical Lawyers*. New York: Avon Books, 1971.

Bloomfield, Maxwell. *American Lawyers in a Changing Society, 1776–1876*. Cambridge: Harvard University Press, 1976.

Carlin, Jerome E. *Lawyers on Their Own*. New Brunswick, NJ: Rutgers University Press, 1962.

Casper, Jonathan D. *Lawyers Before the Warren Court: Civil Liberties and Civil Rights, 1957–1966*. Urbana: University of Illinois Press, 1972.

Chroust, Anton-Hermann. *The Rise of the Legal Profession in America*, 2 Vols. Norman: University of Oklahoma Press, 1965.

Couric, Emily, ed. *Women Lawyers: Perspectives on Success*. New York: Harcourt, Brace, Jovanovich, 1984.

Eisenstein, James. *Counsel for the United States: U.S. Attorney in the Political and Legal System*. Baltimore: John Hopkins University Press, 1978.

Ginger, Ann Fagan. *The Relevant Lawyers*. New York: Simon and Schuster, 1972.

Goulden, Joseph. *The Super-Lawyers*. New York: Weybright & Talley, 1971.

Grossman, Joel B. *Lawyers and Judges: The ABA and the Politics of Judicial Selection*. New York: John Wiley and Sons, 1965.

Gruzenberg, O. *Yesterday: Memoirs of a Russian-Jewish Lawyer*. Lexington, MA: Lexington Books, 1982.

Handler, Joel. *The Lawyer and His Community*. Madison: University of Wisconsin Press, 1967.

Heinz, John P., and Laumann, Edward O. *Chicago Lawyers: The Social Structure of the Bar*. New York: Basic Books, 1983.

Hurst, James Willard. *The Growth of American Law*. Boston: Little, Brown, 1950.

Irons, Peter. *The New Deal Lawyers*. New York: Princeton University Press, 1982.

Kinoy, Arthur. *Rights on Trial: The Odyssey of a People's Lawyer*. Cambridge: Harvard University Press, 1984.

Lefcourt, Robert. *Law Against the People*. New York: Vintage Books, 1971.

Mayer, Martin. *The Lawyers*. New York: Dell Publishing Co., 1968.

Medcalf, Linda. *Law and Identity: Lawyers, Native Americans, and Legal Practice*. Beverly Hills: Sage Publications, 1978.

Melone, Albert P. *Lawyers, Public Policy and Interest Group Politics*. Washington, DC: University Press of America, 1977/1979.

Pound, Roscoe. *The Lawyer from Antiquity to Modern Times*. St. Paul: West Publishing, 1953.

Rosenthal, Douglas. *Lawyer and Client: Who's in Charge?* New Brunswick, NY: Transaction Books, 1974.

Ross, Peggy A. *The Constitutionality of State Bar Residency Requirements.* Chicago: American Bar Association, 1982.

Shaffer, Thomas, and Redmount, Robert. *Lawyers, Law Students and People.* Indianapolis: Sheppard's, 1977.

Smigel, Erwin O. *The Wall Street Lawyer.* New York: The Free Press, 1964.

Spangler, Eve. *Lawyers for Hire: Salaried Professionals at Work.* New Haven: Yale University Press, 1986.

Stevens, Robert. *Law School: Legal Education in America from the 1850s to the 1980s.* Chapel Hill: University of North Carolina Press, 1983.

Stumpf, Harry P. *Community Politics and Legal Services.* Beverly Hills: Sage Publications, 1975.

Twiss, Benjamin. *Lawyers and the Constitution.* Princeton: Princeton University Press, 1942.

Warren, Charles. *A History of the American Bar.* Boston: Little, Brown, 1911.

Wice, Paul B. *Criminal Lawyer: An Endangered Species.* Beverly Hills: Sage Publications, 1978.

Wood, Arthur Lewis. *Criminal Lawyer.* New Haven: College & University Press, 1967.

Zemans, Frances K., and Rosenblum, Victor. *The Making of a Public Profession.* Chicago: American Bar Foundation Press, 1981.

Index

A

Abbreviations, 27, 29–30
Abington Township v. Schemp, see
    School District of Abington Town-
    ship v. Schempp
Abraham, Henry J., 42, 64
Administrative agency reporting, 20–21
Administrative law, 20–21
Allen, W. B., 46
Almanacs
    bibliography entries for, 93
    footnoting, 81
American Association of Law Librar-
    ies, 32, 33
American Digest System, 22, 24
American Journal of Legal History, 32
American Jurisprudence 2d, 13, 14,
    15–16
    sample citation, 16
American Law Reports, 9–10, 16
    sample citation, 10
American Lawyer, The, 11
Amicus curiae briefs, 4
Armstrong, Scott, 72
Atlantic Reporter, 9
    sample citation, 9
Auerbach, Jerold S., 65
AUTO-CITE, 37

B

Baker v. Carr, 5, 116
Bancroft-Whitney Company, 3, 9, 10,
    20, 24, 37
Bankruptcy Reporter, West's, 8
Barenblatt v. United States, 116–
    117
Barron v. Baltimore, 117–118
Bartholomew, Paul C., 42
Battistoni, Richard M., 43
Baxter, Maurice G., 59
Beard, Charles, 46
Becker, Theodore L., 62, 65
Beckstrom, John H., 65
Belz, Herman, 48
Berg, Larry L., 64
Berger, Raoul, 52
Berkson, Larry, 66
Berman, Daniel M., 59
Beveridge, Albert J., 55
Biasi, Vincent, 46
Bibliography, 74, 75, 89–99
Black, J. S., 2
Bland, Randall W., 56
Blaustein, Albert P., 62
Boles, Donald E., 56
Bolling v. Sharpe, 118
Booklets
    bibliography entries for, 94
    footnoting, 82
Books
    bibliography entries for, 89–92
    footnoting, 77–80
    scientific reference form, 102–103
Bowen, Catherine Drinker, 46
Briefs, 4–5
    amicus curiae, 4
    elements of a, 106–112

Briefs *(continued)*
  landmark, 5, 12
  model, 112–114
Briefing cases
  method of, 106–112
  reasons for, 105–106
Brill, Alida, 68
Brown v. Board of Education of
    Topeka I, 118–119
Brown v. Board of Education of
    Topeka II, 119
Buckley v. Valeo, 120
Bullock, Charles, 62, 63
Bureau of National Affairs, Inc., 11
Butchers' Benevolent Association v.
    Crescent City Livestock Landing
    and Slaughterhouse Co., 120–121

C

California Reporter, 8
Cannon, Mark W., 52
Canon, Bradley, 62
Cardozo, Benjamin N., 65
Carp, Robert A., 7fn., 65
Carter, Dan T., 59
Carter v. Carter Coal Co., 5
Case studies, 59–61
Cases
  briefing, 104–114
  table of, 75
  underlining of, 3, 76
Casper, Gerard, 5, 12
Casper, Jonathan D., 66
Champagne, Anthony, 69
Chicago Daily Bulletin, 11
Chimel v. California, 60
Chinn, Nancy, 66
Choper, Jesse H., 52
Citations
  in research papers, 75–103
  parallel, 1–2, 27, 107
  Shepard's U.S., 26–31
Citators, 26–31
Civil Rights Cases, 121–122
Clinton, Robert L., 53
Code of Federal Regulations, 21

Codes, 18–20
Cohen v. California, 60
Collier, Christopher, 46
Collier, James Lincoln, 46
Commerce Clearing House, Inc., 12
Commerce Court of the U.S., 7
Complete Oral Arguments of the
    Supreme Court of the United
    States, 12
Compliance and impact analysis, books
    on, 61–64
Computers, legal research and, 36–37
Concurring opinions, 111
Congressional Information Service, 5
Constitutional Commentary, 31
Cooley v. The Board of Wardens of the
    Port of Philadelphia, 122
Corpus Juris Secundum, 13, 14, 16–
    17
  sample citation, 17
Cortner, Richard C., 59, 60
Cranch, William, 2
Criminal Justice Periodical Index, 35
Current Law Index, 33–34
Currie, David P., 47
Curry, James A., 43

D

Dallas, A. J., 2
Danelski, David J., 66, 71
Dartmouth College v. Woodward, see
    Trustees of Dartmouth College v.
    Woodward
Dennis v. United States, 1, 122–123
Dictionaries, law, 36
Digests, 22–25
  regional, 24fn.
  specialized, 24
Dissenting opinions, 111
Dissertation
  bibliography entries for, 93
  footnoting, 81
  scientific reference form, 103
Documentation, 75–103
Doe v. Bolton, 60
Dolbeare, Kenneth M., 49

Douglas, William O., 56
Downing, Rondal G., 72
DuBois, Philip, 66
Ducat, Craig R., 53
Duncan v. Louisiana, 60
Dunham, Allison, 56
Dunne, Gerald, 56
Duram, James C., 57
Dworkin, Ronald, 53

E

Earle, Edward Meade, 47
Elliot, Jonathan, 47
Ely, John Hart, 53
*Encyclopedia of the American
    Constitution*, 17–18
    sample citation, 18
*Encyclopedia of the American Judicial
    System*, 13, 14
    sample citation, 14
Encyclopedias
    bibliography entries for, 93
    footnoting, 81
    legal, 13–18
Endnotes, 76
Ex Parte McCardle, 123
Ex Parte Milligan, 123
Expository works, 41–45

F

Faber, Doris, 47
Faber, Harold, 47
Fairchild, Erika S., 66, 69
Farrand, Max, 47
Federal Cases, 6, 7
    sample citation, 6, 83
Federal Practice Digest, 24
Federal Register, 21
Federal Reporter, 7
    sample citation, 7, 83
Federal Rules Decisions, 7
    sample citation, 83
Federal Supplement, 7–8
    sample citation, 7, 83

Feeley, Malcolm M., 62
Fellman, David, 43
Ferguson, Clarence Clyde, Jr., 62
Fletcher v. Peck, 60, 124–125
Footnotes, 76–89
    references to former, 88
Furman v. Georgia, 125
Format, research paper, 75
Friedman, Leon, 57
Frontiero v. Richardson, 60
Funston, Richard, 14

G

*Garcia v. San Antonio Metropolitan
    Transit Authority*, 5, 125–126
Garraty, John A., 60
Gibbons v. Ogden, 126
Gideon v. Wainwright, 60, 127
Gitlow v. New York, 127–128
Glick, Henry R., 66
Glossary of terms and phrases, 158–
    176
Goldman, Sheldon, 67
Government documents
    bibliography entries for, 97–99
    footnoting, 85–88
    scientific reference form, 101–102,
        103
Grier, Stephenson D., Jr., 48
Griswold v. Connecticut, 128
Grossman, Joel B., 67
*Guide to American Law: Everyone's
    Legal Encyclopedia*, 13, 14
    sample citation, 14

H

Haines, Charles Grove, 48
Hall, Kermit L., 48
Halpern, Stephen, 43
Hammer v. Dagenart, 128–129
Harbinson, Winfred A., 48
Harrington, Christine, 67
Harvard Law Review, 31

Hastings Constitutional Law Quarterly, 31
Haworth, Charles H., 50
Headnotes, 2, 3, 4
Heart of Atlanta v. United States, 129
Hentoff, Nat, 48
Hirsch, H. N., 57
Historical accounts of the Supreme Court, 45–51
Home Building and Loan Association v. Blaisdell, 129–130
Horowitz, Donald L., 54
Houseman, Gerald L., 54
Howard, Benjamin C., 2
Howard, Woodford, 68
Humanities Index, 35
Hurtado v. California, 130

I

Immigration & Naturalization Service v. Chadha, 131
Index to Foreign Legal Periodicals, 34
Index to Legal Periodical Literature, 32
Index to Legal Periodicals, 32–33
Index to Periodical Articles Related to Law, 34–35
Indexes, legal, 32–34
Information Access Corporation, 33, 34
Information Handling Services, 5
Institute of Advanced Legal Studies, 34
International organizations, footnoting, 87
Interviews
  bibliography entries for, 94
  footnoting, 82
Irons, Peter, 60
Israel, Fred L., 57

J

Jacobini, H. B., 20fn., 21
Jacobstein, Myron, 6fn.
Johnson, Charles, 62
Johnson, Richard M., 62

Jones, Leonard A., 32
Journal articles
  bibliography entries for, 92
  footnoting, 80
  scientific reference form, 102, 103
Journal of Law and Economics, 32
Journal of Psychiatry and Law, 32
Journals, law, 31–32
Judicature, 31
Judicial biographies, 55–59
Judicial Panel on Multi-District Litigation, 7
Judicial process and behavior, books on, 64–72
Judicial review and Constitutional interpretation, 51–55

K

Kadala v. Amoco Oil Co., 7
Kalvelage, Carl, 20fn., 21
Kastner, Daniel L., 63
Katz v. United States, 131–132
Katzenbach v. McClung, 132
Kelly, Alfred, 48
Ketcham, Ralph, 48
Key Number System, West, 8, 22–23, 24
Korematsu v. United States, 132–133
Kramer, Daniel C., 68
Kurland, Philip B., 5, 12, 43, 49, 56

L

LaFave, Wayne R., 43
Lamb, Charles M., 62, 67
Landmark briefs, 5, 12
Landynski, Jacob W., 44
Law & Policy Quarterly, 32
Law and Society Review, 32
Lawyers Co-operative Publishing Company, 3–4, 9, 10, 20, 24, 37
Lawyers' Edition, *see U.S. Supreme Court Reports, Lawyers' Edition*
Legal Resource Index, 34
Legal sources
  bibliography entries for, 95–97
  footnoting, 83–85

Legal Times, 11
Legal Trac, 34
Lerner, Ralph, 43
Lewis, Anthony, 60
Letters
  bibliography entries for, 94
  footnoting, 82
LEXIS, 6, 37
Library, use of, 74–75
Lloyd, Gordon, 46
Lochner v. New York, 133
Lofgren, Charles, 60
Longaker, Richard P., 44
Los Angeles Daily Journal, 11
Louthan, William, 70
Lower Federal Court Reports, 6–8
Luther v. Borden, 133–134

M

Mace, George, 54
McCann, Michael W., 54
McClosky, Herbert, 68
McCulloch v. Maryland, 5, 134
McDonald, Forrest, 49
McDowell, Gary L., 54
Magazine articles
  bibliography entries for, 92
  footnoting, 80
  scientific reference form, 100–103
Magee, James L., 57
Magrath, C. Peter, 57, 60
Manley, John F., 49
Mapp v. Ohio, 134–135
Marbury v. Madison, 135
Mason, Alpheus Thomas, 57
Meetings
  bibliography entries for, 95
  footnoting, 83
Melnick, Shep, 60
Melone, Albert P., 20fn., 21, 54, 68
Mendelson, Wallace, 68
Menez, Joseph F., 42
Mersky, Roy M., 2fn., 8fn.
Microcard Editions Services, 5
Military Justice Reporter, 8
Miller, Arthur S., 44, 54

Milner, Neil A., 63
Millett, Stephen M., 49
Milliken v. Bradley, 136
Miranda v. Arizona, 136–137
Missouri v. Holland, 137
Morris, Richard B., 49
Muir, William K., Jr., 63
Munn v. Illinois, 137–138
Murphy, Bruce Allen, 58
Murphy, Paul L., 49
Murphy, Walter F., 61, 63, 68, 69
Murray v. Curlett, see School District of Abington Township v. Schempp

N

Nagel, Stuart, 69
National Labor Relations Board v. Jones and Laughlin Steel Corp., 138–139
National Law Journal, 11
National League of Cities v. Usery, 125, 126
National Reporter System (West Publishing Company), 8, 10
Neely, Richard, 54, 69
New York Law Journal, 11
New York Supplement, 8
New York Times, 11, 36
New York Times Co. v. Sullivan, 139
New York Times Co. v. United States, 139
New York Times Index, 36
Newmyer, Kent R., 58
Newspapers
  bibliography entries for, 93
  footnoting, 81
  legal, 11
Nixon v. Administrator of General Services, 3
Nixon v. Fitzgerald, 140
North Eastern Reporter, 9
  sample citation, 9
North Western Reporter, 9
  sample citation, 9
Notes, placement of, 75
Nowak, John E., 44

O

O'Brien, David M., 52, 69
Olmstead v. United States, 61
Opinions
  concurring, 111
  dissenting, 111
O'Rourke, Timothy G., 63

P

Pacific Reporter, 9
  sample citation, 9
Palko v. Connecticut, 140
Pamphlets
  bibliography entries for, 94
  footnoting, 82
Parallel citations, 1–2, 27, 107
Parrish, Michael, 58
Peltason, J. W., 44, 70
Periodicals, legal, 31–34
  index to, 32–34
Perry Michael, 55
Peters, Richard, 2
Pinkele, Carl, 70
Plessy v. Ferguson, 60, 140–141
Pohlman, H. L., 58
*Pollock v. Farmer's Loan and Trust
  Co.*, 141–142
Porter, Mary Cornelia, 70
Posner, Richard, 70
Powell v. Alabama, 142
Pritchett, C. Herman, 44, 49, 61, 68
Provine, Doris Marie, 70
*Public Affairs Informations Service
  Bulletin*, 35

R

Radio programs
  bibliography entries for, 94
  footnoting, 82
*Readers' Guide to Periodical
  Literature*, 35
Reams, Bernard D., Jr., 50

*Regents of the University of California
  v. Bakke*, 142–143
Regional digests, 22, 24fn.
Rehnquist, William, 70
Reporters, court, 2
Reports, footnoting, 82
Research, legal, conducting, 1–40
Research reports
  choosing a topic, 73–74
  citations in, 75–89
  documenting, 75–103
  elements of, 75
  format, 75
  writing, 73–103
Reynolds v. Sims, 143–144
Richardson, Richard J., 70
Riley, Richard B., 43
Rodell, Fred, 50
Rodgers, Harrell R., Jr., 63
Roe v. Wade, 144–145
Rohde, David W., 71
Rossiter, Clinton, 44, 50
Rotunda, Ronald D., 44
Rowland, C. K., 7fn., 65
Rules of the Supreme Court, 13

S

*Saint Louis University Public Law
  Review*, 31
Sarat, Austin, 67
*Schechter Poultry Corp. v. United
  States*, 145–146
Schenck v. United States, 146
Schmidhauser, John R., 50, 64
Scholarly resources, 5
*School District of Abington Township
  v. Schempp*, 146–147
Schubert, Glendon, 71
Schwartz, Bernard, 51
Schwartz, Herman, 51
Scientific reference form, 100–103
Scribner's, Charles, Sons, 14
Sheldon, Charles H., 71
Shelley v. Kraemer, 147
Shepard's Citations, Inc., 26–31
Sherwood, Foster H., 48

Silverstein, Mark, 58
Simon, James F., 58
Simons, William B., 71
Sindler, Allan P., 61
Slaughterhouse cases, see Butchers' Benevelent Association v. Crescent City Livestock Landing and Slaughterhouse Co.
Slip opinions, 2–3
Smith, Edward C., 45
Smith v. Allwright, 115, 148
Social Science Index, 35
Sources, legal
   bibliography entries for, 95–97
   footnoting, 83–85
South Eastern Reporter, 9
   sample citation, 9
South Western Reporter, 9
   sample citation, 9
Southern Reporter, 9
   sample citation, 9
Spaeth, Harold J., 45, 71
Sprague, John D., 72
Stare decisis, 1
State Court reporters, 8–9
Steamer, Robert J., 51
Stidham, Ronald, 65
Strum, Philippa, 58
Stuart v. Laird, 148–149
Stumpf, Harry P., 72
Supreme Court, U.S.
   briefs filed with, 4–6
   decisions, summaries of leading, 115–157
   historical accounts of the, 45–51
   opinions of the, 1–4
Supreme Court of the United States Petitions and Briefs, 6
Supreme Court Reporter, 2, 4
Swisher, Carl B., 51
Syllabi, 2, 3

T

Table of Cases, 75
Table of Contents, 75
Tanenhaus, Joseph, 63, 67, 68, 69

Tarr, Allan G., 64, 70
Television programs
   bibliography entries for, 94
   footnoting, 82
Temporary Emergency Court of Appeals, 7
Testa v. Katt, 3
Thesis
   bibliography entries for, 94
   footnoting, 82
   scientific reference form, 103
Tinker v. Des Moines Independent Community School District, 149
Title Page, 75
Topic, choosing a, 73–74
Tribe, Laurence H., 45
Trustees of Dartmouth College v. Woodward, 149–150
Twiss, Benjamin, 51

U

Ulmer, S. Sidney, 72
Uniform State Laws, 15
U.S. Circuit Court, 7
United States Claims Court, 7
United States Claims Court Reporter, 7
United States Code, 18, 19
   sample citation, 19
United States Code Annotated, 19, 20
   sample citation, 20
United States Code Service, 19–20
   sample citation, 20
U.S. Court of Appeals, 7
U.S. Court of Claims, 7
U.S. Court of Customs and Patent Appeals, 7
U.S. Court of International Trade, 7
U.S. District Courts, 7
   decisions, 7–8
U.S. Emergency Court of Appeals, 7
United States Law Week, 11–12
   sample citation, 12, 84
United States Printing Office, 5
United States Reports, 1–3
   sample citation, 3, 83

United States Supreme Court, *see* Supreme Court, U.S.
U.S. Supreme Court Bulletin, 11, 12–13
    sample citation, 13, 84
U.S. Supreme Court Digest, 24
U.S. Supreme Court Records and Briefs, 5–6
United States Supreme Court Reports—Lawyers' Edition, 1, 2, 3–4
U.S. Supreme Court Reports: Lawyers' Edition Digest, 24–25
United States v. Butler, 150–151
United States v. Curtiss-Wright Export Corp., 151
United States v. Darby, 151–152
United States v. E. C. Knight Co., 152–153
United States v. Klein, 3
United States v. Nixon, 153–154
United States v. United States District Court for Eastern District of Michigan, 154
University Microfilms International, 35
University of California v. Bakke, *see* Regents of the University of California v. Bakke
University Publications of America, Inc., 5, 12

V

Vines, Kenneth N., 66, 70

W

Wallace, John William, 2
Walz v. Tax Commission of the City of New York, 154–155
Warren, Charles, 51
Warren, Earl, 59
Wasby, Stephen L., 64, 72
Watson, Richard A., 72
Way, H. Frank, 45
Webb, Vincent J., 66
West Coast Hotel v. Parrish, 155
West Key Number System, 8, 22–23
West Publishing Company, 4, 6, 7, 8, 14, 16, 20, 22–24, 25, 27, 36, 37
West Virginia State Board of Education v. Barnette, 26, 156
Westin, Alan F., 61
WESTLAW, 37
West's Bankruptcy Reporter, 8
West's Federal Case News, 11, 13
Wheare, K. C., 72
Wheaton, Henry, 2
Wilson, H. W., Company, 32
Wisconsin v. Yoder, 60
Witt, Elder, 45
Wolfe, Christopher, 55
Woodward, Bob, 72
Writing research papers, 73–103

Y

Young, J. Nelson, 44
Youngstown Sheet and Tube Co. v. Sawyer, 61, 156–157